WILLIE

Ann Colin

WILLIE

Raising and Loving a Child
with
Attention Deficit
Disorder

VIKING

VIKING
Published by the Penguin Group
Penguin Books USA Inc., 375 Hudson Street,
New York, New York 10014, U.S.A.
Penguin Books Ltd, 27 Wrights Lane, London W8 5TZ, England
Penguin Books Australia Ltd, Ringwood, Victoria, Australia
Penguin Books Canada Ltd, 10 Alcorn Avenue,
Toronto, Ontario, Canada M4V 3B2
Penguin Books (N. Z.) Ltd, 182–190 Wairau Road,
Auckland 10, New Zealand

Penguin Books Ltd, Registered Offices:
Harmondsworth, Middlesex, England

First published in 1997 by Viking Penguin,
a division of Penguin Books USA Inc.

1 3 5 7 9 10 8 6 4 2

The individual experiences recounted in this book are true. However,
in most instances, names and descriptive details have been altered.

A portion of this book first appeared in *Parents* magazine.

LIBRARY OF CONGRESS CATALOGING IN PUBLICATION DATA
Colin, Ann.
Willie: raising and loving a child with attention deficit disorder / by Ann Colin.
p.   cm.
ISBN 0-670-86314-9
1. Problem children—Case studies.   2. Attention-deficit-disordered children—
Case studies.   3. Parent and child—Case studies.   I. Title.
HQ773.H39   1997
649´.153—dc20   96-31312

This book is printed on acid-free paper.
∞

Printed in the United States of America
Set in Electra
Designed by Francesca Belanger

For Peter, Willie, and Nicholas;
and for Cynthia Colin and Jean Herbst,
who taught me the power
of a mother's love

'Tis a gift to be simple, 'tis a gift to be free,
'tis a gift to come down where we ought to be.
And when we find ourselves in the place just right,
we'll dwell in the valley of love and delight.

When true simplicity is gained,
to bow and to bend, we will not be ashamed.
Turning and turning will be our delight,
for by turning and turning we come 'round right.

—"Simple Gifts"
Shaker Traditional Hymn

Acknowledgments

There are many people I'd like to thank for their friendship and encouragement as I was writing this book, foremost among them my agent, Alice Martell, for her faith, enthusiasm, and a wellspring of chocolate desserts. I am also indebted to Mindy Werner at Viking for her sagacious advice and kind concern for me during the editing process, and to Molly Stern for her tenacious attention to detail with this manuscript.

I'd also like to recognize my own personal set of cheerleaders, who urged me on as a writer and as a mother, even though I sometimes doubted my ability on both fronts: my husband, Peter; Susan Squire; Nessa Rapoport; Vicky Ross; Sara Pasternak; Matthew Levine; Shawn Leary; Michael Considine; Judith Ginsberg; Nina Ehrlich-Foley; Jennifer Rimmer; Clare McHugh; Ben Cheever; Marc and Laura Colin Klein; Ed Herbst; Beth Skinner; and Judy Leipzig. I am blessed, too, in having worked with three of the most generous and talented bosses on the planet—Sally Koslow, Catherine Cavender, and Lisa Reilly—who unflaggingly supported me in this project though it (occasionally) diverted my attention away from calendars, comment sheets, and art memos. I would also like to acknowledge the hard work and dedication of Josette Cuvier—our family could not have made it through the past seven years without you.

As for those sterling professionals who were immediately involved with Willie's care during the days and months described in this book, words cannot express the depth of our family's gratitude to you. Norma Doft, Cara Zukerman, Margo Lee, Lois Berman, Judy Gold, Mindy Cossette, Ellen Simon, Alexandra Harbus, Rick Stackow, Canela Panagiotopoulos, Yousefa Kizelnik, Michael Merkin, Alice Barzilay, and everyone at Willie's school—our hearts *and thanks are always with you. To Harry Evans and Tina Brown, thank you for leading us to "the miracle school."*

I am also grateful to the real "Ron," whose wisdom and leadership are advanced far beyond his years; and to Adam Le Clerc, Aaron Abady, and David Wine, for expanding my understanding of friendship—and extending your love to Willie. You are very special people with your own miraculous gifts.

Lastly, I'd like to thank my sons, Willie and Nicholas. Though you both will most likely learn on your own that it can be awfully hard to be a good parent, I hope you will enjoy the company of your children as much as I treasure the time we spend together. Don't ever forget that I consider myself truly lucky to be your mother.

New York City, 1997

Introduction

Attention Deficit Disorder (ADD) is the most commonly diagnosed psychiatric illness among children: Anywhere from 3 to 9 percent of all school-age children are affected. But in 1993, when our three-year-old son, Willie, was diagnosed with ADD, my husband, Peter, and I had never before heard of the disorder. What was this ailment that caused him to be so excitable, impulsive, distractible, and hyperactive? And if it was so pervasive, why was there no mention of ADD in Dr. Spock or Penelope Leach, the Old and New Testaments of child care for our generation?

The situation seemed bleakly ironic: up to this point, everything about having a child had seemed to come so easily to Peter and me. Despite a seventeen-year age difference, we were ideal mates, sharing the same views about everything from furniture slipcovers to politics. We were in the same profession, Peter a magazine editor and I a writer, and our mutual interests and curiosity about new ideas always built useful bridges over the occasional generation gap.

We'd had none of the tortuous self-doubt or anxiety that so many of our friends had experienced when we thought about having children. Peter and I seemed to be completely in sync. Married after a whirlwind, three-month courtship, we knew we wanted to plan a family right away. Sure, I was young and, like all my other twenty-something friends, hadn't found the perfect job or career path just yet. But becoming a mother was something I'd never questioned. In some ways, starting a family early seemed like the perfect solution to my job woes. After all, full-time staff-writing positions were few and far between in the late eighties—many of the magazines and newspapers that often gave a start to young journalists in New York had gone belly-up in the recession. Freelance writing seemed like a good way to work and be involved with the full-time care of a newborn.

Of course, I was lucky to have a choice in when and how I would raise my child—both physically and economically. Though many of Peter's friends who were in their late thirties and early forties were experiencing heartbreaking fertility problems, I was young—twenty-two when I got pregnant—and Willie was conceived the first month we tried. I had a fairly uneventful pregnancy despite horrendous morning sickness—which, in my case, lasted morning, noon, and night. (It was so bad I lost ten pounds during my first trimester.)

But throughout my pregnancy, I was careful. I ate nutritious foods and attended a childbirth class with Peter. My prenatal care had been thorough and attentive—even cautious to the point of making us nervous—with the obstetrician ordering a sonogram at eight months because of my continuous morning sickness. (When all the tests proved normal, the doctor concluded it was probably just my body's hormones kicking in as I went into the final trimester.)

Like any other expectant couple, Peter and I were growing increasingly excited as my due date grew closer. We were comically well prepared, down to the newborn-size diapers waiting in the nursery and the dozens of new and borrowed baby outfits that lay tucked inside the drawers of the already-delivered nursery furniture. When the doctor pronounced me fit as a very large fiddle at the final sonogram, Peter and I stared in awe at the murky image of our son's head projected on the black-and-white screen. He was beautiful, even his insides, which were all we could see of him.

Although Peter and I knew the risks that went along with any pregnancy, it didn't occur to us to be overly concerned about the birth. The doctor said the baby was fine. I was young and in good shape—which meant round as a medicine ball. Perhaps naively, we believed a healthy baby would be our gift for living in New York—a city with some of the most sophisticated medical technology on the planet. To be honest, my biggest fear was that I would *give birth in a taxi. We never imagined that something might be wrong with our child.*

I started keeping a journal about Willie when he was three, first as a way of trying to make sense of his increasingly bewildering behavior. In the beginning, before Peter and I knew what ADD was, I would jot down where and when Willie was getting what I called, for lack of a better word at the time, "fussy." If Willie was losing his temper for seemingly no reason, I wrote it down. In the beginning, the entries were pretty minimal. Though I was hoping to find a pattern, none really emerged. The only thing that was predictable was Willie's unpredictability.

Willie could be infuriatingly hard to reach when we tried to reason with him; he often got angry for no apparent reason; he was constantly fidgeting and interrupting; and he was frequently in trouble in preschool and at home. If excited, his energy could spiral wildly out of control. When we tried to help him calm down, his behavior would often get much, much worse, until he'd wind up having a temper tantrum. He couldn't focus or talk to us when he got wild like this. It was a look in his eye—something completely out of his power to control.

What was wrong with our child? The journal entries were coming fast—and usually furiously. As I looked over them, I realized I was growing increasingly desperate to find some pattern (at one point, I was praying for a milk allergy). But I knew in my heart it was something much deeper and more pervasive than that. What I slowly realized about Willie was that it wasn't one thing that seemed to be slightly "off" with him—it could be everything at once.

Later on, as we became involved with a variety of doctors, I kept my notes on Willie to help remember the information they'd told us and to give them feedback about Willie's behavior. Had he improved? Gotten worse? Sometimes, it was hard to tell the difference. Eventually, in January 1994, the time Willie tried Ritalin (the medication that is commonly prescribed for ADD) my journal became more of a diary—my way of blowing off steam and saving the shreds that remained of my sanity as Peter and I went through a terrible year, one that presented steep challenges in our attempts to help our son.

As a mother, I have mixed feelings about sharing the events here. In some ways, I know it's deeply unfair to Willie for me to tell his story for him, when in only a few years he will be perfectly capable of telling it himself—or keeping his past private. But I'm taking that choice away from him, and I wonder what the repercussions of that will be. Will he be discriminated against because people will know he has ADD? If he wants to run for president someday, for example, will someone whip out this book and his chances be thwarted? (Heaven help us if we're all judged by our behavior in nursery school!) And what about Nicholas, our younger son? As I write this, Nicky is four, an age of keen competition with his older brother. Will he feel less loved because I didn't write a book about him, too? Certainly tales of his endearing good nature could fill volumes, too.

But I believe—and hope Willie and Nicholas will agree as they get older—that my motives are pure. When I realized that so many families go through exactly the same pain and confusion that we did—be it with ADD or any behavioral, emotional, or even physical disorder that affects their child—I felt I had an obligation to share what had happened to us. After all, if our family wasn't going to be part of the solution to lifting the stigma of ADD, then we'd be part of the problem. For better or worse, none of us are the types to stick our heads in the sand, least of all our boys.

I am so proud of Willie and his sheer determination in overcoming his problems. What does he have to be embarrassed about, anyway? That his "wiring" is different? Everybody's wiring is different. That's what makes us individuals. Given recent developments in genetics and human biology, I wouldn't be surprised if we all learned in the next ten or fifteen years that there is a gene or an environmental trait—to say nothing of a name or a label—for all our different intelligences or lack thereof.

Is there such an ailment as Attention Deficit Disorder? I believe the evidence is overwhelmingly clear. Some writers have theo-

rized that ADD is a survival trait in the evolution of our species. According to this theory, thousands of years ago, individuals with ADD were the tribal scouts, their quick reaction times vital in hunting and war. Though the term Attention Deficit Disorder *wasn't used to describe affected individuals until as late as 1980, credit for first recognizing the syndrome usually goes to British pediatrician George Frederic Still, who, in a 1902 lecture series delivered at the Royal College of Physicians, described some of the young patients he worked with as lacking an "inhibitory volition." Rather than attributing their condition to bad parenting, as the Victorian norms of the day might have suggested, Still theorized that the condition was biologically inherited, or a result of brain injury at birth. In the thirties and forties, stimulants (amphetamines) were first used—successfully—to help these children control their behavior.*

Yet researchers had not come far from George Still's notion that overly active or distractible youngsters were "brain damaged" in the classic sense, though the vast majority had never suffered the type of traumatic head injury or birth defects that would account for their otherwise unaccountable behavior. As Edward M. Hallowell, M.D., and John H. Ratey, M.D., point out wryly in their 1994 book, Driven to Distraction: Recognizing and Coping with Attention Deficit Disorder from Childhood through Adulthood *(Simon & Schuster), "Other terms began to appear, some quite descriptive, such as 'organic drivenness,' others rather amorphous and bleak, like 'minimal brain dysfunction.' One had to wonder whether the brain itself was minimal or the dysfunction was minimal or perhaps whether the understanding of what was happening in the first place was minimal."*

By 1960, American researcher Stella Chess had determined that hyperactivity, an involuntary frenetic energy level, had distinctly biological causes. By the next decade, many scientists were investigating the disorder, most notably Canadian behavioral specialist Virginia Douglas, who was the first to distinguish four related traits in many of the hyperactive children she studied: poor attention, impulsivity, overreaction to sensory stimuli, and the need for constant reinforcement or gratification. In large part due to

Douglas's breakthrough discoveries on the syndrome, it was re-named Attention Deficit Disorder in 1980.

Nonetheless, experts are still divided as to the root causes of ADD, or ADHD, as it is sometimes known (the H standing for hyperactivity.) A number of researchers have investigated the effects of sugar consumption on hyperactive behavior (the most recent published studies at the time of this writing indicate that sugar does not increase hyperactivity, though many parents insist that their firsthand experience tells them otherwise). The mother's smoking during pregnancy has also been linked to later behavioral, not to mention health, problems in young children. (No studies, it seems, have been done on the long-term behavioral—as opposed to solely medical—effects of fathers smoking around nonsmoking expectant mothers.) Environmental factors, in utero deficiencies, as well as maternal drug use during pregnancy have also been implicated. The most common source of ADD/ADHD, however, is genetic. Few experts dispute that the disorder runs in families. Between 25 and 35 percent of siblings, 25 to 40 percent of parents, and 20 to 25 percent of other relatives of individuals with ADD also have the disorder.

Scientists are making headway, too, on pinpointing the specific areas in the brain and brain chemistry that are responsible for the low frustration tolerance, poor attention, distractibility, and impulsivity that characterize ADD. While there is no single gene or neurotransmitter that causes this broad range of behaviors, in 1990, Alan Zametkin and his staff at the National Institutes of Mental Health found that individuals with ADD had decreased metabolic activity in the prefrontal and superior premotor cortexes of the brain. (These regions regulate our impulses, memory, and planning ability and also serve as a clearinghouse for the lower brain and limbic system, which help us sort through stimuli and emotions.)

What are the specific brain chemicals that are being underproduced or underutilized by these regions of the brain? As early as 1970, scientists speculated that the catecholamine class of neurotransmitters (dopamine and norepinephrine) were the prime culprits. Stimulants such as Ritalin (methylphenidate) have long been *known to increase the presence of catecholamines. More recently, however, another neurotransmitter, serotonin, has also been implicated as a mechanism in the complex, botched circuitry of ADD. For this reason, antidepressants that boost serotonin levels in the brain, such as Prozac (fluoxetine) or Zoloft (sertraline) can be helpful additions to a psychiatrist's arsenal when stimulants alone are not effective in curbing the symptoms of ADD.*

But beyond trying to understand these technical elements of the disorder, Peter and I—as parents—were also presented with what seemed to be a more immediate crisis regarding Willie's prospects in school. Depending on whose statistics we believed, our son stood a 20 to 50 percent chance of developing learning disabilities attendant to his ADD. Peter and I were confused and alarmed by this information, much as we were relieved to finally have a name for what plagued Willie. What would he need? How would we cope? What could we do to help him get better? Were all the things we hoped and dreamed of for his future already foreclosed? We had hundreds of questions that weren't covered in the few medical manuals we could find.

We worried that the types of problems Willie had been having in preschool would continue to haunt him for his entire academic career. We were concerned that his sometimes violent behavior would "rub off" on and even potentially endanger Nicholas, who was two at the time. It was clear that we needed help, but we didn't know where to go or what to do.

Furthermore, there were deeper, perhaps unanswerable questions—the ones that kept us staring at the ceiling all night in silent isolation. How could an otherwise intelligent, sweet, creative boy like Willie have a neurological problem? Had we done something wrong as parents to inadvertently cause his attention deficit?

As much as I'd been impressed by Willie's creative sense of humor and original thinking (this was a child who knew the meaning of "inanimate objects" at age two), I knew, to the rest of the world, Willie could sometimes sound almost unintelligible. His pronunciation was poor. He had a heavy lisp and a habit of jumping ahead of himself in a sentence, so we often had trouble following his ideas or questions, which would usually frustrate him even more.

As the parent who spent the most time with him on play dates and at preschool, I became Willie's interpreter and defender. When Willie knocked a kid down because he got overexcited in gym, I had to explain to the teachers and other parents that Willie hadn't meant to hurt anyone. Of course, to some people, this sounded like a cop-out. They thought Willie could pay attention, calm down, and keep his hands to himself if he tried. What they didn't see was that he was trying; it just wasn't working. Even close friends accused us of not disciplining Willie properly. We should be stricter— or less strict—depending on who was advising us. But no matter what we tried on our own, Willie wasn't getting better.

When Peter assigned a cover story on Attention Deficit Disorder for the magazine where he worked, the cover line read, "ADD, the scariest letters in the alphabet." Even at the time, I thought this was something of an overstatement. (C-A-N-C-E-R, for example, or A-I-D-S are supremely more terrifying.) ADD isn't a death threat. With early intervention and proper care at home and at school, many affected children become notably successful as adults because of the very energy and intensity that was so problematic in childhood. Since learning of Willie's ADD, we've met countless individuals who admit to being affected: doctors, lawyers, photographers, writers. I only wish that the help and support available now had been accessible to them and their families earlier on. Far too many of them had felt, or been made to feel, lazy, crazy, or stupid because of their "spaciness" or distractibility.

But why are so many people so eager to judge the behavior of such young children? In New York City today, standardized tests are required of four-year-olds whose parents are applying for them to private schools. Even certain "honors track" public schools require standardized tests of prekindergarteners. As expected, parents are anxious that their children's test scores be at peer level at the very least when their skills are evaluated.

But what is normal, and why do we think it so—because a school tells us so or a standardized test given to a child not a year out of diapers? Who is the final arbiter of what we expect from our children? Parents? Our family or friends? To all the parents of children with ADD who still wonder why their child just can't be "normal," I have this to say: What is normal and by whose definition? After all, to be normal is to be average. And who wants a merely average child?

Since I started keeping these journals, ADD has become well known to parents and educators nationwide, to the point where some critics insist that ADD—and learning and behavior problems in general—are being overdiagnosed and children put on medication such as Ritalin needlessly. In just two years, the backlash has already set in. Thomas Armstrong, Ph.D., is one of the most vicious critics (ironically his book, The Myth of the A.D.D. Child, *is published by a division of the same company that is publishing this book). Armstrong charges not only that ADD doesn't exist but also that a generation of mostly male students is being subjected to unneeded drugs as a way for their parents and teachers to exert so-called mind control. Would that Ritalin worked so well that just one dose turned a child with terrible self-esteem and adjustment problems—not to mention learning disabilities—into a well-behaved Rhodes scholar!*

Though I'm not a doctor or statistician, my feeling is that these criticisms, on a nationwide scale, are grossly misdirected. Psychological problems and learning disabilities are historically undertreated, not overtreated. And no responsible doctor would prescribe a pill for a child, then walk away with no further follow-up. Undoubtedly, there are children who are receiving Ritalin who don't need it. But equally true is the fact that there are thousands of children in America right now whose learning and self-esteem are suffering because of an undiagnosed behavioral or attentional disorder. It's my sincere hope that, by sharing my family's experience with ADD, other children and families might be helped.

WILLIE

March 2, 1989

The morning sickness that's been plaguing me throughout my pregnancy came back with a vengeance this morning, on my due date, no less. "Honey, I don't feel so great—maybe you'd better come home," I told my husband, Peter, when he called to check in on me in the late afternoon. After I had vomited yet again, my stomach cramps were worsening. "I can't believe I'm sick on my due date!" I groaned. "What if I'm too sick to give birth? What if I give the baby a stomach virus?"

Around 5 P.M., we noticed something odd. My stomach cramps seemed to be coming in regular intervals, ten minutes apart. "I don't think they're stomach cramps," Peter said. "What if they're contractions?"

A frantic phone call to the doctor confirmed Peter's suspicions. I was in labor! "You'd think I'd know if I were in labor," I grumbled, as we raced to the hospital. Because my water hadn't broken and I was dilated only two centimeters, the doctor on call sent me home to wait.

"Try to eat something," the resident suggested.

"Yeah, right," I said, clutching my stomach. The mere mention of food made me feel even more nauseous. Guiltily, Peter ate a sandwich at a nearby restaurant while I tried to focus on the fact that—despite all the waiting—it was almost time. I *was* in labor, though not active labor. Still, it wouldn't be long, now.

Peter and I went home to wait and time my contractions. By 2 A.M., I was in deep pain, with the contractions coming every five minutes. Though my water still hadn't broken, the pain of the contractions worried me. "We'd better call the doctor," Peter agreed.

My doctor sounded amazingly alert, given the time, when she

called back. (Had she ever slept through a beep? I wondered.) She insisted on talking to me, although I was so uncomfortable that I couldn't speak very well. "Sounds like it's time," she said after I groaned my way through a few contractions. "I can just tell by the way you sound."

We grabbed the suitcase we'd left by the door. The night doorman in our apartment building shouted, "Good luck!" when he realized where we were going. At 2 A.M. in our residential neighborhood, it wasn't hard to get a cab but the ride to the hospital felt surreal.

At the hospital, the delivery didn't progress very quickly but, since I'd opted for an epidural, I couldn't feel the contractions. But this is not to say I was comfortable—between the IV drip and the doctor breaking my water, I felt more trussed-up than a Thanksgiving turkey. I was completely disoriented (I'd left my glasses in my pocketbook, which didn't help). Squinting, I could just make out Peter's brown hair and plaid shirt as he paced nervously in the labor room. I guess I was just too out of it to notice the worried look on the nurse's face when she went to get the doctor at about 5 A.M. after I'd been in heavy labor for three hours.

"There's a problem," my obstetrician said grimly. She was staring at the fetal monitor, which measured the baby's heart rate and my contractions. "Every time you have a contraction, the baby's heart rate goes down. The umbilical cord must be wrapped around its neck. We're going to attach an internal fetal monitor just to confirm your baby is getting enough oxygen."

I glanced at Peter, who looked scared. Maybe it was the painkillers I'd taken, but I wasn't worried. Anyway, things were pretty much out of my power now. I'd done my job just carrying this baby for nine months and getting to the hospital without a hitch. If they needed to do an emergency C-section, so be it. I had complete faith in my doctor. She was a specialist in high-risk pregnancies—older mothers, in-vitro fertilizations, and the like. At twenty-three, I was the youngest and ostensibly healthiest patient in my doctor's practice. She'll know what to do if there's a problem, I thought.

After a bit more poking and prodding, the doctor's face brightened. The tests showed no signs of distress in our baby. Eventually, I became fully dilated and the doctor told me it was almost time to push. My labor nurse told me what to do. "Pretend you're passing a cantaloupe," she instructed. "*Ughh*," I grunted, as much out of disgust at the image as out of effort. "*Stop* pushing!" she said, after I'd pushed a few more times. The baby's head was "crowning," which meant he was ready to be delivered. Thinking I'd take much longer to crown, my obstetrician had left the room. "We've got to get you to a delivery room," the nurse said, wheeling me out hastily to the corridor. She tossed a set of yellow scrubs to Peter, who rushed to put them on before following us to the delivery room.

I, normally a modest person, was spread out on the gurney in front of what felt like about a dozen people: more nurses, the anesthesiologist, and a few other people in scrubs. "Okay, we've got to roll you onto the table," the labor nurse said as my obstetrician raced into the delivery room.

"You're kidding, right?" I said, my teeth clenched. Why couldn't they just get this baby out, already? Isn't that what I was here for?

"Okay, here he comes," the doctor said. "The cord is wrapped twice around his neck."

"Is he okay?" I hear Peter asking nervously.

And then, a new voice enters the squall: William Franklin — all six pounds and four ounces of him giving a healthy holler. I could barely see him through my tears of joy.

March 5, 1989

It's our first anniversary and, as our present to ourselves, we've got a beautiful baby to take home from the hospital. I can't believe how little he is! His whole head fits into the palm of my hand. He's got black hair now, but the doctor says that will fall out and new hair will grow in its place. His eyes are a deep blue, which surprised us because Peter and I both have brown eyes. Our friends and relatives all say that all Caucasian babies are born with blue eyes and that his eyes, like his hair, will change over time, but I'm not so sure.

Other than that, it's hard to tell whom he looks like. He's not exactly a Winston Churchill baby—he's not fat enough to have a lot of extra folds of skin around his neck or eyes. He's got a round head that reminds me of Peter's brother but with my father's eyebrows, thick dark stripes that make his pale skin seem even fairer. He's even cute when he cries—his whole face screws up and turns a remarkable shade of pink. It always makes me laugh, even though he's yelling his head off, his mouth formed in a perfect O.

Peter already has proven himself a doting, devoted father: changing Willie's diapers in the maternity ward and hunting down extra blankets for him when his tiny fingers felt cold. Coming home from the hospital to our apartment on Manhattan's Upper West Side, I have an overwhelming sense of serenity, despite my exhaustion.

My mother and Jolie, the grandmotherly Haitian baby-sitter we've hired to help out, are waiting for us at our apartment. Everyone except Willie and I seems to swing into high gear as soon as we arrive. My mother takes Willie and deposits him in his bassinet, a treasured hand-me-down from friends. Jolie brings me a cup of hot coffee in bed. (Already I am calling her "our" baby-sitter, because she seems intent on taking as good care of Peter and me as she is of Willie.) As soon as I'm settled, Peter rushes off to Zabar's, the West Side's famous gourmet delicatessen, to buy me bagels and lots of iron-rich cold cuts "to build up your strength for nursing," as he puts it. I lie back in bed, happy for all the pampering. Willie and I are off to a great start, I'm sure of it.

July 2, 1989

What's a new baby "supposed" to be like? At night, he sleeps little and is up every two hours for feedings, but we attribute this to his relatively small birth weight. (According to our child-care manuals, it's hard for any newborn to sleep over six hours until he weighs more than thirteen pounds.)

After four months, though, Peter and I are beginning to feel like we're going crazy. At the magazine where Peter works as an editor, he can barely stay awake with his "New Papa-itis," as some of his co-workers call it. At home, I nap almost every afternoon with the help of Jolie, who sleeps over on evenings when I get particularly desperate. I'm exhausted and frazzled from Willie's demanding schedule. Peter tries to help out, but he needs his own sleep to function at work. So much for my idea of writing and taking care of a newborn. The novel I've been working on got put on a shelf. I've been so tired that, when I try to work at the computer, the words blur together and I lose my concentration. It's discouraging and depleting. Not only am I not being a very good writer—with all the help that I need from Jolie, I'm afraid I'm not being a very good mother, either.

If it wasn't for how my heart melts every time I look at Willie, I'd think the whole thing had been a mistake. It's really hard when I talk on the phone to my friends from college. It seems as if they're all out on the fast track studying to be neurosurgeons or financiers, and I'm at home nursing and changing diapers. Peter tells me not to worry; I'll feel better when I get some sleep. But I think it's more than my near-constant state of exhaustion that is making me feel so blue. I didn't expect to feel so isolated or lonely after having a baby. Maybe if I had been working in an office with lots of people around me to have lunch with and to whom I could show off the baby, I'd feel a little more connected to the world.

Still, Willie's sweet face is a pretty great consolation. Sometimes I think I could just stare at him all day, the way his whole body seems to concentrate and gets still while he's nursing; how he kicks and bats at his musical mobile; the striped cotton-ball box he adores and punches at. He seems so smart to me—of course, I'm sure every mother thinks that of her own child. But when Willie is focused on something, it seems to totally absorb him. Even at four months, I can tell he really is special.

August 20, 1989

We take what is supposed to be a peaceful drive in the country. Ha! Between the bottles, diapers, baby wipes, and car seat, it looks as if we have enough in the backseat to travel cross-country. Though we live in New York, a city famous (or, rather, infamous) for its mass transportation, Willie's used to car drives and normally nods off within our first half hour on the road, his round face angelic-looking with its frame of now sandy-blond hair.

Something's bothering him today, though. Could he be teething at five months? He was okay on the ride up but got incredibly fussy on the way back home after we visited our friends at their house upstate. Eventually, he was screaming so much that I had to pull over to nurse him, hoping that would quiet him down. (How could he be hungry, though? I just fed him before we left our friends' house.) There we are, parked near a cornfield on a beautiful summer's day. *Wahh, wahh, wahh!* He starts crying as soon as I stop nursing him. I can't stand the noise, though Peter insists we should keep driving. I'm convinced the racket is going to cause us to have an accident. Who can think with all that screaming?

Peter turns on the radio—loud. It's no good, though. Willie screams the whole way back from Dutchess County before finally falling asleep minutes before we reach the city. My head is throbbing, and I feel totally frazzled. "Remember when we used to have conversations in the car?" I ask Peter. Those days are gone.

January 4, 1990

Willie sure loves his Gymboree class, which is held in the basement of a nearby church. There's a baby-size trampoline and safety bar, padded gym mats set up for tumbling, and a colorful jungle gym, in addition to the circle-time activities which include singing with a Raggedy Andy–style hand puppet named Gymbo. Though Willie likes to race-crawl around the big auditorium with me in hot pursuit (he doesn't walk yet, but neither do most of the other ten-month-olds), he doesn't seem particularly interested in playing with the other kids. Most of the other mothers seem to know one another already—I think one of them said they all live in the same building—and they cluster in the center of the room with their children. The rest of us "singles" sort of orbit around their cozy bunch like satellites.

Not that I mind, really; I'm glad Willie likes to play independently. He's involved enough at home with me and Jolie, and a frequent stream of visiting relatives. He's not shy at all around new people, either—none of the stranger anxiety that seems to plague so many other ten-month-olds. Actually, Willie is quite good-natured about being passed from lap to lap at family get-togethers. That is, if he could sit still for very long. Like any baby, he's pretty curious about investigating every nook and cranny of our apartment. Even with new people, he'll focus right away on their voices, or on a bright watch or necklace they're wearing, and is completely entranced. Other babies his age seem a little more lackadaisical. Willie seems so curious about everything, and once he finds something he likes to do, like ringing the bell on his toy telephone or playing with his Sesame Street pop-up toys, he does it over and over.

His favorite thing to do at Gymboree is to lie, stomach-down, on a cylindrical rubber tube while I roll him back and forth. He kicks his legs from side to side, his feet pedaling in the air and his arms windmilling as if he's trying to propel himself into the air. His eyes are bright with a look of sheer pleasure and the same intensity he used to get while playing with his musical mobile. "This reminds me of one of those movies from high-school biology class where the rhesus monkeys sway back and forth all day," I joke to one of the clique-y moms, who stares blankly at me as her child waits for a turn on the rubber tube. Oops, I realize, thinking about those monkeys again and remembering that they were autistic. No wonder this woman is looking at me funny.

"Okay, Willie, enough," I say, trying to pull him off the tube. We've been here twenty minutes and all Willie's done is roll back and forth the whole time. The main point of coming here, after all, is for a little socialization and to run around a bit more than he can in our apartment. But Willie doesn't want to move. He holds fast to the hand grips on the inner tube and starts to moan. His face looks knotted and his hands are clenched into fists. He's shaking his arms and his whole body's gone rigid. Willie can certainly put up a fight when he wants to. Sometimes he gets so worked up, he even hits or scratches Peter and me, just batting at whoever gets in his way. We've seen this at home but it also seems to happen a lot outside, like at the playground and here at Gymboree. (My mother thinks it's because he gets so frustrated not being able to communicate what he wants besides little words like "Da-da" or "cookie.")

"That's okay," the other mother says, as her child scampers off to another activity, apparently not wanting to get on the tube enough to endure Willie's noise and commotion. I don't know what Willie's problem is, why he gets so turf-conscious sometimes. That rubber tube is big enough for four or five children to play on. We're trying to teach Willie to share but, since he has no brothers or sisters, the message doesn't seem to be getting through. (I guess it doesn't help that, at home, he's got everything to himself.) Well, he's still young yet, I think, as I roll ten-month-old Willie back and forth on the tube for the 187th time in a row. He'll learn.

March 2, 1990

Willie's first birthday; we've made it through one year! He's still not walking but is getting close enough for me to buy a pair of blue Keds for him to wear to his birthday party. When my mother walks in and sees me trying to stuff his wriggling feet into the sneakers, she starts to laugh, reminding me of how, when I was Willie's age, my feet were so wide that I didn't fit into party shoes. This becomes an embarrassing topic of conversation for everyone at the party.

But even if it's just because of my big feet, I'm flattered to be compared to my son. He's getting to be so handsome, with those huge, blue eyes (I *knew* they wouldn't change color!) and his new-as-of-yesterday first haircut. His whole body has the proportions of a strong, young boy, not a baby anymore. If anyone thinks I in any way resemble Willie, the compliment is to me.

It just amazes me that, twelve short months ago, he was inside of me, a part of me. I never thought I'd miss being pregnant with him—all the terrible morning sickness—but I'm sad already to think of how fast the time is going. Peter says parenthood inspires instant nostalgia, and I agree. I miss nursing him even though I'm pleased he's starting to feed himself. We're lucky, he's not a fussy eater and never had colic. He loves to be cuddled and kissed—he was never one of those difficult babies who hated to be touched. But, of course, now all he wants to do is move, move, move.

I see him cruising around the coffee table, not walking, but balancing against it to swing himself around toward a plate of peanut-butter-and-jelly sandwiches I made for all the children at the party. Willie takes a big bite and squeals with pleasure at the unfamiliar taste and consistency.

I have no idea what he makes of this celebration. We went to the birthday party of a friend's child last week, and Willie got kind of anxious, crying and getting fussy when the cake was being served. (He even scratched Peter in the face as we tried to wrestle him into his snowsuit at the end.) It seemed as if the singing somehow scared him. Or maybe it was the applause after the little girl blew out the candles. Come to think of it, Willie has never liked loud noises. A car horn or even Peter's loud sneezes can make him burst into tears. But that birthday party was kind of odd, actually, because it seemed as if he was having fun until the noise. Of course, he's also been battling a cold so perhaps he just wasn't feeling well.

I go over to pick him up as Peter dims the lights to bring out the birthday cake. Everyone sings "Happy Birthday" while Willie looks wide-eyed at the candles.

"Okay, honey," I tell Willie, as my brother-in-law points our video camera at us. "Blow out the candles."

Willie looks hypnotized by the two tiny candles (one for his age and one to grow on). He points his finger dangerously close to the flame. *Whooh!* Instinctively, I blow out the candles and everyone applauds. Willie swivels his head toward me and bursts into tears.

"It's okay," I say, trying to pull him close. Willie is thrashing in my arms, trying to get down.

"Oh," I hear someone say, admonishingly. "He wanted to blow out the candles himself."

What was I supposed to do, I think, let him burn his fingers? Can a one-year-old even blow out birthday candles by himself?

Peter picks up Willie to comfort him, but he still seems fussy. I look at Peter, concerned. I feel bad, as though I ruined Willie's party for him. But this is exactly the way he behaved on our friend's daughter's birthday. Maybe all the noise and excitement are just too much for him, though the other young children at the party don't seem to mind.

My mother-in-law comes over to help and must see I look upset because she says, "Don't worry, Peter acted the same way as a baby when there were lots of people around." I nod. I've heard the stories of Peter's "difficult" infancy before. At four, he got so overwhelmed on his first day of nursery school that he wouldn't leave his mother's side. Eventually, they decided to keep him home for the year and he didn't start school until kindergarten at age five.

So Willie comes by it honestly, I figure, cutting deep wedges in the chocolate cake. I'm just sorry he doesn't seem to be enjoying his birthday.

June 10, 1990

We're meeting some friends with kids at a playground on the Upper East Side. It's not our usual stomping ground—since we're

West Siders, we tend to go to a playground near our house. This park is adjacent to the East River. We can see people walking dogs and pushing baby strollers on the wide pathway that looks over the water. It's a pretty cityscape, with Roosevelt Island and Queens in the distance, and I'd like to get closer since we're not in this neighborhood very often but I don't dare it with Willie. He's so rambunctious these days, I'd be afraid he'd jump in the river or something while our backs were turned.

We're definitely in the "chase stage" since Willie started to walk two months ago. At fifteen months old, he's very independent, but we don't dare leave him alone for a second. Like today, going into the playground to meet our friends, Willie is tugging and straining to get out of his stroller. But there's no way I'm going to let him run in on his own. Willie is too much of a daredevil—always clambering up the highest slide or rushing into the middle of the swings if the gate's not locked. He's already been knocked to the ground once at our playground near home by a moving swing before I could stop him. He seems to have no sense of danger. Is it the age? Other children his age appear to be much more careful.

Our friend's daughter is playing in the sandbox. Thankfully, Willie is more interested in her purple shovel than in putting his life at risk running up to the big kids on the seesaw. Peter and I sit down on the edge of the sandbox and chat with our friends while the two kids parallel-play. Willie is digging a hole and refilling it with sand. Suddenly, our friend's daughter reaches over in the area where Willie's working. I move toward them because I know Willie can get really territorial in the sandbox. I've seen him hit other kids when he doesn't want to share. Our friend's daughter sticks her shovel in the tunnel Willie's building. "No!" Willie cries, balling up his fists by his sides. "Come on, Willie," I say. "Just play nicely with Amanda." But Willie doesn't play nicely with Amanda, and I'm starting to feel nervous. Every time she moves near him, he seems to get more upset. He turns his back on her rudely and Peter and I get red faced, trying to cover up his behavior by acting as if he's just gotten distracted building something on the other side. Now Peter and I are both in the sandbox, hovering around Willie.

"I guess Willie doesn't like Amanda that much," our friend's mother observes.

"Oh, no, it's not that," I explain. "He can get a little weird at the playground. You know how it is."

She looks puzzled. I guess she doesn't know how it is.

"Boys are just naturally more aggressive," our friend's husband says.

I don't know about that. Other little boys don't seem to get into fights in the playground as much as Willie does. Even at the park near our house, he's always swatting other kids when they get too close or if they try to borrow his sand toys. All the other children here are playing quietly, sharing pails and shovels. It's only Willie who's having a problem.

October 2, 1990

I'm pregnant and thrilled, except for the thought that I might get such hideous morning sickness the way I did with Willie. Though I still feel that it's a little early to actually have another child, Peter and I want kids spaced two years apart so they could be close, the way I was with my eighteen-months-older sister and Peter was with his brother, who's three years younger.

I hope it's a boy, though we don't have any brilliant boys' names, yet. We like Phillip and Steven, but Peter has cousins named that already. (We're Jewish, and it's considered bad luck to name a child after a family member who's living.) Peter likes Alexander, but there are a lot of Alexanders around right now and we don't want to be too trendy. We both like Nicholas. For girls, we like Olivia and Nina. Fortunately, we have nine months to decide!

I can't believe I have a little person inside of me. Actually, the baby's just a bunch of cells right now, but every time I look at Willie, I think of the baby's little feet or hands—how it's really *somebody* growing in there. I'm more keenly aware of it this time than I was with Willie.

I'm much more excited this time and less nervous than I was with Willie. Part of it is that I'm not feeling quite so sick. Though they say the second one is always easier, I'm also out and about more than I was when I was pregnant with Willie, and I think that's made me feel better about myself. Though I'm still struggling with my novel and trying to get freelance writing assignments, I've started working this fall at a job in the alumni office of an East Side private school. They were looking for someone to edit and write their publications and organize reunions and fundraising efforts. They're being very flexible with my hours, so I can work mostly from home.

We're also trying to get Willie into a routine so he'll have his own friends and his own activities by the time the baby comes in May. Twice a week, he attends a two-hour play group with six other children who are all nearly eighteen months old. As opposed to Gymboree, which was so challenging for him, this class has a lot less running around and the emphasis is on socialization, which Willie obviously needs.

But even here, he can't seem to figure out how to compose himself, how to make the transition to being in a group. At the beginning of each session, the other kids seem more reticent than Willie. On the other hand, this is how my charming son makes an entrance: He runs all around the room like a wild man, knocking toys off the shelves and interrupting whatever little puzzles or games the other children there are quietly playing. He's like a tornado. Just one foot in the door and he can change the whole tone of the room from one of peace and quiet to total pandemonium.

He can't even seem to focus on the teacher, who tries to help him settle down with one activity. If she says hello or tries to show him something, he doesn't even look at her; he just keeps twisting his head, trying to look behind her toward the toy shelves. Usually, I spend the first half of the class trying to put everything back that Willie's knocked down. "Oh, never mind," the teacher says, about the mess. But I don't want Willie to think he can just toss things all over the place and not have to clean up. But when I try to get Willie to help, it becomes a tug-of-war with me going toward the mess and Willie wanting to go in the other direction to make more.

He just doesn't seem to know what to do in these situations, and I don't know how to help him. Everyone likes him, though. It's hard not to, despite his whirlwind behavior—he's so enthusiastic about everything in the class, be it finger painting or doing some crazy dance with scarves. What he likes best is at the end of the class when the teacher puts on a Raffi tape, loud, and we all march around in a circle smashing cymbals or maracas. Willie whirls around faster and faster until he collapses in a heap on the floor. He gets so excited, his whole body shakes and he covers his face with his hands. But, when I peek through, it's as if he hardly recognizes me. His eyes are glinting wildly. It's not until we get outside to the street that the cold air seems to finally calm him down. I guess he's having a good time. It's hard to tell, though; he doesn't slow down long enough for me to really see him do much of anything but move.

February 16, 1991

Jolie has made a discovery: an indoor kids' play space that she was introduced to by another baby-sitter. With the bad weather, I thought it would be a lifesaver to have a place where Willie could run around. Now that I'm trying to write *and* work from home, it's really distracting to have Willie at home all the time, and it's still far too cold for Jolie to take him to the park.

The play space is in the auditorium of a local community center. There are lots of the same jungle gym–type equipment they had at Gymboree: climbing toys, a mini-trampoline, and also lots of art supplies, a toy kitchen, and a plastic castle with a slide that Willie loves. The only problem is the way Willie handles being around the dozen or so other kids that push and shove to get onto the same equipment. When I'm there with him, he climbs onto one piece of equipment, as he did with the inner tube when he was a baby, and fights everyone else who tries to play near him. Though I've explained to him countless times that he has to take turns, it doesn't help. He's not territorial like this at his play group. I thought he had grown out of this stage already.

What I don't understand about it is that I can tell he'd really like to make friends with the other boys his age. I see him standing near where they cluster together by the jungle gym. But it's as if he doesn't know what to do to get their attention. He'll just get right up in their faces. It's intimidating to them. Why can't he just sit at the art table and color like some of the other children? I envy the other moms and baby-sitters who can sit on the sides, just chatting and relaxing. I can't ever do that with Willie. If I leave him alone, pandemonium will break loose.

There's so much else I *like* to do with him at home—sing songs, bake cookies, and watch him make what he calls his "ghost paintings"—one of his more creative ideas where he drips Elmer's glue on colored paper and lets it dry. I love spending time just with him on our own. Who needs the aggravation of a crowded auditorium and a hundred kids running wild? Maybe it's also my temperament as a huge, pregnant lady. Since I've hit my last trimester, I just don't have the energy to constantly chase after him. If Jolie can deal with him here, fine. She has three grown boys of her own and never seems to find anything strange about Willie's behavior. Maybe it's me. Have I gotten more grouchy since I got pregnant?

May 6, 1991

Nicholas Frederick was born three days ago, a much easier delivery than his older brother. I'd had none of the debilitating morning sickness I had with Willie, gaining weight all too easily this time around. The delivery itself was much less frightening, too, perhaps because I was a veteran at it but also because Nicholas suffered none of the traumas that attended Willie's birth.

His vital signs were all strong during my labor; we needed none of the intimidating internal fetal monitoring equipment that Willie's dipping heart rate had required. I knew enough to plan ahead before going to the hospital. I put in my contact lenses so I could see exactly what was going on and I felt much more in control. I was so relaxed, in fact, that I spent most of my time in the labor room discussing favorite books with my very affable obstetrician.

The two experiences were so different—this time around, there was none of the edge of panic and fear that accompanied my labor with Willie. It was hard to believe there wasn't going to be some catch with Nicky's birth. "That's it?" I asked, when the delivery nurse told me it was time to push. Peter and I didn't have to wait long, though, to see for ourselves that our baby was fine. After only half an hour of pushing, Nicky's head was crowning.

I couldn't help but laugh when the doctor pulled him out. To me, he looked like a perfect little duck, brown with blood, squawking and flapping his arms in displeasure at his welcome to the world. In what seems like a supreme act of sibling one-upmanship, Nicky's umbilical cord was wrapped three times around his neck. It sounds impossible, but Peter swears he saw it himself. Nonetheless, there was no crisis despite his rather elaborate necklace. He seemed so tiny but actually weighed six pounds and nine ounces—five more ounces than Willie at birth. He had the same head of dark hair with a whorl in the back in the exact same place and hazel eyes the same color as my own. (So much for the theory that all Caucasian babies are born with blue eyes.) What amazed me most about Nicky, though, were his long, elegant fingernails that had been growing in utero. *My easy boy,* I thought, as Nicky nuzzled my neck and promptly fell asleep on my chest in the recovery room.

Already I'm feeling nostalgic for pregnancy. Since Peter and I want only two children (since each of us comes from a small family, that's what feels right to us), Nicky is the last baby we're planning on having. No more kicks inside of me; no more proud stares at myself sideways in the mirror, amazed at what my own body could do. In a year, I would be finished with nursing, never again to have that feeling of nourishing my child in such an immediate way. I stared at Nicky's tiny fingers, the thin, translucent nails I would need to trim in the nursery. How could I love anyone as much as I love Willie? I almost feel disloyal thinking about it, but Nicky's completely won me over.

I'm a big show-off with him later in my room, expertly nursing and diapering him, much to the pleasure of his grandmothers, who seem to magically appear before official visiting hours. (Sadly, there are no grandfathers here to share the occasion. I never knew Peter's father, who died in 1980, long before I ever met Peter; and my father and stepmother moved to Santa Fe last year.)

My bluster fades when we arrive home from the hospital. Willie is napping and, while Jolie and Peter take Nicholas, I go into Willie's room to see him—he wasn't allowed to visit me at the hospital, and I've never been separated from him for this long before.

For his birthday in March, my mother gave him a "big-boy bed." (We tried to make a big deal out of it because we knew we'd need the crib for Nicholas but didn't want Willie to feel he was getting displaced by the baby.) Seeing him stretched out asleep, I think he looks so peaceful but HUGE compared with Nicholas. I'm so happy to see him, I start to cry. My crying wakes him up and he jumps into my arms but, because my stomach muscles are still so stretched out from the pregnancy, I almost drop him.

I've been preparing for this moment. "Look, Willie," I say, leading him into my room. Before I went into the hospital, I got Willie a special treat: a Teenage Mutant Ninja Turtle made out of candy. "Wow!" Willie says, delighted, munching off a piece of its head.

"Would you like to meet your baby brother?"

Willie nods eagerly.

We go into the nursery, where Jolie hands me Nicky. I hold him down gingerly, not really knowing how Willie's going to react. Willie is very excited, standing on his tiptoes, which he does a lot, lately. He smiles broadly at the white, blanket-clad package being held down for his inspection.

"*Auugh,*" he says, shocked at Nicky's tiny, pink face.

"Willie, say hi to Nicholas," I tell him.

"Doesn't he talk?" Willie asks, looking concerned.

"He's too little to talk. You're the big boy now. You're almost two and a half, and he's just three days old. See how little his hand is compared to yours?" I move Willie's hand closer to Nicholas's, which is just peeking out of his swaddling.

"Gimme five, Nicholas!" Willie says.

I move Nicky's hand in the direction of Willie's, who lightly taps it. I'm amazed by how good he is around the baby. So far no rivalry, though I suppose it's a little early to tell.

"Maybe he wants a block," Willie says, running off to his room to get Nicky some building blocks.

I call after him that Nicky is too young to play with blocks, but Willie comes back with an armload of them anyway. "Here," he says, tossing them toward me and Nicky. I pull Nicky away from the airborne, wooden blocks. Willie runs away giggling, knowing he's done something mischievous. Maybe I spoke too soon about that rivalry business. . . .

August 4, 1991

Why are two children four times the work of one? I'm still on maternity leave from my job at the school (it was very convenient that I gave birth right before summer vacation, when the work in the alumni office is very light). Between Nicky's feedings and Willie's still getting up so early—5 A.M. is still his average—we're exhausted. I didn't think I could be more tired than I was with Willie, but having two kids stretches me to new heights of fatigue.

Peter is still at the same magazine and fortunately, his hours are pretty predictable. Still, just making dinner is a major production. Nicky always needs to nurse around 6 P.M., just as Willie wants my attention because he's starting to get bored waiting for Peter to come home (and Jolie is long gone by then). I thought I'd found a good solution when I'd let both of them sit on my lap while I gave Nicky a bottle of expressed milk or formula. Nicky is fine with this arrangement but Willie always gets too wriggly and slithers off. Why can't he just sit still like Nicky? Even at three months, Nicky in some ways seems more composed than Willie. Of course, Willie is older. Isn't it natural for him to want to run around all the time?

November 30, 1991

After a summer at the same play group where he went last fall (I wanted the continuity, given all the disruptions of having a baby in the house), Willie's enrolled in a new play school two afternoons a week. We looked at a couple of preschools in our neighborhood and, although there were many more programs for two-year-olds on the East Side, we thought it would be better to have him at a local school, given that we'd also have to think about Nicholas's schedule. I didn't see commuting with a six-month-old and a two-and-a-half-year-old, if I could help it.

Willie's school this year is a little more "school-like" than the play group. It's bigger, for one thing, with sixteen children in the class, a head teacher, and an assistant. It's a drop-off program, so I don't stay with him. I was very proud of Willie that he separated so easily. He didn't cry or fuss at all, unlike many of his classmates.

Nonetheless, I was hoping "real" school would calm Willie down a bit. He's fine when he's playing by himself with Legos or toy people, but he still has trouble settling down in a group. When I drop him off, he rushes around the room the same way he did in his play group while the other children seem to have a much easier time sitting down at the tables set up with crayons and puzzles.

The teachers seem to like him, though, especially the assistant, who is a woman in her fifties who says he's "full of vinegar." She raised four sons of her own and says they were "active" like Willie. I don't know how she stood it.

Willie gives us very little trouble at home, though he's still getting up early. We're tired all the time and Willie seems to be,

too. He'll take long, two-hour naps every day after lunch. (I've noticed his behavior is a lot wilder at school if he hasn't gotten
enough sleep that day.) Yet he continues to be very indulgent of
Nicholas, despite the fact that Nicky has started to crawl and,
therefore, gets into all of Willie's toys and precious Ninja Turtle
collection much more than before.

With me and Peter, Willie is usually a true joy to be
around—none of the "terrible twos" our friends complain about.
He's grown into a sturdy, happy little fellow, curious about everything and eager to learn. The other day, we were walking back
from the playground, and he became fascinated by some flowers
in a garden. Though he'd been particularly difficult in the sandbox that afternoon, fighting with another two-year-old about who
could build a castle in a certain corner, squaring off with him finally and pushing him to the ground, Willie seemed to change
into a different person as he stared at the flowers, caressing their
petals carefully so they wouldn't be damaged. At home, he can be
unusually considerate and emotional, hugging and thanking us
repeatedly for simple things like getting a bubble bath. I don't understand Willie's strange behavior, or the Jekyll-and-Hyde way he
seems to snap in and out of it.

When we go to the store or while we're waiting for the bus,
he's got a terrible habit of following interesting-looking strangers,
wanting to touch their clothes or hair, or trying to get their attention by yelling out things like: "Hey, fat lady!" or "Tall man in the
cap!" Not only is this dangerous to do in the middle of New York
City, it's also embarrassing for Peter and me. People often frown
and stare at us wondering why we can't control our child. He
doesn't do it to be mean, I want to tell them. It's as if he doesn't
understand the boundaries of where his own body ends and theirs
begin.

Recently, as a special treat, we took him to look at the suits of
armor exhibit at the Metropolitan Museum. But instead of looking at the various swords and helmets, he spent most of his time
trying to attract the attention of the older boys nearby. "Hey, kid
in the green shirt!" he'd say, getting right up in the other boy's

face. Though some of them seemed to think this was funny, if not exactly pleasant, Willie never knew when to take the hint and back off. Peter and I would try to attract his attention to something else, but once Willie fixated on children he wanted to play with, he was locked onto them, even if they obviously weren't interested. The more they'd try to walk away from him, the more Willie would pursue them.

It was heartbreaking to watch. The other kids thought he was so weird and even started to make fun of him, imitating him to their friends. But the worst thing was, even as they were teasing him, Willie *still* didn't get it. I could feel my face getting hotter and hotter. Finally, I told Peter I wanted to leave. We didn't even discuss it. Peter wanted to get out of there, too, I could tell.

We don't know why Willie acts this way, let alone how to control it. Though we haven't really talked about it, I know Peter thinks Willie's behavior is odd, too. None of our friends' kids behave so erratically, nor do any of the children in his play groups. But Peter and I don't have enough time to sleep, let alone get into a big discussion about Willie. What with Nicholas, my job at the school, Peter's work, and everything else in our lives, we feel as though we've been under siege. Is there some secret to getting kids to behave and, if so, how come we're the only parents who haven't discovered it?

May 10, 1992

We've been getting calls from the teacher of Willie's play-school class that Willie's having what she calls temper tantrums, kicking and screaming at the teachers and other children. "Is something going on at home that might be making him angry?" she wondered. A death or divorce? Had we hired a new baby-sitter? Peter and I almost laughed: Willie was still getting up one or two times a night and rising for good at 5:30 A.M. With another baby in the house and Willie's demanding schedule, most nights, we're too tired to talk, let alone argue with each other, and Jolie was our lifeline. I'd rather fire myself than get rid of Jolie.

I told the teacher I thought the problem was mostly logistical. To get Willie to school on time those two afternoons a week, we have to cut short his nap, which he still desperately needs because he gets up so early. "He's probably just tired and cranky," I say.

"He really loves school," the teacher admits. "When he's in a good mood, he's really a pleasure." Alarmed, I look at Peter. Is it really so bad the rest of the time?

October 17, 1992

Despite Willie's problems last fall, his school was happy to enroll him again for the morning "threes" class, which lasts from 9 A.M. to 11:45 every day. I figure Willie won't be so tired with a morning schedule. Last year, I had to wake him up from his nap to get to the afternoon class on time. I always wondered if he wasn't particularly difficult because he was always tired then.

Willie's teacher is new to the school and new to teaching, a woman in her forties who has three daughters of her own and decided to change careers after fifteen years selling real estate. Though I'm worried about her relative inexperience, she'll have an assistant teacher with her all day and there are two other specialists for music and art. Out of the class of sixteen, there are only four other boys, none of whom seem particularly active or outgoing to me, but I try to look on the bright side. Maybe the unusual ratio of girls to boys might force Willie to play with some of the girls more often instead of being so rough-and-tumble on his own.

But Willie stuck out like a sore thumb in the waiting room the first day. While all the other children clung to their mother's or baby-sitter's skirts, Willie was tracing brisk circles around the room, singing the Oompa-Loompa song from *Willie Wonka and the Chocolate Factory*. Some of the other parents and I thought this was pretty cute but when the teacher came in, she looked straight at Willie and said sternly, "Who's making all the *noise?*"

Last night, I got a strange phone call from his teacher. Peter and I were just returning from a rare evening out to dinner and a movie. "Why is she calling so late?" Peter mouthed to me, when he realized who it was. Her voice was anxious and tense. "We're having a problem with Willie," the teacher said, explaining that Willie was getting "wild" in the gym. "I understand this is a pattern with him."

"What do you mean?" I ask, confused, not liking the way she seemed to have already branded him a "bad" boy. "I never heard about any problems in the gym before."

"He's playing Crash Dummies. That's not allowed. He crashes into the other children while they're riding their scooters."

Aha, I think, nodding. The Crash Dummies have been popular this fall. Based on the real crash test mannequins that car companies used to test safety features, a series of Crash Dummy toys and comic books were recently released featuring the funny-looking characters that children break apart and put back together.

"Willie loves the Crash Dummies," I explain.

"Well, I don't like violent toys for children," his teacher said, primly.

"They're not exactly violent," I say, getting annoyed. "They're supposed to teach auto *safety*." Obviously, Willie's behavior in the gym was unacceptable, but it was not this woman's place at 10:30 P.M. on a weeknight to be giving me a lecture about what toys to give my child.

"Nonetheless," the teacher continued, "you need to explain to Willie that he will have to sit out if he crashes in gym."

I stare at the phone, a little surprised. Why was she being so hostile? Didn't most teachers try to work with parents instead of trying to pin blame? I tell her I'll talk to Willie about the crashing and explain to him that crashing is not for people.

"She's got a real attitude," Peter said, when I hung up. I agree but she's still Willie's teacher and I don't want Willie to be crashing in the gym, either. Why does he have to be so wild? Why can't he just play like all the other kids?

November 17, 1992

Willie's problems at school have gotten worse. He fusses and fights with me almost from the minute it's time to get ready to the minute I drop him off at his class. The late-night calls have increased to twice a week, and his teacher is getting increasingly negative about Willie. He's having tantrums, she says, when it's time to put away toys and when he plays in the gym. Additionally, she tells us, Willie's shouted at her and the assistant teacher.

"I think Willie has a problem with authority," she tells me during one of her late-night phone calls. I think she has a problem with assertive little boys. Apparently, last week, Willie called her and the assistant teacher "stupid idiots." When she told him he wasn't permitted to use that kind of language, he improvised, calling them "a plant" and "an old wallpaper" instead.

"Isn't that an improvement?" I ask. "At least he didn't say 'stupid.' "

But Willie's teacher is not impressed by my son's copious vocabulary. "Willie's behavior is scaring the other children," she says avidly. "They don't want to play with him—he can be so aggressive."

The longer she speaks, the more frustrated and impatient I become. Surely other three-year-olds in the history of the school have yelled in class, too. Had their parents been called and told their children had a problem with authority?

November 25, 1992

I decide to mention Willie's behavior in school to the pediatrician when I'm in with Nicholas for his vaccinations. "Does every child yell like this?" I ask, embarrassed.

The pediatrician tells me not to worry. "Oppositional behavior," as he calls it, is common among three-year-olds and should go away on its own. He laughs when I tell him how Willie substituted "old wallpaper" for the offending "stupid idiot."

"He's obviously very creative," the pediatrician says, still smiling.

I stare at him blankly. They never call Willie creative in school. In fact, his teacher rarely says anything positive about him. Why is it so hard for her to appreciate the good things about my son—his sense of humor, his vocabulary, his wonderful singing?

November 30, 1992

I get another phone call from Willie's teacher, this one at 6 P.M., right while I'm in the middle of making dinner. Why doesn't this woman have the common courtesy to call in the afternoon instead of in the evening when I'm always so busy? I turn off the burner and try to get the boys involved in some coloring books so I can talk on the phone. Nicky, who's eighteen months now, has a different idea about what to do with his crayons. He tears off the paper wrappers and shreds them on the kitchen table. Willie, on the other hand, is happily obedient, using bold, broad strokes to color a dinosaur in his coloring book. Unlike the other kids in his class—something his teacher has pointed out with almost gleeful foreboding in one of her many late-night phone calls—Willie never manages to stay inside the lines.

"I want to let you know something," the teacher says, as I brace myself for another litany of all the terrible things Willie's done wrong that day.

"We've been having this problem in circle time," the teacher says.

"What problem is that?" I ask.

The teacher explains that she's been trying to get each child to stand up and make a three-minute speech each day.

"Aren't they a little young for public speaking?" I say, surprised. Most adults I know couldn't talk extemporaneously for that amount of time. Why does she expect it of three-year-olds?

"Willie talks in circles," she complains. "It's totally age inappropriate. Yesterday, for example, he got up and said, 'On the way to school I saw dog poop...I saw dog poop...Dog poop . . . Poop.' He started to laugh and was laughing so hard, I finally told him to sit down."

"Sounds age appropriate to me," I say, smiling in spite of myself. I reach over to stroke Willie's face. "Mama," he says sweetly and kisses my hand.

What was happening in school that brought out the worst in Willie? Or what was happening with this teacher that she just saw this catalogue of bad behavior? She doesn't know anything about my child, and I'm beginning to doubt she knows anything about three-year-olds in general. Certainly, she has to be out of touch if she doesn't know that toilet language passes for witty repartee among the preschool set.

"I'm not sure you recognize the seriousness of the situation," the teacher chides. "This could be a very grave problem with your son. I just got back from a teachers' conference where they discussed something called 'sequencing.' I think this is what Willie has so much trouble with. His sentences don't flow logically from each other. He can't answer 'why' questions. It's all part of a package. . . ."

I try to digest this. Willie certainly has a problem with his pronunciation—he seems to be suffering from the same kind of lisp I had as a child—but I'd never noticed that he had a problem with "why" questions before.

"What can we do about it?" I ask, concerned.

"You need to redirect him onto the next thought or sentence."

"Redirect him?" One conference and suddenly the teacher is throwing all this jargon at me.

"How it works is he says something; then you ask him a question; then he says something else; then you ask more about the subject."

"Oh," I say, wondering why she thinks this is such a big discovery. "You mean *talking* to him?"

I get off the phone with her as fast as I can. "Willie," I say, before getting back to our dinner, which is slowly smoldering on the stove. "Why do you need an umbrella when it's raining out?"

Willie looks up, surprised, from his coloring book. *Don't you know?* he seems to think. "Because da rain is fallin' and you get wet!" he shouts, laughing at the thought of his silly mommy in the rain.

"Good answer," I say.

I know Willie can be difficult, even disruptive, in school, but what is this woman's problem? He can answer a "why" question.

December 17, 1992

Peter and I have been called in for a conference with the preschool's director. Her office is attached to a big room with cubbies that doubles as a waiting room and art room for Willie's class. Peter and I sit on child-size chairs as we wait for the principal to get off a phone call with another set of parents. We can hear her voice rise and fall in a friendly tone that is completely foreign to us from all the discussions we've ever had with her about Willie.

When she's done with her phone call, she sits down at the minisize art table. She's young, and this is only her second year at the school. Her long maroon dress seems overly matronly, as if she's trying to look older to gain authority.

"I'm not going to beat around the bush," the director says. "Willie's teacher says she can't handle him in class anymore." The director says she thinks it would be best if we didn't bring him back after Christmas vacation. Because the school is so small, there's no other threes class to switch Willie into, assuming the school would even be willing to try.

Peter and I stare at each other, our faces mirror images of fear and panic. "Well, what are we supposed to do with him for the rest of the year?" Peter says.

"We think you ought to look into some testing," the director tells us, evenly. "There are some troubling signs that you ought to have examined."

"Such as what?" I ask, numbly.

"The tiptoe walking, for example," the director tells us.

As long as Willie had been walking, he'd had a tendency to go on tiptoes whenever he got excited. "What's wrong with tip-toes?" I ask defensively, remembering that I walked on my toes for years as a child. I could still remember the shocked look on my mother's face as I bent my feet over and walked on point at age six without the benefit of toe shoes.

The director looks at Peter as if to find a more sympathetic listener. "It's not just the tiptoe walking; it's the water play, too."

"What's wrong with water play?" Peter asks, in the same surprised tone as mine.

"It's the way he gets so caught up with the textures and the shapes—as if he can't stop playing with them. It could be a sign of brain damage."

"*Brain damage?!*" Peter and I shout. This would seem like a very bad joke if she wasn't describing our child.

"Let me get this straight," I say firmly. "You think Willie has brain damage because he likes to play with water and walks on his toes?"

"They're two very distinct signs."

I shake my head. The table and cubbies are a blur of light wood. I want to grab my coat and run out of here as fast as I can. Peter, on the other hand, is completely, chillingly still. In our hearts, we both know Willie's behavior isn't entirely normal: the temper tantrums; the wild look he gets in his eyes when he's overexcited; the way we feel that we sometimes can't reach him no matter what we do or say. Though the director and Willie's teacher had bungled things miserably this year, even I have to admit that maybe they see something in Willie that I am denying.

"What do you recommend?" Peter asks, gravely.

The director gives us the name of a school on the Upper East Side and shows us its catalogue. I flip through almost half the brochure before I realize it's a school for children who are emotionally disturbed.

"I know what you're thinking," the director says, seeing my face fall. "But don't dismiss the place before you see it. They're very smart there about all different kinds of children."

I scan the admissions form. "It says here that you have to be five to apply."

"Well, that's a year from now," the director says.

"No, it's not," I say, trying to swallow my disgust. "Willie will be four next year, *not* five."

I don't know which I'm more offended by—the fact that they're trying to shunt us off to a school for the mentally handicapped or the fact that Willie's been at this school for two years already and they don't even know his age. How can they think they have a right to any opinion about his intellectual or behavioral capacities if they don't even know the basic, defining fact of his age? Moreover, if they don't know how old he is, how can they be judging what's age-appropriate behavior for him during activities like circle time and gym?

I look at Peter, expecting him to be ready to storm out in a wake of expletives but, to my surprise, he's taken out a notebook from his jacket pocket and is writing down the name of the school the director recommended and two doctors' names the director is giving us: a pediatric neurologist and a child psychologist. He stands up and shakes the director's hand before we leave the building. I feel paralyzed, unable to breathe, let alone be polite.

"We've got to talk to these doctors," Peter says, when we get outside.

"They don't know how old Willie is, why should we trust their neurological opinions?"

"How can we not go?" Peter asks, plainly. "If there's something wrong with Willie, we need to know the truth so we can do something about it."

The truth—what's the truth? That Willie is impulsive, sometimes impossible with his peers but also so endearing and sweet with his brother that he could make me cry when he sings him a lullaby? Is it a physical problem, as the director is implying? Willie has enough small motor control to be able to build fantastic block buildings but can't keep his hands to himself in a play group. What's the truth about a child like that?

"I'm willing to believe we screwed up by putting him in a

school that was inflexible and incompetent," I tell Peter, defensively. "I'm even willing to believe that we're bad parents, that we never set proper limits for Willie or that we've been too indulgent. But brain damage? You're never going to get me to believe it."

Peter shakes his head, as determined as I am to do what he thinks is right for Willie. "We have to at least see these doctors."

January 11, 1993

To please Peter, I've set up an appointment for Willie with the psychologist that the school director recommended. Her office is near the Metropolitan Museum—the scene of Willie's suit of armor fiasco. The psychologist greets us in the waiting room of her office, which is decorated with art posters from the museum's gift shop. She is an unusually tall woman with high, poufy hair, which makes her seem even bigger than she already is. Her voice sounds similarly overblown and breathy with the saccharine, excessively comforting tone many people use with children when they're unaccustomed to them.

She tells me she's spoken on the phone with the director, who explained about Willie's many problems at school. Willie, who is playing with a puzzle in the waiting room, looks up as he hears the name of his former school and its dreaded director. I'm surprised at the psychologist for talking about Willie so negatively while he's right in the room with us. Hadn't she ever heard the one about little pitchers having big ears?

But she's all bouffant and smiles as she takes Willie's hand and leads him into her inner office. I get up to follow, but she holds her hand out like a school crossing guard. "No, Mommy," she says, in her syrupy voice. "Parents *aren't* allowed."

I watch with mild alarm as Willie follows the psychologist out of the waiting room. Despite her expensive designer suit and framed Ph.D. on the wall, it strikes me as odd that she's keeping me out of the testing room. I'm not going to like her, that much is clear. (Why should I like anyone who calls another grown-up "Mommy?") But as long as Willie feels comfortable enough to go with her, that's more important.

The tests last about an hour and a half, and afterwards the psychologist deposits him back with me, Willie tiptoeing nervously and the psychologist smiling as widely as ever. Uncharitably, I think her mouth must hurt by the end of the day. I wonder if it gets on the nerves of her other patients but, then again, I don't see any other patients in the waiting room. I wonder if her practice has been hit by the recession that's affected almost every business in New York right now. Every day in the paper we read about some new corporate layoff. Many people can't afford to go to psychologists anymore, even if they need them. We don't even know if the health maintenance organization that has just recently taken over our insurance at Peter's magazine will pay for this appointment, but there's no question in our minds about going. We need to see if this doctor thinks the claims of "brain damage" by Willie's old school are as patently ridiculous as I think they are.

January 28, 1993

The follow-up appointment for me and "Daddy" comes a week later, and the news isn't good. The waiting room is once again empty as the psychologist ushers us into her office, smiling as broadly as ever. A framed de Kooning poster of a bandaged woman hangs over her desk, all deconstructed into pointy teeth and boxed bosom. It's an odd artistic choice for a doctor who works mostly with children, I think.

"I've done various motor and visual exams in addition to a standard battery of psychological tests," she says. Peter and I are too nervous to ask what these entailed; we just hold hands tightly, praying she'll say Willie doesn't have brain damage.

The psychologist clears her throat. I notice that for once, she isn't smiling. "Based on what I've seen in the tests and what the school's told me," she continues, "I think we should have Willie assessed for some organic impairment."

"What does that mean?" Peter asks, alarmed.

"There is the possibility of minimal brain damage. A neurologist will have to look at him."

"But what about the tests?" I say.

"It's the school's report that disturbs me more."

"Well, we don't necessarily agree with everything *that* school says," I say, sharply.

"What I saw with Willie was consistent with what the school described," the psychologist says, as if trying to convince me. "I think if you came in on a regular basis we could explore in session the family dynamic that is producing Willie's anxiety."

I glare at her rudely. If Willie has brain damage, how could she blame our "family dynamic" for causing his problems? Besides, this woman knew nothing about our parenting skills—she'd spent just one hour with Peter and me. She was just blindly accepting everything the preschool had told her. With the attitude we encountered there, why should we trust any so-called expert they recommended?

It was raining by the time Peter and I got back outside, thick drops of water hitting our umbrellas with cold, heavy thuds. "This can't be happening," Peter says. "This is Willie, our gorgeous boy."

I look at Peter. In one hour, the hair near his temples seemed to have turned entirely gray. The expression on his face is one of indescribable pain. I feel awful for him, for both of us. Here he waited so long to get married and have children and now this doctor seems to be throwing everything away in one instant— condemning us as bad parents or genetic freaks. I feel like I'm suffocating.

"I don't believe it," I say, almost shouting on the street. Sure, Willie could be difficult at times, but his behavior didn't jibe with anything I understood as being remotely connected to brain damage. Certainly, Peter and I had occasional disagreements about breast-feeding and toilet training, but the idea that our parenting *caused* Willie's behavior on a biological level was absurd.

"There's something suspicious to me about that psychologist,"

I say. "Did you notice the way she kept trying to encourage us to sign up for family therapy, like she just wanted the business or something?"

"I don't know, honey. Maybe Willie's worse off than we think."

February 3, 1993

We make an appointment with the pediatric neurologist, Dr. Rujillo, whom the psychologist recommended. Though we could have looked for a doctor on our own, it didn't occur to us to try to find another specialist. We've been in such shock that we actually need a doctor like this, shopping around for our own seems beside the point. Surely, if Willie is brain damaged, any doctor will see it.

The past few weeks have all revolved around what this new doctor will say about Willie. We haven't been sleeping or eating well; we're constantly bickering with each other about stupid things. But underneath it all, I know we're both on the same side and scared to death about what this man will say about Willie. If he's got brain damage, what can we do about it? We assume that that kind of diagnosis means he'll never be able to function at a high level of intelligence or independence. Will he need special schools? Can he ever go to college? Get married? Have any semblance of a "normal" life?

And if Willie doesn't have brain damage, the scenario seems equally bleak. His aggressive, erratic behavior will be considered totally voluntary, the result of psychological problems or worse.

Sometimes I catch myself hoping it's a biological issue because, inside, I know Willie can't help the way he acts. He's not *choosing* to have these bizarre mood swings and tantrums. Two hundred years ago, they might have said he was possessed by evil spirits. And maybe he is, in ways we just can't understand.

What have I come to, though, when I catch myself *wishing* my child has brain damage? Still, I know there's something not entirely normal about Willie's behavior. Nicholas is nearly two now and is nothing like the way Willie was at that age. At the twice-weekly play group to which I take him, he has no trouble following the teacher's instructions. He can be in the middle of a rowdy game of tag with the other children but when it's time to stop or move on to another activity, I get none of the same wails or kicks and screams as I did with Willie. And when Nicky enters the room, he picks one activity and goes directly to it, instead of bouncing from the art table to the puzzles, to the toy kitchen and back again, leaving a trail of scattered toys in his wake.

Before we take Willie to the neurologist, we tell him he's going to get a checkup. He doesn't need to know why we're seeing yet another doctor. As far as Willie knows, all these "checkups" and testing are perfectly normal. Peter and I, on the other hand, feel completely unstrung. What if the doctor finds something? What if he doesn't?

The neurologist's office is located in one of the large hospitals on the East Side. Because Peter's office is nearby, he suggests we meet him at work for lunch, and then go to the hospital together. Willie thinks this is a big treat, to go to Daddy's office *and* McDonald's. He clutches his Happy Meal toy in his mittened fist as we go to the doctor's, swinging him over the curbs, much to Willie's delight. His legs wriggle in excitement and he's grinning from ear to ear. His innocence is, at the moment, utterly heartbreaking. In his bulky down jacket, Willie looks like a miniature version of the Michelin man. The outing would have been a lot of fun, I realize, if we were going anywhere else but here.

The doctor's receptionist welcomes us with a surprising greeting. "How are you today? Probably not too good, if you have to see us, right?"

"We've definitely been better," Peter agrees, relaxing. I'm grateful for the receptionist's candor. Finally, someone is acknowledging how hard this is on *us*. Maybe for the doctors and therapists, these examinations are just routine, but from a parent's perspective, they're sheer torture.

The receptionist shows us into the doctor's office and tells us to wait, that the doctor will be in to see us in a few minutes. Willie entertains himself while we wait by picking up a pop-up book. He opens and closes its pages about a hundred times in a row while making up battle scene dialogue that seems to consist entirely of one character saying "*Auugh*, I'll get you!" and the other one saying "No, you won't!"

Willie is moving so quickly that the flaps are getting bent in the wrong direction and starting to tear.

"Willie," I say, finally getting annoyed. "Enough."

Willie stares up at me, looking tiny in the adult-sized office chair. Tears start to well up in his eyes at my criticism.

"I'm sorry, honey," I say, quickly, hugging him and stroking his cheek. Of course, Willie must be nervous, too.

Peter goes out to see how much longer the doctor will be. He comes back a second later. "Not too much longer," he says, sounding uncertain.

"The sooner we get this over with, the better," I say.

The doctor comes in finally, shaking our hands and apologizing for making us wait. I'm surprised to see on my watch that it's only been ten minutes. It felt much longer than that. The doctor bends down to look Willie in the eye, totally focusing on him, instead of on us.

"Hi, there," he says, kindly.

"Hi," Willie chirps back, letting the pop-up book drop to the floor.

Because he got the case history from us on the phone, the doctor can get right down to the physical examination. I like the doctor's gentle, genuine manner. He's pleasant with Willie and with us—not all phony smiles and jargon like the psychologist. I also like the fact that Peter and I aren't being banished to the waiting room so we can see for ourselves how Willie's doing on the tests. I trust this man, whatever the test results will be.

"Willie, we're going to play some games," the doctor says, handing him a peg board. "Is that all right with you?"

"Oh, sure," Willie answers, characteristically self-confident.

The peg board has colored shapes on it. The doctor takes the shapes off and tells Willie he's going to give him some instructions and he should do the best he can to follow them exactly. Willie nods obediently. He's so eager to please. Why couldn't any of the people at that school see *this* side of him?

"Can you put the red square in the square hole, Willie?" the doctor asks, gently.

Willie looks at the board for a second, then makes the right match.

"Now the blue circle in the round hole."

Willie does it correctly and looks up again, smiling.

"The yellow triangle in the triangle-shaped hole."

Once again, no problem.

"Good," the doctor says, reaching over to take the peg board away.

"Wait a minute," Willie lisps, looking sweetly at the doctor. "What about the white pentagon in the pentagon hole?"

Peter and I look at each other and laugh in relief. At that moment, we know our child is just stubbornly, achingly normal.

"Okay, do the pentagon," the doctor says, smiling.

After the tests in his office, the doctor takes us into an examining room where he asks us to get Willie undressed down to his underwear. I don't know why he needs to see Willie's body when it's his head he's supposed to be examining, but I figure the doctor knows what he's doing.

Peter helps Willie while I put his things on a chair, staring at him in his Superman underwear. "You're doing great, sweetie," I tell him, tousling his hair.

"*Mom*," he complains, brushing me away as if I'm embarrassing him.

The doctor proceeds to do a number of tests: hearing tests; balance tests; tests where he pricks Willie's toes lightly with needles to see if Willie can gauge sensations; tests where Willie walks a straight line with one heel in front of the other to see if he can walk with flat feet; tests where Willie touches his nose with his eyes shut; tests where Willie has to string beads together. It seems to go on forever.

"I'm glad to inform you that your son is neurologically perfect," the doctor says, when he's finally finished.

"*I told you!*" I say to Peter, unable to stop myself from gloating.

"But what about the toe walking?" Peter asks.

"It's not a neurological problem," the doctor says. "Willie *can* walk normally. You saw him do it yourself. You only worry when they can't put their heels down at all or if they get off balance walking on flat feet."

"What about the beads and water play?" I ask.

"Maybe he just likes beads and water."

Downstairs, Peter and I are so happy we don't know what to do. We buy Willie a toy in the hospital gift shop and get all the way outside before remembering the uneasy balance of peace in our house. If we buy something for Willie, we'd better go back and buy a gift for Nicholas, too, if we want to stave off full-blown civil war. It's a small oversight but significant in my mind. Here we've been in a panic mode about Willie for so long it sometimes threatens to eclipse all other needs: Nicky's, mine, Peter's, ours as a couple and a family.

Peter has to go back to work. "I couldn't get a thing done all morning, I was so nervous," he admits, as he hails a cab for me and Willie. We speed up First Avenue, the city passing us by in tall, bright colors. I'm almost dizzy with happiness. This nonsense about brain damage is finally over, I think, and Willie is fine. We can go back to our old lives again, where everything feels safe and familiar. The life where we have two healthy, normal children.

February 8, 1993

We've fibbed to Willie about why he isn't going back to his old preschool, telling him it's a new year and kids go to different schools in the new year. (How could a three-year-old know that the academic year actually runs from September to June?) Of course, since Willie was kicked out midyear, we've run into the problem of finding room at another threes program—none of the schools we call has a space. Most say they're already running over full capacity.

Another problem, we realize, with Willie's getting kicked out of that nursery school is that it might cause problems with his getting into another school for next fall. We'd already sent in applications for private schools (the public schools in our neighborhood are known for their large class size, which would be a disaster for Willie, given how hard it's been for him with fifteen other children this year), but the old preschool—and his dreaded threes teacher—were supposed to write recommendations to help us get him in. We know that the schools we're applying to will definitely contact Willie's former nursery school to learn more about him, and us as a family. What kind of negative things will they say about Willie? That he's disruptive in circle time and crashes cars in gym? That he can't answer "why" questions and they sent him to a shrink to test for brain damage?! What school in the world will let us in once they learn about that?

I've managed to patch a schedule together for now, though. Willie was already taking an after-school gymnastics class once a week, so I signed him up for an extra daytime session. I'd like him to learn some of the internal self-control and body awareness that's required in gymnastics—like if you get wild and rush around while trying to walk on a four-inch-wide balance beam, you'll fall on your face! But I get a sinking feeling when I watch Willie in class.

While the other three-year-olds can handle the class fine, Willie is always poking or prodding some other child, usually the other boys. I can tell no one wants to stretch or stand in line next to Willie. The other kids have started to act scared of him, trying to avoid getting too near him as they get ready for the class, or afterwards when we get our coats on. Watching him interact with the other children, waiting for him to impulsively strike, is gut-wrenching. I don't know what to think. His teachers don't make a federal case out of it like they did at his preschool, but I know it's not normal. Why can't he just keep his hands to himself?

In addition to the gym class Willie also goes to an art and music class two mornings a week. This is a drop-off program more like a formal preschool. The class is small—only eight children—and fairly structured in the sense that specific materials like clay or beads are laid out for the children, whom the teachers carefully supervise. Willie has one female teacher and one male—rare in the preschool world. They both seem laid-back enough, a welcome change from the stern, almost unfriendly demeanor of Willie's former teacher.

Because I'm so worried about the way things are going, based on what I've seen in the gym class, I check in frequently with his teacher. When I called most recently, he tells me everything is fine. His whole manner is upbeat. He tells me Willie's a great kid.

Something about his honesty inspires me to tell him the whole truth. I explain the problems Willie had in his first school—how the teacher said he was always screaming and fighting. "Well, I don't really see that at all," he says. "Sure, some of the boys get into arguments, but it's not just Willie. It's the age."

I'm relieved, but also more confused than ever. Why does Willie act so calm and cooperative in his art and music class but get so difficult and aggressive in gymnastics? Is it the cavernous gymnasium that gets him overwhelmed? (It was also the gym where he had so many problems at his old threes class.) Is it something about the large room or the frenetic activity that makes him get disruptive? Obviously, he can handle himself fairly well with a small number of his peers at the music and art class. But no matter how many times we go over the rules with him before gymnastics, he can't keep his hands to himself. I used to think that he tried but just couldn't help it. Now I don't even know if he tries anymore. He seems to concentrate hard on our instructions to behave but, five minutes later, he acts as if he's totally forgotten.

February 10, 1993

Some friends are over for Sunday brunch. Their older son, Steven, is seven and their younger son is nearly four, just two months younger than Willie.

It's unusual for Willie to have a play date at home. Since he left his preschool, none of those families have ever called to see how Willie is doing or to set up play dates. Though Willie doesn't seem to notice, it makes us feel awful. Lots of four-year-olds are starting to have best friends, but Willie doesn't have any kids his own age with whom he's particularly close. Even friends' children have gotten distant. We notice our friends call us only for "adult get-togethers" now. Has Willie just smacked their kids once too often for them to feel safe around him?

Of course, there are other reasons that situations and friend-ships change. We used to see our friends who are over today once a week or so, but since they moved to Long Island recently, we get together with them much less often—once every three or four months now, at best.

We've had a busy morning, and Willie hasn't had a nap yet. When we tell our friends this, they look at us strangely. Their four-year-old gave up his nap a year ago. Willie still sleeps at least an hour during the day, more on the days when he has gymnas-tics, and seems particularly stressed out afterward.

Peter and I are in the kitchen when we hear screaming in the living room. It's our friends' older son, crying that Willie's scratched him. Steven has a pink scratch running from the top of his cheek to the bottom of his chin.

"What happened?!" Peter and I say simultaneously.

The mom—who'd seen everything—shakes her head, more stunned than angry. "It was really strange. They were playing soc-cer and Willie lost a point, then started fighting and scratching. Steven didn't *do* anything. He was just standing there."

We see Willie running away on tiptoes to hide behind our living-room curtains. He's red-faced and giggling nervously, as if he thinks it's a joke. His whole body seems electrified with the power and violence of what he's done. Our friends' child is whimpering, holding his cheek.

"*Willie!*" Peter booms, chasing after him.

Willie's whole body seems to stiffen when he realizes that he's in serious trouble. His shoulders square off, ready for a fight; his fists are balled up, quivering as if he's about to let loose. Peter drags him out by his wrist from the corner of the living room. He scoops him up and gives him four or five quick whacks on the bottom. "No! No!" Willie screams. His legs are cycling wildly as Peter carries him off for a time-out in his bedroom. Peter is white-hot and Willie is getting more and more hysterical by the second. "*I'm sorry! I'm sorry!*" he screams, grabbing at the walls to hold Peter back. "*Please, don't lock me in there!*"

"But you hurt Steven!" Peter says, trying to remind Willie why he's in trouble.

"*Let me down! Let me down!*" Willie screams, turning his full wrath on Peter. "You idiot! Idiot! I-di-ot!" He repeats the word with an obsessive fury.

In the living room, our friends' child is starting to wail in earnest, more from Willie's screaming, I think, than from real pain. Nicholas and our friends' younger son are staring blankly at the whole scene as they play with balloons. Our friends stare at us in horror. We know the looks on their faces. At the moment, I'm sure we look horrified, too. *What's wrong with Willie?*

February 12, 1993

Peter insists we must find another therapist, someone who can help us figure out what to do about Willie. Steven's parents— who, amazingly, are still talking to us after Sunday—suggest we talk to Steven's former teacher who recommended a wonderful doctor to the family of one of Steven's friends who was, as they put it, "sort of like Willie."

Though I'm reluctant to get involved with any more psychologists after our last experience, I know we don't have a choice. "Okay," I tell Peter. "Go ahead and call her."

The teacher recommends Dr. Andersov, a psychologist on Central Park West, someone whom she describes as an expert at working with "difficult" children. Dr. Andersov's office is only a few blocks away from our apartment building, and I meet Peter there after work for our first appointment.

I've got no idea what to expect from a new therapist, or how anyone can help with Willie's bizarre behavior since there seems to be nothing medically wrong with him. But I have to admit, my idea of child therapy mostly comes from television and the movies: kids lying on a couch discussing how much their parents have messed them up. How can Willie benefit just from talking when his problems never seem to come out one-on-one with grown-ups, anyway?

Dr. Andersov comes into the waiting room and ushers us into her office. Whereas the first psychologist was all shoulder pads and brisk smiles, Dr. Andersov is dressed like a college professor in a long, straight skirt—no power suit, fortunately—and an over-sized sweater. I can't tell exactly how old she is, probably late forties. The only tip-off is her hair, which has a few streaks of gray.

Unlike the first psychologist, who seemed so phony and judg-mental, Dr. Andersov puts us immediately at ease. We make so-cial chitchat for a few minutes but then get down to business. Dr. Andersov is sympathetic when we tell her about Willie's experi-ence at his first nursery school and the way the school director and first psychologist kept suggesting he had brain damage.

"That's an awful thing for any family to go through," she says. "It must have been so hard on all of you." Her voice is soothing, not smarmy like the first therapist's.

"We know we're not perfect," Peter says, "but we feel that we handle Willie pretty well. We set clear boundaries. We give him a lot of love and support and, with us, he generally seems pretty happy and well behaved. But we don't know. . . . He obviously has serious problems with other kids. We think that he might need family therapy."

"Not every child with problems needs family therapy," Dr. Andersov explains.

She asks us to describe Willie's problems, and we start talking. Peter and I take turns explaining everything that happened at his preschool; what the neurologist said; what his new teachers say at his gymnastics and art classes; even the scratching incident last weekend with Steven. More than that, we reveal how rough Willie can be with his brother, whom we know he loves. We'd once watched the boys playing outside and saw Willie, who'd gotten particularly frustrated that he couldn't get Nicky to do something his way, haul off and hit his younger brother hard in the face. Peter says he sometimes fears that Willie is capable of real violence. Are we raising a thug?

We tell her we're concerned that Willie's temper tantrums seem so spontaneous, their triggers so unpredictable. He genuinely wants to have friends, we explain, but it's almost as if he doesn't know how. Even as a baby, we recall, he could act suddenly aggressive, like at family gatherings or birthday parties. It takes us over forty minutes to tell her everything that's wrong: Willie's impulsivity; his low frustration tolerance; his inability to "read" social cues; his excitability and constant commotion.

After this litany, I'm half expecting Dr. Andersov to show us the door. The situation is hopeless, I'm sure of it. There is no cure for Willie.

But Dr. Andersov just lets out a low breath and shakes her head sympathetically. She doesn't look shocked. In fact, she looks encouraging. "While I'd have to meet Willie and do some more tests to be sure, it sounds to me like Willie might have Attention Deficit Disorder, or ADD, as it's called for short."

"Attention Deficit Disorder?" I say, having never before heard of it. "But Willie doesn't have poor attention. He can sit and play with his Legos for hours."

"Having ADD doesn't mean a child can't *ever* focus," Dr. Andersov explains. "Some children pay extreme attention to certain activities in order to block out other stimulation." Dr. Andersov explains that ADD isn't voluntary behavior—affected children aren't trying to be difficult or oppositional. They just go on overload and can strike out or react in a self-protective way. Though people used to think that children "outgrew" ADD, the prevailing wisdom now is that people just get better at compensating for it as they get older. Most importantly, ADD is ultimately treatable. Medications such as Ritalin, she tells us, are also quite effective in managing the symptoms.

"But if it's a medical problem, how come the pediatric neurologist didn't catch it?" I ask, confused.

Dr. Andersov explains that ADD does not show up on a standard neurological screening. "I'd need to see Willie in my office to be sure—and probably send him to another therapist to do some tests I can't do here. But it sounds as if Willie has ADD."

I find myself nodding in relief and recognition. From what she says, I know instinctively that ADD is what Willie's got. For the first time, all his behaviors make sense: the giddiness and fidgeting; his underinhibitedness and temperamental short fuse; the way he can seem so distant and inaccessible when overexcited. It's not our fault, or the fault of our "family dynamic," as the first psychologist put it. He was just born this way, apparently. It was in his wiring, as I've always suspected.

"Will Willie be able to achieve academically with ADD?" Peter asks, looking nervous.

"There are brain surgeons, scholars, and heads of state with ADD," Dr. Andersov says. There seems to be some link between the disorder and creative achievement, she tells us. A number of well-known artists, actors, and writers have ADD. "I'll be honest with you, though," she adds. "Children with ADD can often have problems in school that have nothing to do with their intelligence. They can have trouble sitting still and paying attention. Some have learning disabilities, though we still don't really know why. Still, there's no reason these can't be treated as they come up."

"Wait a minute," I say, surprised. "You mean this isn't a new diagnosis—people have known about it for years?" If ADD was so obvious from Willie's case history, why didn't the first psychologist catch it?

"We've known about ADD for decades. Before the seventies,

however, it used to be called 'minimal brain damage' or 'minimal brain dysfunction.' "

"You're kidding," I say, feeling the blood drain from my face. So the first psychologist hadn't been wrong—just a frightening twenty years out of date!

"Will you need to see him on a regular basis for therapy?" Peter asks.

"Well, first let's get the diagnosis," Dr. Andersov advises. "We don't even know if this is what he's got. And besides that, he's quite young. Most ADD symptoms don't really kick in before a child turns five."

"You mean it will get *worse?*" I ask, alarmed.

"Believe it or not, it doesn't sound as though Willie's even got it very badly. At worst, he's probably borderline—not bouncing off walls, but definitely worth taking a look at."

As we make the appointment for Willie to come in, I feel as if a huge weight were being lifted off my shoulders. Finally, someone is going to help Willie—and help us learn how to help him.

Sitting in Dr. Andersov's office, listening to her calm and comforting voice, I feel palpably relieved for the first time in months. Whether we settle on a treatment for Willie right away seems less important than understanding what the trouble really is. And surely, understanding Willie's problems will be the first step toward solving them.

February 15, 1993

Willie's first meeting with Dr. Andersov is today. I made sure to schedule our visit on an afternoon when Willie doesn't have gymnastics, so he won't be overly tired or stimulated. I want Dr. Andersov to get a fair picture of him, not of a child who's exhausted or totally hyped up. She's prepared me in advance for what we can expect (and I, in turn, have been able to prepare Willie by saying he'll be going to meet a new doctor to play some games and just talk). They'll play together first with blocks or dolls. Later in the session, if she thinks Willie's ready for it, she might suggest a more structured activity, like a board game, to see how he follows rules and handles small frustrations like waiting his turn or losing the game.

The session is going to be pretty informal, she says, because she doesn't have the right materials in her office to do the standard battery of aptitude and psychological tests that would diagnose the ADD more specifically. If she thinks Willie displays enough of the symptoms, she's going to recommend that we get tests done at another specialist's office—most likely this summer, when Willie will be a little older. (Though I'd rather find out now, Willie's still not quite four, too young to make a definitive diagnosis, Dr. Andersov explains.) Six months would give Willie more time to develop, she says, and allow the new doctor to get a more accurate reading.

While I'm less than thrilled to think that we'll have to take Willie in to yet another doctor (the fourth person we will have talked to, including the two therapists and the pediatric neurologist), I trust Dr. Andersov's opinion. We're pursuing a diagnosis that makes some sense to me—as opposed to the nonsensical idea that Willie has brain damage—and I'm willing to do whatever we have to do to get answers about Willie.

Willie comes with me willingly, even when I explain that we're going to a doctor's office. "Is Dr. Andersov a friend of Dr. Rujillo?" Willie asks, naming the pediatric neurologist on the East Side we liked so much.

"She's very nice like Dr. Rujillo," I say, noticing that Willie didn't ask about the East Side psychologist, whether Dr. Andersov was a friend of hers, too. Had he forgotten all about her already?

"Dr. Andersov's office is near McDonald's *and* Baskin-Robbins," Willie observes, impressed.

"Would you like a treat after we're done?" I offer, but then immediately regret it. I don't want Willie, or Dr. Andersov, to think I was bribing Willie to come.

Inside Dr. Andersov's waiting room, I hang Willie's little down parka on the coatrack. I see the head of one of his plastic Ninja Turtles dangling out of his pocket. Willie is so little to be going through all this; I hate the fact that, at age three, we've had to drag him all over town for psychological testing. This was not how I thought I'd be spending his preschool years, to say the least.

Instead of sitting on one of the comfortable-looking chairs or sofa in Dr. Andersov's waiting room, Willie has plopped himself cross-legged on the floor, rubbing his hands repeatedly over the plush maroon carpet. The humidifier in the corner seems distracting to Willie, as well. Every few minutes, he looks up from the carpet when the machine sputters or ticks. "What's that? What's that?" he keeps asking. Before the issue of ADD was raised, it never occurred to me how distracted Willie gets by various noises and sensations.

Dr. Andersov opens the door, and Willie pops up from the rug.

"Why don't you come in?" Dr. Andersov says, in her soothing voice, after introducing herself to Willie. He holds her hand and starts out of the waiting room without even a backward glance, not like most children his age, who would be more fearful of strangers.

I move back to the couch to read a magazine, assuming I can't go with them to watch the session like at the first psychologist's office. But Dr. Andersov says I should join them, and I'm only too interested.

Inside, Willie is Mr. Polite—saying please and thank you for everything. At first, Dr. Andersov doesn't push him too hard. She lets him play the way he wants to at the dollhouse. He pretends it's a birthday party and there's a mischievous boy who wants to steal the cake. (*Does it mean anything, I wonder, that Willie's picked a birthday party—a situation that's always been challenging for him?*) As the game continues, Dr. Andersov tries to get Willie worked up a bit, introducing more rules as to what the birthday boy in their game can and can't do.

Willie starts to get more excited as the game continues— acting babyish, biting and pulling on his shirt—but he's able to follow the game much better than I'd have predicted. She continues with him at the toy house for fifteen more minutes or so.

They play with blocks but never get to the board game. Throughout the whole time, though, Willie's demeanor is essentially the same: courteous, if a little excited, but essentially in control.

Ironically, I feel a little disappointed. If Willie doesn't act out in her office, how will she ever know how to help him?

"Okay, Willie," Dr. Andersov says at the end of the session. "Thanks for visiting me today."

"Am I going to come back?" Willie asks.

"Maybe," I say, intentionally skirting his question because, until I talk to Dr. Andersov on the phone later, I won't know, either.

"Thanks, Dr. Andersov," I say, buttoning Willie's coat in the waiting room.

"Can I have my ice cream now? You promised," Willie reminds me.

I turned as red as the rug.

"It's not a bad idea to give Willie a treat when he comes here," Dr. Andersov says, graciously. "It's very Pavlovian. It will help him build good associations with my office."

Though I'm sure she's saying it mostly to help me save face, the Pavlov theory makes sense. Maybe I shouldn't consider it bribery and instead think of it as Willie's reward for being such a good sport about going to all these doctors in the first place.

February 16, 1993

Dr. Andersov picks up after her answering machine already starts its message. "Hi, you've reached Dr. Andersov on tape . . ."

I ask her what she thinks about Willie's visit. "Is it ADD?" I ask, eager to finally have a diagnosis.

"He's clearly excitable and distractible," Dr. Andersov agrees. "But he held himself together well, even when I tried to provoke him. Of course, it was just the three of us in here."

"That's been a problem all along. One-on-one, he's great. It's when he gets in a big group of kids his own age that he has trouble."

"Well, maybe that's when I should see him. Could you arrange for me to observe him at his art and music class?"

"It's more the gymnastics class where he has trouble, though."

"But a big gymnastics class is naturally stimulating," Dr. Andersov says. "Most children get worked up in that kind of setting. I'd rather see him in a place that's more like a formal nursery school."

"I don't know if that's allowed," I explain. "It would be pretty disruptive for them."

Dr. Andersov suggests I call the school and explain that I'd like to have someone come observe Willie's class. "You don't have to tell them I'm a psychologist if you don't want to," she says. "There are lots of different reasons people want to observe children in preschool. Teachers and school admissions officers do it all the time. Most schools are perfectly happy to accommodate."

"Most schools," I repeat, remembering how Willie's first nursery school never let me sit in on a class to observe Willie in the classroom or in gym where he was having so much trouble. Looking back, I realize I should have insisted on observing for at least an hour or two. It was a private school, after all. Wasn't accessibility supposed to be part of what we were paying for? In retrospect, maybe my sense of a secretive, closed-door atmosphere there should have been a warning sign that something was going drastically wrong for Willie. The whole time he was in that threes class, I felt completely shut out by the principal and teachers.

We agree that I'll try to set up an appointment for Dr. Andersov to observe Willie's art and music class. I get off the phone with her and call Willie's teacher. Fortunately, he seems quite pleased about the idea of someone observing. "Please let me know if there's something more I could be doing to help Willie," he offers. "I'd love to hear what this person thinks of the class."

I tell him I appreciate how much he's done for Willie already. Willie loves going to his art and music class—a far cry from the days when I had to drag him kicking and screaming to his threes program at that awful preschool. Aside from that, I'm relieved beyond words that we've finally found a place where the teachers seem to actually appreciate our son.

What I don't say to the teacher, however, is that *I'm* quite nervous about the idea of Dr. Andersov's going to observe Willie. *What if she doesn't think he's got ADD?* On the one hand, it would be great to learn that he *doesn't* have a disorder but, on the other, I know Willie's behavior—the temper tantrums, the self-defensive way he lashes out when he gets overexcited—is just not normal.

If it's not ADD, then what is it? Will we have to go back to square one again if Dr. Andersov thinks it's something else? I'm not sure how many more doctors or tests we all can take. Even if there's not a name for what Willie's got, he clearly needs help.

And Peter and I do, too. Already, I feel as if I'm losing my mind over this. People ask me how I am and I answer with some new anecdote about Willie—as if I as a person have ceased to exist. "Oh, I'm not so good," I'll say, when a friend will call. "Willie scratched a kid in the park."

Maybe it's because I had children at such a young age that I feel so particularly frantic. If I'd had more experience with babies before I had my own or had helped raise young nieces or nephews, maybe things would be different with Willie. Peter says I'm too hard on myself, that anyone facing problems with a child would naturally be worried and blame herself.

But there is a definite shortcoming to my having been the first of my friends to have a baby. Much as they try, even my closest friends don't understand what I'm going through. Most of them aren't married yet, and have no idea what it's like to be a parent. Solving a problem with your child, after all, is nothing like navigating dilemmas in the workplace.

I think the sad truth is that nothing could have prepared me for this, no matter how long I waited to start a family. Stupidly—ignorantly—I just expected that everything about my child's life would be fine. No, more than fine—*better* than what Peter and I ever experienced.

While Peter had never been a particularly successful student and always felt somewhat ashamed that he didn't go to a better college than the red-brick university he attended in the late sixties, we were determined to send Willie to the finest schools we could afford. We wanted to make sure he developed into a child who loved school and learning. And on my end, I was resolved that my children would grow up with a loving, active father; that my marriage would in no way replicate the doomed, explosive union of my parents, whose twenty-four-year relationship ended with a divorce so bitter that, as far as I know, their lawyers still aren't speaking to each other.

In our ignorance, Peter and I thought that, if we could avoid making the same mistakes our parents made in the past, everything would be fine. What we have instead is a child with potentially grave psychological problems who can't function in school and whom—happily married though we are—Peter and I can't reach. I'd almost laugh at the irony if I didn't feel so desperate.

February 23, 1993

A strange storm is heading our way, a kind of mini-hurricane called a nor'easter that is dumping inches of rain from Bangor to Orlando. I'm supposed to call Dr. Andersov this afternoon about her observation of Willie's class. Since I'll do almost anything to keep busy until it's time to call her—including going to Bloomingdale's in the middle of a hurricane—I head out to buy a quilt that we need at a white sale. (*When the going gets tough*, as the saying goes, *the tough go shopping.*)

Amazingly, the store is jam-packed. Can there be *that* many other crazy people in New York who save their errands for the worst rainstorm of the year? I find the pay phones first and check to confirm that I'll have enough quarters to call Dr. Andersov. I try not to let myself focus on what she might say, staring instead at the quilts, which are a blur of star and floral patterns. I think about the mothers in the eighteenth and nineteenth centuries who would have sewn quilts like these by hand while chopping firewood, harvesting wheat, doing farm chores, and tending four or five children.

Two hundred years ago, Willie would have been educated in a one-room schoolhouse with a single teacher and a handful of local students. He'd have sat at a desk instead of sitting in "circle time," done the "three Rs" instead of doing "free play." They wouldn't have dreamed of children as young as two or three starting school back then. Of course, Willie would also have probably been hit with a switch or made to wear a dunce cap if he scratched other kids in class or talked back to the teacher. Still, I can't help thinking that today's standard nursery school format really does some children a disservice. Maybe Willie would have learned more in a small, mixed-age classroom instead of a place with fifteen other three-year-olds.

I pick out a plaid quilt and go to the register to pay. I start to give the cashier the address for delivery, but when she tells me it'll take four to six weeks I decide to take everything with me. I've got no idea how I'm going to hold the two enormous shopping bags and my umbrella on the bus home (there's no way I'm going to get a cab in the rain, I know). I check my watch as I stumble out of the bedding department with my huge packages. Finally, it's time to call Dr. Andersov.

Peter is already waiting on the other line for the conference call when I reach Dr. Andersov. I guess I'm not the only one who's anxious. "So, how did Willie do?" Peter asks nervously.

"I observed Willie in his art and music class for almost an hour," Dr. Andersov says. "From what I can see, he's not a terrible discipline problem there."

I'm relieved, but I remind myself that Willie's art and music teacher always sounded very positive about Willie.

Dr. Andersov essentially reiterates what Willie's teacher's already told me about the class: It's a small group of seven other children—four boys and three girls. In addition to the male teacher, there's a female co-teacher in the room with them. A few other boys in the class get rowdy besides Willie, Dr. Andersov says, and it's usually not Willie who starts the trouble—when there is any. However, she observed that Willie *does* seem to get more excited than the other children and it's more challenging for him to calm down once aroused.

"He's not used to being with other active boys besides his brother," Peter points out. "At his old school there were only three other boys, and they were fairly passive."

"Willie's behavior was different from what I saw in my office, though," Dr. Andersov says. She explains that she observed more attentional problems and "nonpurposeful activity" like fidgeting or twitching his legs, which indicates hyperactivity. "Still, at this level, it would be considered very borderline. The teachers are very good with him, and Willie clearly enjoys being there."

"So do you think you can help him?" Peter asks.

"Right now, since the teachers are handling him well at this program, I'd like to wait until he's a little older," Dr. Andersov says.

"I don't understand," I say, gripping the receiver tightly. "Why can't you help him *now?*"

"He's still very young," Dr. Andersov explains. "I'd like to send him for those tests we talked about over the summer when he's had a chance to develop more. If it's ADD, he's not going to grow out of it. If it's partially or entirely developmental, it will be important to see how his issues have changed—*if* they've changed as he gets older."

"What happens if those tests come out positive?" Peter asks.

"Then we can think about trying one of the medications we talked about that have been so successful with ADD. We'll keep an eye on him next fall, and I can visit his class again to see how he's doing."

"*If* he gets into a fours class for next year," I say.

"What do you mean?" Dr. Andersov asks.

I explain that Peter and I worked with Willie's old nursery school to make sure that the letter of recommendation they sent out for Willie wasn't too negative. At first, they wanted to send out just a transcript stating that Willie had been registered at the school but no longer attended. (They had already given us our tuition back, prorated for the time Willie had spent in the school. I'd expected a big battle over the money, but they were surprisingly forthcoming.)

However, without a good letter of recommendation for Willie from his teachers, he'd never get into any private nursery program (because it was already December by the time he was kicked out, we were already too late to get on the waiting lists for the scarce public school enrichment programs for four-year-olds in our district even if we thought Willie could cope with the larger class size). Eventually we got the old school to say something nice about how much he liked singing and running in gym, but the overall tone of the letter was so lukewarm that—on top of the fact that we'd already removed him from the school—we doubted Willie's chances of getting in anywhere else were very good.

"Why don't you just leave him where he is?" Dr. Andersov asks.

"They don't have any daytime classes for four-year-olds. Everyone else is already in nursery school," I explain.

My supply of quarters is just about gone, so I tell Dr. Andersov we'll check in with her after we get Willie tested this summer.

I haul my shopping bags out into the rain to get home to cook dinner and relieve Jolie. The wind has picked up even more than before, as has the rain. As I expected, trying to get a cab is an exercise in futility and the bus is completely jam-packed because it's the middle of rush hour. People send me dirty looks because my quilt and throw pillows are taking up so much space. I'm so sick of the city, all the pushing and competitiveness: for schools, for a bus seat, for just about everything worth having.

Sometimes, I think Peter and I made a big mistake trying to raise our family in New York. If we lived in the suburbs, maybe we wouldn't have felt so compelled to put Willie into preschool at age two, like everyone else. Maybe Willie would have had an easier time fitting in if he'd had a chance to mature more. Maybe he wouldn't even have had the same problems he's having now.

Maybe, I'm just dreaming.

August 2, 1993

Today I speak with Dr. Levine, the tester to whom Dr. Andersov referred us. Unlike most psychologists, Dr. Levine isn't going away for the entire month of August, so I could get an appointment fairly quickly.

"Why don't you send me a copy of the tests from the first psychologist?" Dr. Levine suggests.

"I have the neurologist's report," I tell her, "but that first psychologist never sent us anything in writing."

"That's odd," Dr. Levine says. "What tests did she do?"

"I'm not sure. Visual and motor, I think. But I don't know what else."

"She didn't tell you?"

"Well, no." I was beginning to feel really stupid. How were Peter and I supposed to know we should have asked for Willie's test results? The more we were dealing with people we like and trust, the worse this first psychologist looked.

As soon as I get off the phone with Dr. Levine, I call the first psychologist. Her high, saccharine voice immediately sets my teeth on edge.

"How's Willie doing?" she asks, after getting his chart. (Before that, I notice, she doesn't use his first name. I wonder if she even remembers it without looking us up.)

I struggle to keep my voice calm. This is the woman who said she thought Willie had brain damage and never mentioned ADD. "Willie's doing just fine," I tell her, evenly. "I need a copy of the tests you ran on him because he's being evaluated for Attention Deficit Disorder. Do you know what that is?"

"Of course I do," she says, sounding defensive.

"Well, if you do, why'd you tell us you thought Willie might have minimal brain damage? Isn't that what they used to call ADD years ago?"

There's a pause and the rustle of papers as she flips through her notes. "Willie didn't strike me as having the classic profile of ADD."

"But he struck you as having the classic profile of brain damage?" I shoot back.

"When I test a child in my office, I'm only getting a picture of his behavior that day. Perhaps Willie's profile has changed. What I saw was a lot of anxiety and a number of physical issues that I thought should be examined by a neurologist."

If I didn't hate this woman so much I might almost be impressed by the way she's trying to cover her tracks. "What about the tests you did? I'd like to see a copy."

"I don't know," she stalls. "I really didn't do a standard battery of tests. I did a few parts of a number of different tests."

"Well, I'd like to see them anyway."

"All right," she promises, sounding eager to get me off the phone. "I'll send them to you."

August 16, 1993

I've waited two weeks for the tests from the first psychologist, but they still haven't come. My many phone calls to her office have all been answered by her service, and she's never returned the numerous messages. When I complain about this to a friend who's a lawyer, she says we can sue; we've got a right to our child's medical records. But dragging this out in court is the last thing I want to do, much as I want to punish the psychologist for terrifying us with the thought that Willie might have brain damage. But what kind of message would a lawsuit send to Willie? After all, we're trying to teach him to let go of his anger and deal with his feelings more constructively.

I'm not all kindness and forgiveness yet, however. After about my twentieth unanswered call to the psychologist's office, I call an organization Dr. Andersov told me about, NYC-CHADD, a local chapter of Children and Adults with Attention Deficit Disorder, a national ADD support group. Dr. Andersov said NYC-CHADD kept a list of doctors' names—those they encouraged families to see and those they warned parents away from.

(Both Dr. Andersov and Dr. Levine were on the recommended list, it turned out.)

"I want to report a doctor for the 'don't see' list," I tell the man who answered the phone at NYC-CHADD.

"Really?" he says, sounding somewhat doubtful. "What happened?"

I tell him our story and, when I'm finished, ask him if he's going to put the first doctor's name on the list.

"In capital letters," he says.

I feel a bit better, but not as much as I expected from my meager revenge. I just keep thinking about all the families who, like us, still need to find the right help for their children. Even though I'm feeling confident about Dr. Andersov and Dr. Levine, I'm a long way from feeling that our own problems have been solved.

August 23, 1993

Dr. Levine's office is near the Guggenheim Museum, the dramatic Frank Lloyd Wright design of which enthralls Willie as soon as he sees it.

"Is *this* it?" he asks, sounding impressed. I explain that Dr. Levine's office is actually in a smaller building nearby.

"I see ice cream," Willie says pointedly, gesturing at a Good Humor truck parked near the museum. I think of Dr. Andersov and her comment about Pavlov. All I'd have to do is ring a bell, and Willie would probably be drooling.

Dr. Levine opens the door herself when we buzz. She has gray hair and a dangly African necklace that seems to fascinate Willie. "Hi, Willie," she says, in a friendly tone. Willie doesn't seem surprised that she knows his name, as other children might be. He reaches out for the pendant on her necklace, fascinated. Already I'm starting to think like a psychologist, knowing that Dr. Levine must have also noticed how distracted Willie was by the shiny object and how impulsive he was to just grab at it without asking permission first.

"Do you like my necklace, Willie?" she says in an encouraging tone. She's got a slight New York accent and a tendency to speak loudly. I'd think her voice might interest Willie but he's already switched his attention to a puzzle in the toy box. Dr. Levine leads us both into a narrow hallway. Her office is actually a small, two-bedroom apartment cleverly converted into a series of small exam rooms. We pass a kitchenette that seems to be stocked entirely with popcorn and cans of red Kool-Aid.

"Can I have a drink?" he asks.

Dr. Levine looks at me. "Is it okay with you, Mom?"

Like the first psychologist, Dr. Levine has addressed me as if she were a child, or a grown-up parody of how a child would talk. But coming from her, there's more of a sense of humor about it that doesn't set my teeth on edge.

"Go ahead, sweetie," I tell Willie. "Just be careful with the cup." I quietly explain to Dr. Levine that Willie has a habit of chewing on things: paper cups, his plastic toys. I don't care so much if he eats the paper but the thought of the neon-bright Kool-Aid spilling out all over the testing papers didn't seem like an auspicious way to start these sessions.

"When you're done with your drink, draw a picture of yourself, cutie," Dr. Levine says to Willie.

Holding the pen in his fist, Willie scribbles a face with some legs and arms—the usual floating heads I've seen him draw dozens of times before.

"In general, it's better for the faces to have bodies," Dr. Levine notes. "It's one of the things they look for on the ERBs." ERB stands for Educational Records Bureau tests, the standardized tests for admission to private school.

"What do you mean, 'better'?" I ask.

"The testers like the faces to have bodies," she explains. "It's a sign of maturity."

"I thought drawing was supposed to be a form of self-expression," I tell her. By those standards, half the art in the Guggenheim Museum around the corner would be considered "immature."

"I know the standards might seem harsh," Dr. Levine agrees. "But if you want to help him to do better on these tests, his heads should have bodies."

"These pens smell good," Willie says, sticking his nose into a green magic marker.

Distractible, I think, watching Dr. Levine make a note.

"Good job, Willie," Dr. Levine says, handing Willie a sticker. "Now we're going to play a game." She gives him some diamond-shaped blocks and makes a pattern out of some of them. "Now you copy it," she tells him.

Willie does the pattern easily, and Dr. Levine makes another. The shapes are getting harder and harder, with Willie being required to manipulate them into triangles, squares and diagonal patterns. This is clearly some kind of test of Willie's spatial ability. He gets stumped on the last shape, where he has to turn a block sideways. He taps the block against the tabletop and twitches his foot. I am sitting on my hands so I won't be tempted to reach in and solve the puzzle for Willie.

"Aha!" Willie says, finally turning the block the right way.

"Good!" Dr. Levine says, in her loud, enthusiastic voice.

I can tell already that I'm going to be a nervous wreck by the time these tests are through.

We need to come back twice more to complete the standard battery of Dr. Levine's three hour-and-a-half sessions. The tests today include peg boards—more complex than the one at the neurologist's last year—inkblot tests, and lots of flash cards. It doesn't seem to me that Willie is doing particularly well on any of them except the vocabulary section, where he answers so many of the questions correctly that Dr. Levine finally runs out of flash cards. I can see Willie's low frustration tolerance kicking in as the tasks become longer and more complicated—one of the hallmarks of ADD. Willie gets impatient having to do the games "her" way and, eventually, loses interest in the tests altogether.

"What's missing?" Dr. Levine asks during one test, pointing to the flash card of a rocking chair with a missing leg.

"Oh, nothing," Willie answers, not even looking at the flash card. "Can I have some more popcorn?"

After all the tests are done, Dr. Levine tells me that she'll be going on vacation but will send us a written report when she gets back.

"But what about the ADD?" I ask plaintively. "Do you think he's got it?"

Dr. Levine moves away from the table where Willie is playing with his stickers. I know the answer before she even says it, have known from the minute we walked in the door.

"Oh, yes," she says, typically matter-of-fact. "And that's not even tabulating the test results. What's more significant to me is the way he took the test, the impulsive answers, the way he'd get so excited and giggly, which increased when he let down his guard and felt more comfortable with me. But he's a wonderful little boy, a real sweetie pie."

"So what do we do?" I ask. Though I've been expecting this moment for seven months, to hear someone finally saying my son has ADD leaves me feeling somewhat shell-shocked.

"What you're going to want to do is look into a trial dose of Ritalin. Dr. Andersov can recommend you to a psychiatrist who'd probably want to do his own evaluation."

"*Another* doctor?"

"Well, you need an M.D., someone to write the prescription. There are a number of psychiatrists we both work with who are wonderful. The other thing I would recommend is a consultation with a speech therapist. Willie definitely has some expressive and receptive language issues beyond articulation that need to be looked into."

"What do you mean?" I ask, confused by her jargon.

"He sometimes mishears words as well as misspeaks them," she tells me. Willie has a large vocabulary, but simple concepts like categories totally elude him. She explains that there is a test where Willie had to give the name of pictures on flash cards. He could name a grapefruit, pineapple, and even a pa-

paya, but when asked what they all had in common he said "vegetables."

"I never noticed that before," I tell her, surprised.

"It could be a reason why he gets so frustrated at school, especially when he gets overexcited, and it's hard for him to slow down to get all the words out," says Dr. Levine. "You know how the mantra in nursery schools is for kids to use words. Well, that's particularly hard for a kid like Willie who knows that, even if he can calm himself down long enough to find the right words, he's probably going to be misunderstood, anyway, because of his articulation."

"I never thought of Willie's pronunciation as being that serious," I say, feeling guilty. Is this something Peter and I should have picked up on earlier? We always knew he had a lisp, but it never occurred to me that there might be a problem in the way his language was fundamentally organized.

"It still might be something that works itself out developmentally," Dr. Levine explains. "This is the kind of thing teachers tend to notice once school has started. Most parents of kids this age spend so much time with their children that they understand their kids perfectly, even if the rest of the world doesn't."

Dr. Levine gives me the name and number of a language therapist she recommends. "It was a pleasure to meet you," Dr. Levine says to Willie.

Willie shakes her hand. He has a pink Kool-Aid mustache and is clutching the stickers she gave him in his fist.

"Can we get ice cream now?" Willie asks me as we leave.

"Are you still hungry, cutie?" Dr. Levine asks, surprised. Since he's been here today, he's had two helpings of popcorn and three cups of Kool-Aid.

"No," I tell her, cryptically. "Blame it on Pavlov."

September 23, 1993

As we feared, we had a hard time getting Willie into a school for this fall. Of course, we'll never know the exact reason why:

whether it was because of the decidedly tepid recommendation of the school last year or because so many pre-K classes elsewhere were already filled with children who'd been attending since age two. Did the teachers and admissions officers see something negative in Willie—or in Peter and me—when we went to visit for Willie's interview? Could they tell from just watching him play with a small group of other children that he had ADD? At the time we were applying, we hadn't gotten the diagnosis yet. Could they have known the problem, even as we were just discovering it ourselves? I'm still not sure. When you get rejected, they never tell you why: only that it's a pity there's not space for all of the wonderful children who apply.

Of the seven or eight pre-K classes that we looked at, Willie got into only one outright and was waitlisted at two others. Essentially, we were looking for a school that was the exact opposite of where Willie had been so miserable before. Whereas his teacher there had been new and inexperienced, this time we wanted educators with years in the field. Because that school had a poor ratio of boys to girls, we wanted to make sure his new class would be more evenly balanced. We wanted a big enough school so that if we didn't like the way his teacher was handling him, we could try to switch him to another class (which hadn't been an option the first time around: his class was the only one the school offered for three-year-olds).

But we didn't want a school that was so big or loosely structured that Willie would feel overwhelmed or uncomfortable. We had the feeling we'd know the right place when we saw it. But even in New York, where there are literally dozens of excellent private schools for older children, I felt that the choices were slim for four-year-olds. I remember being told about a supposedly wonderful school that I eagerly visited only to find the pre-K class so poorly supervised and overcrowded that one boy was chasing another classmate around the room with *scissors*, threatening to give him a haircut—and no one but me and the other parents on tour seemed to notice! (Our tour guide eventually wrestled the scissors out of the child's hand.)

Fortunately, the school Willie got into—a nursery school on the Upper West Side—seemed to offer most of what we were looking for. Though their fours classes were a little larger than we'd like (sixteen children with a head teacher and an assistant), it was smaller than some of the other pre-K classes at private schools we visited with twenty-two or even thirty kids. Though the nursery school director was new, the head teachers all had had at least three years' experience before getting their own classrooms, their brochure said. Some of the teachers had been there for ten years or more. Most importantly, it was the only school Willie got into. Our choice seemed to have been made for us.

There are sixteen children in Willie's fours class this fall—an even mix of eight boys and eight girls. As of the second week, Willie seems to have fit right into the flow of the class, with his typical lack of anxiety about separation. The day is long compared to his art and music program. He arrives at school every morning at 8:45, eats lunch there, has a half-hour nap, and has afternoon activities until dismissal at 2:45. Twice a week, he goes to a language specialist after school, the one recommended by Dr. Levine, to work on his pronunciation. The other days, he's had play dates with a few of the little boys who live in our neighborhood. So far, I haven't heard any complaints about his behavior at school or with his friends.

At first, I debated whether or not to tell his teachers about Willie's ADD—I didn't want to prejudice them or interfere with their forming their own opinions. But it occurred to me that they also might be upset if they found out on their own. Also, it would be important to make sure they knew the best ways to help Willie—and this included telling them about the negative experiences he had at his old threes program. Peter and I were so eager to make sure that Willie would have a good year at his new school that we did a little research and requested a specific teacher, one whom friends had recommended as being great with "active" boys (the reigning euphemism, it appears, for *hyper*active boys). This woman had been a teacher at the school for twenty years, we were told, and had sons of her own. We were thrilled to think Willie would be in such good hands.

The second day of school, after I drop Willie off, I ask to speak with the head teacher for a moment in private.

"I just want to alert you to something that we're going to ask for your help with this year," I explain once Willie is out of earshot. "We're having Willie evaluated for ADD. Do you know what that is?"

"Oh, sure," the teacher says with a nod. "A boy in my class last year was on Ritalin."

"Great," I tell her. "Your input is really important to us as we continue to have him evaluated and, perhaps, do a trial of Ritalin this fall."

"Willie seems like he's settling in fine," the teacher repeats. "He really doesn't seem that much more active than the other boys." I'm glad to hear Willie hasn't been a problem, but I know the way things seem to work for him. Willie's still probably on good behavior with all the new adults and teachers in the room. It's only the second day, after all. And, as I explain to his new teacher, hyperactivity doesn't seem to be Willie's main problem: the impulsivity, excitability, and low frustration tolerance were more what we wanted to work on. I explain that, because of his lisp, he is working with a speech therapist, which should help him feel more comfortable using language (as opposed to his fists) to solve his problems.

The teacher looks skeptical, as if she thinks Peter and I are overreacting. "I noticed he's got a bit of a lisp," she allows. "But then again, a number of children at this age talk funny."

I bite my lip, unhappy with the way this conversation is going. "Well, we won't do anything without talking to you first," I promise, trying to be diplomatic. "But I think we owe it to Willie to check out Ritalin if it can help him."

The head teacher still looks distinctly unconvinced. I tell her I'll bring in Dr. Levine's report, which we just received last week. The head teacher says she'll discuss it with her assistant, a woman in her early twenties who, coincidentally, worked as a special ed assistant in a public school last year. But I know that she thinks I'm crazy to worry about a child who, to her, looks completely normal. I can almost read it on her face. *New York parents. Why are they all so neurotic and pushy?*

October 1, 1993

We haven't heard much from Willie's school except for the occasional phone call that Willie's been roughhousing in the gym. Still, the head teacher insists that he doesn't seem so much different from the other boys in his class, many of whom get "time-outs" for rowdiness, too. She keeps urging me to reconsider his ADD diagnosis. The constant negative reinforcement and the personality clash could have been most of the problem at his first school, she says.

While I agree that Willie and his threes teacher were a bad match, I still know in my heart that ADD is what Willie's got. I see how he acts compared with the other kids in his class, the way one part of his body is always moving, his feet and hands usually, twitching and tapping away. I see how fidgety he gets when the teachers try to gather the children in a circle for morning meeting—how he has to have a lot of space around him at all times or else he feels "squooshed." Even Nicholas, who's in the throes of his "terrible twos," has a lot easier time keeping his hands to himself. It's ironic, I think, that after all the time I spent praying someone would say Willie was "normal," *I'm* the one who's insisting now that he's got an underlying neurological problem.

I'm meeting with the school psychologist to discuss the situation with her. In advance, I've sent her Dr. Levine's report and that of the pediatric neurologist, hoping that these will help convince her—not that I think we need the school's consent for a diagnosis but, after our experience at Willie's old school, I'd rather have all of us working on the same side. Actually, I'm hoping that the school psychologist can be our ally in this. Though Willie's teacher may be reluctant to agree about the ADD, surely the psychologist will recognize the telltale signs from all his tests.

The psychologist ushers me into her office and proceeds to ask me about Willie's background, although all that information is in Dr. Levine's report. I ask her if she's observed Willie at all in class and she says that, since it's the beginning of the year, she didn't want to disrupt the class with a lengthy observation.

This sounds a little odd to me. How will she be able to tell if he has ADD or not if she hasn't spent any time with him?

"Did you get a chance to read Dr. Levine's report?" I ask.

"I don't know about ADD," the school psychologist says, not really answering my question. "You want to be sure you're not pigeonholing him with negative labels too soon."

"I agree," I say, trying not to sound too confrontational. "That's why we've pursued so many people's opinions."

"But have you *really* considered the alternatives to ADD, like an oppositional-behavior disorder or performance anxiety?" she persists.

"If it's too early to 'pigeonhole' him with a 'label' like ADD," I say, getting annoyed, "it's certainly too early to label him as oppositional, or performance anxious."

We continue the meeting without making any headway. Like Willie's teacher, she seems intent on downplaying Willie's symptoms, despite the fact that everyone agrees he's been having problems in class. She encourages me to keep trying to think of other reasons why Willie might be "acting out," as she calls it.

I finally give up trying to convince her that I might know my son a little bit better than she does—even though she admits she hasn't observed him for more than ten or fifteen minutes firsthand. *Why is everyone here arguing with me about the ADD diagnosis?*

November 13, 1993

As winter vacation approaches, I've been getting more phone calls about Willie. He's been roughhousing in the gym, having problems keeping his hands to himself in circle time, and sometimes hitting or scratching the other boys during free play, particularly when he can't get his way in the block corner.

"It's not that he's doing it out of aggression," his teacher says, bewildered. "He'll see a friend and give him a hug, then the hug turns to a squeeze, and then they're both on the floor, fighting."

"You don't have to explain," I say, morosely. "He's been doing that since he was two years old."

I call Dr. Andersov later that day to explain what's going on with Willie, and she suggests that she come in to observe his new class. I don't know what the point of an observation is, I tell her, when we know what the problems are with Willie. "It's the same thing he always struggles with," I say, frustrated. "Gym. Circle time. Hitting his friends over the head with wooden blocks."

Maybe somewhere inside myself I was secretly wishing that Willie's teacher was right—that he didn't have ADD; that it was all a bad dream.

"Still, the last time I saw him was nearly six months ago," Dr. Andersov points out. "I can't help him if I don't see him now."

I can see I have no choice in the matter. All the doctors—even Dr. Andersov and Dr. Levine, whom I like and trust—keep stretching everything out with more referrals and tests and observations than I thought were possible for a four-year-old boy. He's got ADD. What else do they need to know? Why can't they just figure out a way to help my son?

December 16, 1993

Peter and I meet with Dr. Andersov in her office after she's observed Willie at school. It's 8 A.M., not the ideal time for any of us to be talking about something so important. We're both exhausted from getting up so early for this appointment and I forgot to bring a cup of coffee with me, although coffee, like so many foods lately, is really starting to upset my stomach.

This was the only way to get all three of us together, however. Willie is not alone in having an eventful fall. Recently, I've gone back to work on my novel. I take Nicky to his play group twice a week, but the rest of the day he's at home with Jolie. Though I've tried to work in a small back room off our kitchen, Nicky has a habit of storming up to my computer and shouting imperiously, "Turn it *off!*" The writer's studio where I now rent space is ten blocks from Willie's school—a room set up with little carrels in an office building—and no phones allowed, for maximum peace and quiet.

Additionally, Peter has just been named the acting editor of the magazine where he works after his boss of thirteen years left this fall. The magazine company is considering whether they'll appoint him as permanent editor in chief, which is something he has worked for all his career. Of course, this new situation means much more pressure, and his once-flexible schedule is now completely chaotic.

Dr. Andersov says she observed Willie during the morning free-play time, when he went to the block corner with some other boys. There were a few instances of the pushing and fighting we'd described from his threes class. The main problem, she says, is that there are simply too many children in the class for Willie. "There's too much visual activity, too much noise," she insists. "It's way too stimulating for him to manage."

"What can we do about that?" Peter asks.

"We need to give his teachers strategies to help Willie better: to recognize when he's starting to feel out of control and intervene before he gets out of hand." The block corner, Dr. Andersov explains, is particularly challenging for Willie. The activities are unstructured, and it's hard for Willie to get settled. Working with building blocks also requires a lot of communication and cooperation—both of which are hard for him because of his speech problems and his tendency to react physically instead of verbally to the other children.

"Most of the situations where Willie gets into trouble are avoidable," she says. "You can see Willie's frustration brewing like a teakettle until it finally erupts."

She tells us an anecdote from her recent visit. Willie and two boys were building a block tower that the other boys said was a farm but that Willie insisted was the Empire State Building. When the boys started putting plastic farm animals on the structure, Willie got upset and started to raise his voice, insisting it was the Empire State Building. The boys wouldn't change their game and Willie started looking angry, clenching his fists and squaring off, as if ready to fight.

If the teachers had intervened then, Dr. Andersov said, they could have defused Willie's anger and helped the boys figure out a solution to the problem, like taking turns with the building being a barn, *then* the Empire State Building. Instead, what happened was that Willie started shouting and crying when the boys wouldn't change their game and eventually broke the building, getting everyone even more angry and upset with him.

My stomach feels tight as I hear her story and I glance at Peter, who looks anxious, too. Poor Willie! He must always feel that something goes wrong when he plays with kids his age. (And it usually does, because of his problems.) How is he ever going to learn to have friends, let alone feel good about who he is on his own, when things like this always happen?

Dr. Andersov says she talked with the assistant teacher, who'd been near the block area while all this was taking place. The assistant said that this type of incident was fairly common for Willie and that once he got upset, it was hard to calm him down again. Obviously, stepping in before Willie gets so worked up will be crucial to his success. Punishing him for his impulsive reactions wouldn't teach him anything, everyone agreed.

"The goal," Dr. Andersov explains, "is to eventually make Willie aware of when he's starting to feel angry and teach him how to calm himself down."

"Can he learn that at four?" I ask.

"I think Willie's old enough now to come in for weekly sessions," Dr. Andersov says, adding that what she'd try to do with Willie is have him role-play the frustrating situations that he encounters in class—like playing games in the block corner where he doesn't always get his own way. Over time, she explains, he'd get desensitized to those kinds of emotional triggers. Dr. Andersov suggests that I come into the sessions with Willie, acting as a kind of co-therapist. "It's a little unusual, I know, but it would allow for us to do more than what would be possible one-on-one."

"But I don't know anything about psychology," I say, nervously. "What if I do the wrong thing?"

"I'll be in there with you," she says encouragingly, explaining that, normally, she'd try to put Willie in group therapy but all the other children she's working with right now are too old for him. Besides, working with me, she points out—someone he knows and trusts—will probably be more productive than working with new kids who he might feel would be more of a threat.

"It's a great idea, honey," Peter says, obviously all for it.

It *is* a great idea, but it also means leaving work before 4 P.M. every Monday in order to get Willie to Dr. Andersov's office on time. I don't know how I'd be doing all this if I worked in a regular job. As it is, I'm not getting much done on my novel. The rewrite I promised my agent last August is still sitting half finished in my computer.

"Okay," I say, hesitating only a minute. How can I say no? It's our child. Willie means more to me than any novel.

Dr. Andersov is talking about teaching Willie a behavior modification technique called "Stop, Relax, and Think," which would help him with his impulsivity, but I'm not really listening as carefully as I should.

A year has gone by since Willie was kicked out of his first preschool. It's hard to believe that we are finally taking the first steps toward getting him help. Our sweet boy. I can picture his face in the nursery school, the look of bewilderment dissolving to anger as he tries to play with the other children.

All we want for him is what every parent wants: for him to learn, to have friends, to be happy. It must be so hard to be Willie—such a little guy—to be unable to control his own body or actions; to know that he's done the wrong thing and feel bad about it; to know that everyone always gets upset with him.

I think about Willie when he was an infant. I would get up in the middle of the night to nurse him, and his red face would look as if it were made out of one huge, open mouth. It was so easy to take care of him then, to give him what he needed. I can't pick him up now and whisper "Everything will be all right," without feeling like a liar. I hope it will be all right. Anything more, I can't promise.

January 3, 1994

We've met Dr. Miller, a pediatric psychiatrist who evaluated whether or not Willie would be a good candidate for Ritalin. This is the seventh specialist we've been to for Willie. When I visit Dr. Miller, of course he asks for Willie's case history and, for the seventh time, like a robot, I hear myself spit out all the relevant facts and figures: the problems with my labor and delivery, how the umbilical cord was wrapped around Willie's neck (reduced oxygen to the brain in delivery, I've learned, is a possible cause of ADD, as well as genetics and environmental factors).

I tell Dr. Miller about Willie's infant sleeping and eating habits, the way he was always frightened by loud noises—reacting violently with slapping or scratching. Dr. Miller shakes his head when I tell him about the first nursery school. It's still depressing and makes me angry to go over the details, but the doctor needs to know to get a full picture of Willie's symptoms.

Dr. Miller asks if there is any history of facial tics or heart ailments in the family. I must look surprised as I tell him no, because he quickly explains that Ritalin can aggravate those conditions. This gets me a little suspicious.

"Has Ritalin been thoroughly studied for use with ADD?" I ask, alarmed. Peter and I don't want to risk trying any experimental drugs for Willie. We don't want to use our child as a guinea pig.

Dr. Miller assures me that Ritalin is the most-studied drug in the world, after aspirin. How it became used for ADD, he says, is that originally, they were testing it for other medical uses in children, but the researchers noticed it made the hyperactive children much less fidgety.

I tell him that I've heard Ritalin can suppress a child's normal growth, but Dr. Miller shakes his head. Ritalin is perfectly safe to take over a long period of time, he tells me. There are no known permanent side effects. If growth is occasionally inhibited, they'll take the child off the drug and he'll reach his normal height. "Of course, it's not going to turn a Willie Shoemaker into a Kareem Abdul Jabaar. It's not a growth hormone."

"What about addiction? I've heard it can be dangerous," I say.

Dr. Miller explains that Ritalin is nonaddictive. In fact, recent studies have shown that teenagers who use Ritalin for Attention Deficit Disorder were *less* likely to experiment with drugs or alcohol. Best of all, it's extremely effective—curbing hyperactive, inattentive, and impulsive behavior in 80 percent of the children who take it. Though he says it might seem paradoxical giving a psychostimulant—speed—to children who are already overly active, the drug seems to act like a radio transmitter, with the Ritalin strengthening the frequency of the transmissions and cutting through the "static" of irrelevant stimuli.

"Why does that help?" I ask, confused.

"You see," Dr. Miller explains, "the problem with these children isn't that they get too much neurological information, it's that they get too much all at once."

I nod as it all sinks in. Finally, I understand why Willie's behavior could seem so erratic. Willie overreacts to some things, like noise and frustration, but underreacts to others, like social cues.

"Would you put your own child on it?" I ask, as a kind of litmus test.

"My own son *is* on it," he says, nodding. "That's how I got interested in treating ADD in the first place."

"If Willie checks out," I tell the doctor, "I'd like to give Ritalin a try."

"How does your husband feel about it?" Dr. Miller asks.

I'm not going to lie to him: Truth is, Peter's less than thrilled about the idea of giving psychostimulants to a four-year-old. When Peter was growing up, his family was skeptical about the way many medicines seemed to be overprescribed. When Peter got a cold, his mother gave him chicken soup while his friends popped antibiotics. I, on the other hand, went twice weekly to an allergist for shots—I was allergic to everything from cow's milk to chocolate, dogs to dust mites. Without Western medicine, I'd probably have died of an asthma attack long ago. Even now, I still take a fistful of drugs every morning: steroid inhalers to treat my asthma, iron for anemia, and antacids for the almost-constant burning in my stomach, which I attribute to stress about Willie's school and Peter's work situation. Still, Peter and I agree about Ritalin for Willie. If it can help him, Peter agrees that we owe it to Willie to try. "My husband is willing to do it if you think it might help," I explain.

I schedule an appointment with Dr. Miller for him to meet Willie. If he thinks that Willie has ADD, he'll prescribe Ritalin. In the meantime, I'm going to mail him a copy of Dr. Levine's report (he says he wants to see it *after* he meets Willie so he can form his own opinion of him). Additionally, he gives us some forms that he wants us and his teachers to fill out and mail back to him. The teachers' answers should be confidential, he says, because it encourages them to be more honest. I scan the forms, which ask parents to rate how much, or how little, their child has been affected by certain problems during the past month. The list of behaviors seems to go on and on: "Picks at things (nails, fingers, hair, clothing); excitable or impulsive; gets into more trouble than others same age; restless in the 'squirmy' sense; mood changes that are quick and drastic; problems with sleep (can't fall asleep, up too early, up in the night)." Without even reading very far down the list, I can't believe how many of these describe my child.

January 13, 1994

This morning, I meet with the director of Willie's nursery school to discuss the possibility of trying Willie out on Ritalin. The director, a willowy woman with curly red hair, looks relieved when she hears we want to try medicating Willie. In fact, she tells me, if I hadn't brought it up, she was going to suggest the subject of drug treatment herself. She's familiar with Ritalin: Other students in the lower school take it. The director nods supportively when I explain how we'd work the drug trial: a small dose of 2.5 milligrams at first, working up to 5 milligrams if it seems successful.

The director says that they have been concerned about Willie's behavior, which seems to have gotten worse since he came back from winter break. As with his first nursery school, he still is hitting and getting out of control during the unstructured activities like free play and gym. "The other children need to feel safe at school," the director says, primly, and I can't disagree.

Still, I'm frustrated that it took them so long to agree to the Ritalin trial. Just because ADD is a behavioral disorder, they felt free to second-guess us from the minute we brought it up; whereas if I'd come in saying I wanted them to help us try a medicine for my son's diabetes or epilepsy, they never would have disputed the underlying diagnosis.

The important thing now, however, is that the school is willing to cooperate with us on the Ritalin trial. As it turns out, we need their help giving Willie the drug because Willie's teachers would need to give him his second dose at lunchtime.

The meeting is going well, despite its rough points. The nursery school director is smiling at me, happy that everyone finally agrees. Her phone rings and, a few seconds after answering it, her face falls.

It's the assistant teacher in Willie's class, requesting urgent help with Willie. Getting up from her desk, the director tells me tersely that Willie was having some kind of fit—hiding under a table, spitting and kicking. His teachers tried to get him out, but nothing would work.

I'm shocked. Willie's been disruptive in school before, but he's never done anything quite like this. I feel like Linda Blair's mother in *The Exorcist*, half expecting the director to tell me Willie is vomiting pea soup.

I follow the director downstairs through the outside play area as a shortcut to Willie's class. Though it's the middle of January, we haven't bothered to put on our coats. In the twenty yards or so it takes to cross the playground, my hands and face get numb in the wind, but I barely notice. On some irrational level, I think that the more I suffer, the more suffering will be taken away from my child, as if my dying of frostbite would have any effect on Willie's ADD.

On the stairs going up to the classroom, the director elaborates on the phone call. Willie became upset when a substitute teacher tried to work with him in the block corner. The head teacher is out sick, she says. This is beginning to make sense now.

Like many other ADD kids, Willie has a hard time adjusting to new people and places, I explain to the director. Even small, unavoidable changes in his routine, like a substitute teacher, can really unnerve him.

"Even so," the director says, "Willie's violence is disturbing. The substitute teacher was afraid he might kick her in the stomach." I must have looked confused because then the director explains that the substitute teacher is pregnant.

My vision changes from *The Exorcist* to *Rosemary's Baby*, with my son as the devil-child, the threat to procreation.

I feel increasingly anxious and nauseous as we climb the stairs to Willie's classroom. On the walls of the stairwell are happy, Day-Glo drawings, which make the situation feel even more surreal. As far as I can tell, I'm the only parent in the entire six-floor building. Everyone else has left after dropping off all their happy, normal, well-adjusted children. The other mothers have all gone home or to work, where I'd be right now if my child wasn't hiding in a bunker like some kind of junior David Koresh in Waco.

I try to lighten the mood because I'm afraid of the numbness growing deep in my stomach, that I might faint or throw up if I don't force myself to talk soon. I try to joke with the director as we walk up our fourth flight of stairs that at least we won't have to go to the gym today, after climbing all these stairs. She smiles, empathetically, as if to remind me she's not the villain in all of this. She's got children, too. She knows how hard it is to be a parent.

When we finally reach Willie's floor, I see the assistant teacher leading the children out of the classroom in a single-file line. Like the stairs, the hall is bright and full of colorful artwork, but it's drafty and narrow, so I'm surprised when I see her sit the children down on the landing and read a story to them.

"What are you doing out here?" I ask. I expected to see Willie banished to the hallway, not the rest of them.

The teacher reminds me that they can't get Willie out from under the table and that the other children were starting to be afraid of his yelling and fighting.

Under the circumstances, she seems amazingly friendly and calm. I glance at the fifteen other children sitting in the hallway because of my son. They don't even seem to notice me, I've become such a permanent fixture in their classroom, always staying after drop-off to help Willie negotiate the block corner until the assistant teacher can come over, always picking up Willie early to herd him off to one doctor's appointment or another.

Inside, I see Willie, looking scared but angry. He's hiding under the table and shaking his fists. The assistant teacher talks to me out in the hall while the substitute reads the story to the children. The director goes inside and somehow—I don't know how—manages to coax Willie out.

The director opens the door to the class and Willie runs into my arms. His soft face is tearstained and hot as I kiss it. I wonder if he's coming down with a fever, which might explain why he's so irritable.

I cuddle him, whispering "I love you," in his ear. Willie gurgles like a baby, saying "Mama, mama." His voice sounds like a china doll's, high-pitched and fragile. He tucks his head into my neck, the way he did when he was little and I rocked him to sleep. I want to sing him a lullaby, sweet simple words that will make it all better.

The school psychologist arrives and suggests that I take Willie out in the hallway so the rest of the class can come back inside.

It's hard to carry Willie in my high heels and tailored skirt—I'm dressed to go to a meeting with an editor today about some potential freelance magazine articles, not to spend the morning in preschool. Eventually, I manage to get us both out to the stairwell. I'm trying to comfort him and, at the same time, find out in his own words why he went under the table and started fighting in the first place.

Willie doesn't want to speak. He won't even meet my glance. He just lies in my arms, exhausted from his tirade.

I'm very conscious of the fact that a psychologist and two educational experts are on the other side of the doorway listening to everything we say. This is my least-favorite aspect of the morning's events: parenting on parade.

Willie seems tired but willing to go back inside the classroom. (I'm more surprised by the fact that the teachers are willing to have him stay after all this.) I remain outside, talking to the director and the school psychologist, who has just gotten off a previously scheduled phone call with Dr. Andersov. I think about how much work an ADD child causes the school staff. Between the phone calls and the meetings—emergency and otherwise—20 percent of their day has already been taken up by my son. And this is only one ADD child in the school.

We hear shouts in the classroom, so we go inside. To no one's surprise, the shouts have come from Willie. He's in the block corner, in another tangle with the second-most-difficult boy in the class, who wants to change the architecture of one of Willie's buildings.

This child is Willie's nemesis—athletic and smart but with a history of teasing Willie because of his speech impediment. Willie is flailing his arms and shouting in frustration. I wonder why, considering the morning he's had, there isn't a teacher working directly with Willie to help ease his transition back to the classroom and intercept problems like this before they start. He shouldn't have been left unsupervised or allowed to play with this boy, in particular.

I sit down in the block corner in my short-skirted business

suit, trying not to flash my underwear to the roomful of four-year-olds. Willie has knocked down his building rather than do it the other boy's way.

"It's garbage now," Willie says, referring to the damaged building.

I don't like to hear him call his own work garbage, so I decide to take his comment literally.

"It's a garbage dump," I say, trying to involve the two or three other children who have gathered around us, curious. "What are some of the things you might find in a garbage dump?"

"Rats and worms," the nemesis says, typically mischievous.

"Maybe seagulls," a girl offers daintily.

We all start to act like the animals they've just mentioned. Even Willie is flapping his arms like a seagull, making little throaty bird sounds and smiling happily.

The crisis is over, I think, as I see the teacher approach. "Willie's had a pretty rough morning," she whispers to me. "I think it would be better for everyone if you took Willie home to relax."

Better for everyone, maybe, but Willie and me. Now that he's calm, it seems unfair to send Willie home at midday.

Outside, Willie throws snowballs at the parked cars as we walk home. Though he seems carefree and happy, singing Christmas carols in his high-pitched soprano, I know he's becoming increasingly aware that he gets in trouble more often than the other children in his class. And while I always try to make the decision to go home a positive, not a punitive one, I worry that, if things don't get better for him on Ritalin, his self-esteem will be damaged, and he'll start to be stigmatized as the "bad boy," as he was at his old nursery school.

When we get home, I call the psychiatrist even before I take off my coat. The doctor recommends that we start the Ritalin immediately, at a low dose, initially 2.5 milligrams today, working up to 5 milligrams over the weekend.

I've been warned about the side effects such as repressed appetite and sleeplessness—just what we need, I think, not looking forward to either possibility. Just this year, Willie graduated from the peculiar diet he favored as a three-year-old, which consisted almost exclusively of chicken nuggets, strawberries, and macaroni and cheese. How much more finicky could he get on Ritalin?

And that's not even the worst side effect, the doctor warned.

What I'm dreading is the "rebound effect." In a rebound, the child crashes like a speed freak, becoming anxious and irritable as the medicine wears off.

Dr. Miller says not to worry too much about "rebounding," as he calls it. Usually, a third dose in the afternoon helps so the drug doesn't wear off until the child's regular bedtime. He encourages me to call him in the evening and over the weekend if any problems come up, even though it's a holiday on Monday.

There's only one thing left to do now and that's give Willie the medicine, which I've been saving in a cabinet since Dr. Miller gave me the prescription. The pills are tiny, smaller than a Jujube, and surprisingly brittle.

One pill is 5 milligrams, so I have to cut it in half, which isn't easy, because of its consistency and size. The first one I try comes out completely uneven. I wash it down the sink so Nicholas won't find it in the garbage can and eat it, mistakenly thinking it's candy.

I go into the living room where Willie is watching a videotape of *Bedknobs and Broomsticks*. I watch for a little while with him, wishing that the things challenging him were as laughably inept as the bungling Disney Nazis in the movie.

I wait until after lunch to give him his first pill, so he will have some food in his stomach in case the drug suppresses his appetite later. I'm very conscious of the fact that Campbell's chicken soup with stars, an American cheese sandwich, and carrot sticks are an unusual appetizer for amphetamines.

Everything about giving my son Ritalin makes me feel like I'm a criminal. There were the pharmacist's careful whispers to me after she read the prescription, as if what Willie had was too awful to say aloud. (Every time I go in there now, I feel as if the whole staff is looking at me. I imagine them thinking: "There's that woman who gave Ritalin to a four-year-old.") On the bottle is a warning label telling me it's a felony offense to dispense the medication without a prescription.

Willie swallows the pill without any trouble: proud of himself that he was able to do it on the very first try. His innocent willingness to please is almost heartbreaking, given the circumstances.

At 12:30 P.M., our baby-sitter returns with Nicholas asleep in his stroller. I force myself out the door, feeling guilty for leaving, thinking I should stay home to observe Willie, in case anything happens. But there's not much to watch. The drug won't peak for another two hours.

When I finally get to the office, I'm too upset to work on my novel or prepare for my meeting with the magazine editor. The situation strikes me as bleakly ironic. I started writing to make sense of my past—the mystery of my parents' difficult marriage and my childhood in New York—and here I keep getting pulled back into the reality of the unrelenting present: my own children, my own marriage, the family Peter and I have made together.

On my bulletin board, I've got a picture of Willie and Nicholas together in the bathtub: It almost makes me cry now to look at their shiny, wet faces. I used to think a happy childhood was something I could give them so effortlessly, like a loving hug after a bath, or a fluffy, dry towel. Now I realize what Willie needs is so much more complicated than I expected and I'm afraid of failing with him—of failing him—when it's so vital that we succeed.

Peter has warned me not to get my hopes up too much about the Ritalin, but I can't avoid it: I'm convinced that somewhere there is a drug to help Willie. To me, trying Ritalin is like opening a door in a sideshow. What's behind it for him: the lady or the tiger?

January 15, 1994

It's Saturday morning, the start of a long weekend: Martin Luther King, Jr.'s birthday. Outside, the weather is below zero, a record-breaking cold spell, and people are advised to stay indoors all day. I thought we were prepared for the contingencies of this weekend: we made at-home play dates for the boys and stocked up on junk food and Star Trek videos, which they're both too young to really understand but enjoy anyway.

But cabin fever has struck already (real fever, too—I wake up with 99.5°F), and I can tell it's going to be a *long* long weekend. It's not even 9 A.M. yet and Peter and I are snapping at each other as he sits in the middle of our apartment, trying to assemble a complicated mail-order sled.

"We're not going sledding when it's colder than Antarctica outside," I say critically, as Willie chases Nicholas around the living room.

It's Willie's third day on Ritalin but I can't see any improvement in his behavior. If anything, I think the medicine makes him worse: more defiant and emotional, as if he were constantly rebounding. His sleeping and eating have gone off-schedule, as the doctor warned they might.

He was wakeful last night, up a few times between 11 P.M. and 2 A.M., and up for good at 6 A.M. We are all exhausted and feeling sick.

Even Willie looks like he's coming down with something. He's flushed and sweaty as he dashes back and forth, trying to get our attention by being loud and disruptive: sitting on the sled as Peter tries to work on it; jumping on Nicholas and me, toppling both of us over. I'm desperate for a shower and a cup of hot coffee, but I'm afraid of what will happen if I leave the room.

I glance at the newspaper headlines for what can only be a few seconds, but it's enough time for Willie to grab a screwdriver from the open tool kit. I tell him to put it back and Willie laughs at me, mocking and defiant. Peter ignores him, but I can't: he has willfully disobeyed me in a way that is both rude and potentially dangerous.

"Put the screwdriver down, Willie," I repeat, more firmly.

Willie zips toward the dining room, his tousled hair a sandy-blond blur. His hands are shaking with excitement. He's running on tiptoes, as if his body can't possibly contain all his energy. The screwdriver flashes in the morning light. Its Phillips-head tip is sharp and pointed—I'm imagining puncture wounds, permanent eye loss.

This giddiness and disobedience is totally out of character. He hasn't acted like this since he was three years old. I shout after him, angrily now. "Willie, get back here this instant!"

I chase the boys into the dining room, trying to apprehend the tool thief, who has crawled under the dining room table and is giggling madly.

Nicholas is underneath the table, hiding and laughing, too, imitating his older brother. I stare at my younger child's face. His dark, almond-shaped eyes are wide-open in delight at this ingenious new version of hide-and-seek Willie has invented. I know Nicky has no idea that Willie's behavior is at all out of the ordinary: all he knows is that what Willie's doing looks like fun and is exciting. As I crouch down on the floor to try to sweet-talk Willie out, I worry about the kind of example we are setting for Nicholas, that he will think this kind of mischief is accepted and normal.

My inclination, at the moment, is to yell furiously at Willie, but we've found that shouting only makes him more defensive and angry—possibly because of his sensitivity to loud noises. Besides, the point of our discipline, as Dr. Andersov has explained, is not to force Willie to do what we want, but to help him learn how to behave the right way on his own.

I try to keep this in mind on mornings like this, when it's hard enough to calm my own temper, let alone that of my son. What I want to do is grab the screwdriver and hurl it back in the tool chest, then collapse in my bed and sleep twelve more hours.

But what I do, instead, is to take a deep breath and try to keep my voice (and rising temperature) in check. The incident has come to a critical point. If I yell at Willie now, he could start fighting under the table, screaming and writhing around. The screwdriver is just too close to Nicholas's face to risk it. I look at Willie, still huddled under the dining room table, his soft, still-pudgy little-boy hands vibrating with excitement compared with Nicky, who, as excited as he is at this newfound "game," is nonetheless perfectly still, watching Buddhalike as I negotiate with Willie.

I try to think about what it feels like to Willie under there. His pajamas must feel smooth compared with the pointed metal screwdriver. The light is dim and exotic in the makeshift hideout. Nicholas pushes closer to Willie with his small, warm body, then Willie fidgets away, hungry for more space.

Outside, the sound of people shoveling snow is as steady as a metronome. I start to feel exhausted and feverish so I lie down on the cool, wooden floor. I wonder what my friends without children are doing right now, and why my husband is still in the living room playing with his sled.

"Willie, give me the screwdriver," I tell him, softly. My voice is calm but firm, the way Dr. Andersov has suggested.

Still with his hands over his face, Willie giggles with a high-pitched trill and tries to hide the incriminating tool under Nicky's yellow blanket.

"I see the screwdriver, Willie. Can you hand it to me or should I get it myself?" This is a variation of the mantra Dr. Andersov says we're supposed to use whenever Willie gets wild: "Can you get back in control, or should I help you?"

There is a scratch, then a slide along the brown parquet floor. The rolling screwdriver stops just before it hits me in the leg. It glints silver in the light, reminding me of buried treasure: Willie's true angelic sweetness, hidden deep under his symptoms.

All morning, Willie needs almost constant attention. He's chattering persistently—another side effect of the Ritalin—and getting very anxious if he's left alone, although everything Peter and I do, from getting him dressed to reading stories, seems to just annoy him more. Willie's behavior toward Nicholas hasn't changed, however. In typical older-brother fashion, he seems alternatively oblivious and protective. By noon, we've managed to get Willie seated at the kitchen table for his next dose of Ritalin.

He waits, swinging his legs rapidly over the edge of the chair. It's the longest he's been able to sit (relatively) still all day.

We give him the second little yellow half-pill and, as soon as we do, I've a panicky, almost uncontrollable impulse to smack him on chest so he will spit it back up.

Suddenly, Willie is furious, jumping off the chair and yelling that he wanted a white cup, not the blue one we gave him with water for his pill. He looks tired and slightly dazed, but his color is rising as he finds a focus for his anger.

"I wanted the white one! The white one!" he says, becoming inconsolable.

On Ritalin, he's been repeating himself a lot, like a broken record, when he gets angry. He's standing up now, shouting at Peter and me, still upset about the misunderstanding with the cup. He's repeating himself so many times in a row that I finally stop counting after eleven. I'm too shocked to do anything but stare at the back of his balled-up fists as he storms out of the kitchen.

I look at Peter anxiously, knowing we should call the doctor. This is more than a rebound from his morning medication. I think that Willie might be having one of those rare "paradoxical" reactions the psychiatrist warned us about, where the Ritalin actually makes some of the ADD symptoms worse.

Before, Willie tended to be oversensitive and short-tempered, but he could usually be humored out of any bad mood in a matter of minutes. On Ritalin, when he's angry, the tantrums go on for almost half an hour, as if the Ritalin has improved only his ability to pay attention to his own anger.

When I suggest this to Peter, his face tightens noticeably. He warns me not to "overreact" on the basis of just one morning. I stare hard at the dull, red floor tiles in the kitchen, more perplexed than annoyed by Peter's reaction. I decide my husband is in denial. To me, it's clear that our trial of Ritalin has been a total disaster.

I try to use the same psychology that worked before with Willie, thinking what this situation feels like to Peter. I know he's annoyed because he couldn't finish building the sled this morning. He worked hard to find this exact brand and model and was looking forward to using it in the park today with the boys but can't because of the below-freezing weather.

I'm sure he's just as worried about the Ritalin as I am; he only shows his anxiety differently—by repressing it completely. He says that he's got as much right to his opinion about the medication as I do—which is true, of course—but I tell him I'm certain that the Ritalin should have worked by now, if it's ever going to work at all. The parents in the ADD support group meetings I've attended—even Dr. Miller, himself—say that when Ritalin works, it does so after the very first dose.

I suggest we ask the doctor about switching Willie to Dexedrine, a time-released drug (also a psychostimulant) that is the second most commonly prescribed drug for ADD. As Dr. Miller explained it, Dexedrine metabolizes more evenly, meaning fewer of the "speedy" peaks and crashes we've been seeing with Willie.

"You just talked to the doctor last night," Peter says, sharply. "It's unlikely he's changed his mind about the Ritalin in the last twelve hours."

"I'm not sure he appreciates the full extent of Willie's side effects," I say, my tone getting caustic. Last night when I talked to Dr. Miller, he said it was too early to tell whether Willie's reaction was paradoxical. It can occassionally require days for children to get used to the drug, he explained, especially a four-year-old whose metabolic system is still naturally uneven. He recommended a third dose at 4 P.M. for the evening rebound and told us to "stay the course," sounding as doomed and hopeless to me as a preelection George Bush.

"We haven't tried the third dose yet," Peter says, as we bicker in the kitchen.

Since it's only the men who are pushing to continue, I wonder if it is a particularly male trait to be more concerned with the procedure of an experiment than with the actual results. Before Ritalin, we had a sweet if excitable boy who had problems with his social skills at school. Now, we have a child whose behavior I hardly recognize.

I'm afraid to go back in the room with him. All I've heard since the time I got home last night is the sound of Willie whining and screaming. We agree to call Dr. Miller, but he's out of the office—not surprising, since it's the middle of Saturday afternoon on a long weekend.

In a fast, frantic voice, I leave a message for him to call us, knowing I sound desperate. I glance at Peter, and see him frowning at me from the other side of the kitchen. More female hysteria, I'm sure he's thinking: the archetypal nervous mother. But at the moment, I'm feeling too hysterical to care whether or not I sound hysterical.

By 1 P.M., the psychiatrist still hasn't called us back, so Willie and I brave the cold weather to go out to a local restaurant for lunch. Though he'd been whining and fussy in the lobby of our building, once outside, Willie's mood improves immediately, just as it did on Thursday when he got sent home from school. I wonder if fresh air—such as it is in New York—helps Willie snap out of tantrums, for he seems happy enough, if not quite his usual cheery self, as we walk the frigid five blocks to the restaurant. He seems particularly interested in the way the wind feels on his face but, considering that it's sixteen degrees below zero outside with winds gusting up to thirty miles per hour, I don't take this as a sign of any abnormal, Ritalin-induced physical sensitivity. You'd have to be a polar bear not to notice that it is freezing out.

At lunch, Willie says he's starving and devours most of the rolls in the bread basket before our food comes. Despite the fact that it's now 1:30 P.M., an hour after his usual lunchtime, it still seems strange to me that he'd be so hungry on the Ritalin. His 12 P.M. dose is nearly peaking. If anything, it should be suppressing his appetite.

While Willie eats the rolls, he turns his head from side to side, as if he's looking for something. "Do you hear that, Mommy? Do you hear that?" he keeps repeating, finally pointing toward a pink neon sign in the window, where an electrical transformer is buzzing slightly. Amid the noise in the restaurant and the traffic outside, the buzzing sound is infinitesimal. It takes me a moment to even distinguish it. Willie, however, is entranced. He starts to stand on his chair to touch the pink lights. So much for the Ritalin helping with his aural distractibility and impulsivity.

I get an angry glance from the table behind us, and I know what the people sitting there are thinking: *Why can't that woman control her child?* We eat our food quickly and take a doggy bag home with the leftovers.

Back in our apartment, Willie makes me search the entire household for a one-inch plastic Star Trek toy. He follows me around the house, maniacally talking, until I suggest we split up and look for it.

Peter has gone out to do errands with Nicholas, so there's no one else here to help. I've been with Willie most of the day, while Peter has had two breaks outside. I consider calling one of my friends from the ADD support group for advice, but I'm too tired and depressed to talk to anyone right now.

I hide in the bathroom, pretending to look for Willie's toy, sitting down on the edge of the tub to close my eyes. If I have to live through another day like this with Willie, I will lose my sanity, my marriage, or both. Willie asks to watch a video, and I'm only too happy to oblige. If he's in front of the TV, maybe I can finally get a break, or at least a minute or so to compose my thoughts and cheer myself up. But as soon as Willie sits down in front of the VCR in the living room, Peter and Nicholas come home. I tell Peter to keep Nicky in the kitchen with him while he's unpacking groceries. Soon, Willie falls asleep but, five minutes after that, our dinner guests arrive with their four-year-old daughter.

There are loud shouts of "Hello," and "Where's Willie?" in the foyer as Nicholas and our friends' child bounce around the apartment.

They start to head for the living room, where Willie is sleeping. I want to move him off the couch fast, before the other children find him.

I notice that Peter is once again conspicuous in his absence:

He's retreated to the kitchen with the other adults to unpack the food and dessert they brought with them. I've been looking forward to seeing these friends all day, but now that they're here I'm furious with them. There they are, discussing the fat content of raspberry sorbet, oblivious to the fact that I'm in a crisis mode, racing to the living room to prevent everyone from waking up Willie.

I can't figure out why Peter and I are reacting so differently in the same situation. Is it because of all the stress at his office? Do Peter's very real concerns about keeping his job drain his energy away from thinking about me and Willie? And is it fair of me to expect him to bear an equal load of anxiety when his nerves are already frazzled from work?

I don't have much time to ponder these questions as I try to distract Nicholas and our friends' daughter from waking up Willie. I'm too late, of course. They are all over his slumped body like Lilliputians on Gulliver. I'm livid. Willie's been up since 6 A.M. and could have used the rest and I, frankly, could have used a break from Willie's difficult behavior today.

The brief nap seems to have left Willie a little disoriented. Although he seems happy to see his friend and they start playing in his room, he still looks tired, with puffed circles under his eyes.

I'm expecting the worst from this ill-timed play date, especially since the last time this little girl came over to play, Willie got unusually turf conscious, unwilling to share with her his favorite talking robot, which she'd decided was the only toy in the house she liked.

Sure enough, our friends' daughter goes right to the robot, but Willie doesn't blink an eye. Nicky flits in between them singing loudly and off-key. Willie starts to sing a different song and gets angry that his brother won't sing the same song that he wants.

"*Make* him sing mine," Willie orders. I remind him of our rule about not forcing people to do things and to try to play their way. Willie looks at me, betrayed.

Between the arguing and the talking robot, the decibel level is rising. Yet, surprisingly, Willie's not flying off the handle, as he might have in the past. Instead of hitting his brother angrily to get him to stop singing, or impulsively turning off the robot while the other child was playing with it, Willie stomps around the room, muttering to himself that Nicky's song is "stupid" and the robot should "shut up."

It's not ideal, but he hasn't hit anyone and I want to praise him for his efforts. "I like the way you're not forcing, Willie. Excellent control." I try to kiss him on the forehead but he shrugs me off quickly, still angry that I wouldn't help him get his own way.

While our friends are watching the Giants game, the psychiatrist calls back. Peter hands me the phone. I hand it back to him. Since it's Peter who doesn't believe that Willie's having a bad reaction to the drug, I figure he ought to hear it from the doctor himself.

"You talk to him," I say, as our friends look at him expectantly.

"All right," Peter says, getting up from the sofa. My guerrilla tactic has worked (so much for our rule about not forcing). As we walk into the bedroom to take the call, Peter gives me this pained look, as if to say he had no idea when he married me that I could be such a witch. I feel immediately guilty about making him get up from the football game. The situation with Willie could not have come at a worse time, given all the stress of Peter's job situation. We each feel pulled in two separate directions with no room in the middle to help each other.

I hear Peter asking Dr. Miller about switching to Dexedrine. He listens for a few minutes, then tells me Dr. Miller didn't recommend it—Dexedrine lasts only a half hour longer.

"I told you it takes time to do a medicine trial," Peter says, after he gets off the phone.

"How long are we supposed to give it?"

Peter shrugs. "He didn't say."

I feel more hopeless than ever. Back in the living room, we explain to our friends what's been going on with the Ritalin, having warned them in advance that Willie was trying out medication and that his behavior with their daughter might be a little unpredictable.

We figure that full disclosure is better than trying to pretend everything's fine. The wife's twelve-year-old nephew has ADD, too, I know. She tells me her nephew was doing fine on Ritalin until he hit puberty, but now his symptoms are getting worse and the medicine's stopped working. She fears her nephew is developing emotional problems. In school, he's a loner with very few friends and is stigmatized by the learning disabilities he has in addition to his ADD. "I feel so bad for my sister," our friend says, sadly. "It's every parent's nightmare."

"What are they going to do with him?" I ask, trying not to project the situation with Willie onto the one our friend has just described.

"They're thinking of sending him to a special school," she says. "It's ruining his life."

As we sit down to dinner, I'm feeling sorry I asked.

January 18, 1994

Willie's experience on Ritalin continues to be uneven, although today at school seems to be better than the weekend. It seems as if he's happier being with his peers than with adults right now. I have no idea if this is medicine-related.

Over the weekend, he continued to have periods of anger and uncooperativeness with Peter and me but was a fabulous companion to kids his own age, less rigid and bossy than we'd ever seen him before Ritalin.

His teachers say his behavior in school has improved for the most part although, with the long weekend, it's only their first day back. Because it's hard to find both the time and the privacy to talk with the teachers about Willie's progress on medication, we've started a notebook to monitor Willie's behavior. His teachers write down events of the day; Peter and I write down anything significant that happens with him at home.

The notebook is useful but, already, I've noticed a tendency for his teachers to focus on the negative, such as how many times a day Willie yelled or acted up, as opposed to the positive, such as how many situations like this Willie was able to avoid by using words or getting the teacher's assistance.

We never made it clear, I realize, what we wanted from the journal. Perhaps the teachers have included so much about the hitting and yelling because this was the behavior that stood out most in their minds. Or, without resorting to conspiracy theories, maybe the nursery school director had instructed them to document any violent episodes so there would be a record of evidence in case they us asked to withdraw Willie midyear, like at his first preschool.

Either way, it's clear we're on different tracks about the notebook, so, in order to get more descriptive information from them, I write out a list of questions for the teachers to use:

- What were the day's scheduled activities?
- Which activities were hardest for Willie? Why?
- Which activities were the easiest? Why?
- Did he nap at rest time?
- Did he have an appetite at lunch and snack?
- Are there still episodes of yelling and hitting? If so, are they shorter in duration on Ritalin or longer?
- Does Willie seem less "hyper" or fidgety?
- Is the medication making him extremely talkative? If so, is this mostly positive or negative?

Whenever I hand in the notebook, I make sure to thank his teachers for their constant attention and hard work. I know that it takes a lot of time to write in Willie's notebook every day, and I try to always remember that there are fifteen other children in the class besides Willie who need the teachers' attention.

January 19, 1994

My suggestions have paid off. Today's journal entry from the school is much more helpful and informative. The assistant teacher writes:

Fewer episodes of yelling, but he's still easily upset. The most difficult time today occurred between 9:30 and 10:30. He was unable to sit during meeting. He was talking and touching the children next to him. Gym time (11:30–12:15) went *very* well. It was difficult to calm him down after his Lego building broke. We had to leave the room and read a story about building a house. He became hypertalkative between 9:30 and 10:00, meeting and sharing time. This was negative; he eventually left the circle and played at the Lego table, quietly and alone. He rested but didn't sleep at nap time. The easiest times of today were snack (11:00–11:30), gym, lunch, and rest. In the afternoon, however, he ran out to the halls and hid in the bathroom and then in the cubbies.

I'm not thrilled to hear about Willie running out of the classroom. This kind of impulsivity is just the thing that the Ritalin is supposed to control. Is the drug having any effect on him? Clearly, it must be doing something—although what we've seen so far has mostly been negative. The hypertalkativeness and temper tantrums are particularly disturbing.

At home, I worry that the medicine is affecting his personality. He's much less cuddly and affectionate with Peter and me than he was before, although I was encouraged tonight to see that he still has his old, familiar flair for the dramatic. While we were watching an old television rerun of *Zorro*, Willie pretended to swordfight, jumping up from his seat to twirl an imaginary, black cape over his shoulders. Adding to the hilarity of the scene, as usual, was Willie's trusty sidekick, Nicholas, who was relegated to the important supporting role of Zorro's horse.

For Peter and me, it's always been fascinating to see the way Willie's ADD expresses itself in such ordinary activities as watching TV. While Nicky can sit still, however noisily, Willie seems biologically propelled into action, his ADD-related impulsivity and suggestibility causing him to reenact scenes and dialogue.

Not to say this is bad—Willie's cute imitations and precocious theatricality are usually pretty charming. But now that he's on Ritalin, Peter and I have to face the disturbing idea that what we've always taken for granted as being fixed pieces of Willie's personality—his imagination and energy—are, in fact, correctable symptoms of an underlying disease.

It makes me wonder about the very nature of Willie's identity: *Is the disorder a filter or a kind of lens that lets through or slants certain aspects of his personality? Which behavior is intrinsic to Willie being Willie and which to the fact that he has ADD? Would he be a different boy if he were neurologically normal and, more importantly, should we want him to be?*

Zorro cuts to a commercial for a seventies disco album, and Willie starts laughing uncontrollably at a picture of the Village People. "Who are *they?*" he asks, fascinated by the idea of adults acting out as dramatically as he ever does. For the next half hour, he's singing the chorus to "YMCA" and pestering me to find his hard hat like the one the guy in the construction-worker costume is wearing. So much for the Ritalin curbing Willie's suggestibility and hyperactivity—he's more unpredictable and frenetic than ever. Willie sings and dances around the kitchen—which, between him and Nicky, now sounds like children's hour at Studio 54.

After dinner, I talk to Willie about how the medicine is making him feel. He already knows about side effects from a special children's book about ADD that Dr. Miller gave him called *Otto Learns About His Medicine.* In the story, Otto is a nice little car who takes pills because his motor runs too fast and he has trouble paying attention in driving school. When we ask Willie if he's feeling any of the same side effects that Otto did in the book (not feeling hungry at lunchtime, not feeling tired at nap time and bedtime), Willie blinks his eyes hard, as if he's been implicitly criticized.

"Oh no, Mommy," he says, obviously remembering the biology section of his much-loved *Children's Encyclopedia.* "My white blood cells are helping the side effects get out. The side effects and the white blood cells are friends."

I've got no idea what this means to him. Does he feel that the medicine is a negative agent, to be fought like a virus, or does he mean that he's trying so hard *not* to fight the side effects that he feels the effort down to his very cells? He says he wants to draw a picture for me, and, though I think he's just trying to change the subject to something a little more psychologically comfortable, I give him a piece of paper. I'm expecting one of his usual floating heads, like the kind he drew in Dr. Levine's office—a large, mournful-looking face with alien-shaped eyes and blunt, horizontal lines for a mouth—so I watch in amazement as Willie produces a picture with arms, legs, a body, a belly button, and even skin.

"This is me," Willie says, proudly.

Maybe he's just answered my question about the Ritalin. Perhaps the drug is helping him in ways we can't entirely see. For the first time, he's drawn himself as more than just a raging head lost in its own inner space. Maybe, on Ritalin, he's finally starting to feel like a whole boy—normal like everyone else, with all the same parts.

January 20, 1994

I've bought a beeper so the school can keep in touch with me while I'm at my writing studio (the one with no phone). I get beeped twice in a row at work, both times with no identifying, return phone number. I know it must either be the nursery school director or the school psychologist because they are the only ones—the M.A. and Ph.D., that is—who still haven't figured out how to use my beeper. I call back from the hallway, pacing the floor.

"Is anything wrong?" I ask when the secretary answers.

The secretary lulls me into a false sense of security by telling me there's no emergency—the school psychologist just wanted to talk to me. I click my tongue, annoyed. This is the same ash-blond woman who suggested back in the fall that we shouldn't "pigeonhole" Willie by thinking of him as ADD; that perhaps he might have "OBD," an oppositional-behavior disorder, though he had none of the premeditated outbursts or general all-round non-compliance that characterizes conduct disorders, as I discovered when I looked the term up in psychiatric manuals.

The secretary puts me on hold while I wait for the psychologist. I've got a regular phone number and an answering machine at home for this kind of thing. Why did she use the beeper? It's supposed to be for emergencies only.

While I'm waiting for the secretary to transfer the call, I try to modulate the irritation in my voice. Whining at the psychologist won't help me write my novel any faster and, besides, it's the psychologist's job to follow up in these situations. I imagine she just wants to touch base about the medication and am, therefore, surprised when she picks up the phone sounding tense and official.

"I'm very concerned that the Ritalin isn't working," she says, adding that she observed Willie's class this morning and saw he was still having disruptive outbursts, crying and screaming, especially in the block corner. "In my opinion, the other children are becoming afraid. They don't feel safe with him in class, nor do the teachers. Yesterday, Willie scratched the assistant teacher and pulled her hair while she was trying to get the class lined up for dismissal."

I am shocked. *None* of this was mentioned in his teacher's journal entry yesterday.

"I'd like to have a meeting to reassess the appropriateness of this setting for Willie," the psychologist says in her typical jargon. "Besides myself, Peter, and you, I'd like the meeting to include Willie's teachers, the director of the nursery school, and the headmaster."

I can guess what she's trying to say underneath all that euphemistic mumbo jumbo. A meeting with the headmaster must mean they want to kick Willie out.

I start pacing rapidly in the hallway, staring straight at my feet until their movement makes me dizzy. If Willie gets kicked out again, what school in the world will accept him for next year?

And what would we do with him the rest of the winter? He's too old for any of the play groups, and the special remedial schools probably won't have room for him in the middle of January, assuming he would even be admitted at one of those. Some inner rage forces its way up through the frozen reaches of my shock.

"Have you talked to the psychiatrist?" I ask, surprised at the petulance I hear in my own voice. "Because all I've heard from the school in the last two days is that everything's going fine. Willie's teachers wrote in his journal that there's been less hitting and yelling."

"Oh," the psychologist says, knowingly, "*I* wrote in the journal myself today. I decided to start a star chart in class for Willie where he will get a star for every half-hour period he doesn't scream."

I start shaking my head in exasperation. *Who does this woman think she is?* It's so typical that she would interfere this way. The journal was for the teachers to write in, not the psychologist. Besides, I thought we had an understanding with the school that they weren't going to do any behavior-modification programs, like star charts, before checking with Dr. Andersov to pick an appropriate "target" behavior.

"I think that might have been a little premature," I tell her, sternly. Though I was ready to take Willie off the Ritalin myself on Saturday, now that we are committed to doing a drug trial, it seems a little early to be making sweeping judgments on the basis of only two days in school, let alone on the "appropriateness of the setting" for Willie.

The psychologist goes on to say that she's already made the appointment with the headmaster for early next Tuesday morning, to accommodate Peter's work schedule — as if this tiny shred of consideration is supposed to make me happy.

I'm furious that the psychologist has taken what seems to me the incredible liberty of scheduling an appointment with the headmaster without clearing it first through Willie's teachers or the nursery school director, who have observed him firsthand much more than the psychologist. If the situation is so serious that the school is thinking of expelling Willie, shouldn't I be hearing about it from one of Willie's teachers or the nursery school director? Could it be that there is some misunderstanding between them about the severity of Willie's behavior?

"Gee, I don't know about Tuesday," I say, trying to stall the psychologist. "I'll have to check Peter's calendar and get back to you."

I hang up and immediately call the nursery school director, telling her exactly what's happened and how angry I am about it.

The director does not sound very conciliatory—perhaps because I've just put her on the defensive about one of her staff members whose judgment she seems to value highly. When I point out that it might have been better if she had called me about Willie herself, she makes it clear that she authorized the psychologist to call.

"We often work in a powwow," the director says casually.

"Well, I'm still surprised. All I've read in Willie's notebook is that Willie is coming along fine on the drugs."

"Oh, *no*," the director insists. "The head teacher agrees. As a matter of fact, she was just in here for a meeting about Willie."

I start pacing again. This is like a nightmare version of that children's game Operator, where one person says something and it has to be repeated so many times that, by the end of the game, it sounds like gibberish.

I've got no idea what to think about Willie's behavior. According to the notebook, he sounds as if he's improved in some areas on Ritalin, even though it's only been two days. Now, the school psychologist and director are giving me a completely different story. I go back to my office with no hope of actually working. Instead, I make a list of what I think the school should do before they kick Willie out:

1. Find out more about the medicine from the psychiatrist.

- How long does it take to work? Do we need to fix the dosage?
- Should we switch to something else?

2. If the other children are getting scared of Willie, have a meeting to explain that his problem is medical.
   - Say that Willie isn't being "bad" or "mean." Explain that he has something that sometimes makes him feel angry and sad.
   - It's never too early to teach a little tolerance — wouldn't the school say something to reassure the other children if a student had been having epileptic seizures in class?

3. Let Willie opt out of certain activities that are hard for him now, like nap and circle time, until the situation is under control with the medication.

4. Get a specialist or one of the substitute teachers to stay in the classroom when Willie needs extra attention.

I don't know if these ideas are the best ones possible or if they're even feasible but at least I'm thinking about ways to solve Willie's immediate problems, which seems like more than the school is doing right now.

I call Peter from the hallway to tell him what has happened. He gives me more bad news: The magazine company picked someone else for the job of editor in chief. By the end of the month, he'll be out of work for the first time in his adult life. There is silence on both ends of the phone as the reality of what Peter is saying sinks in. He's been at the magazine for over twelve years, working his way up the masthead until he finally reached the top.

Running his own magazine was the one thing he wanted professionally, and now it is gone. It seems impossibly unfair that Peter is going to be replaced — and stupid, too. But, of course, I'm biased. I feel a pain in my chest as if my heart is literally breaking for Peter.

"I'm so sorry," I say, feeling just like Job's wife. We stay on the phone for a few minutes longer, not saying much but not wanting to hang up, either. I think back seven years ago to the moment I realized I had fallen in love with Peter. We were eating dinner at an Italian restaurant, and he was telling me about a peace march he led during the sixties. His idealism and convictions impressed me, but even more than that was the fact that Peter was an incredibly moral person, with his own code of ethics that never bent under pressure. I realize that if we can teach Willie and Nicholas to have half of Peter's character, we will have done our jobs as parents, regardless of how they fare in nursery school.

Still, the mood is sober when Peter comes home from work. We don't have much time to console each other: the phone is ringing nonstop with people calling to offer condolences about Peter's job. In the middle of the chaos, Dr. Miller calls back. So much has happened since the morning, I forgot that I left a message for him to call me about the school psychologist's report. Hurriedly, I explain my concerns about the situation with Willie.

"I guess it's time to switch to Dexedrine," the psychiatrist says, matter-of-factly.

I'm amazed. "I thought you told Peter last Saturday that Dexedrine lasts only half an hour longer than Ritalin?"

"No," Dr. Miller explains. "What I said was that Dexedrine has a longer *half-life*. It lasts two to four hours longer than Ritalin."

I let the phone dangle, feeling like an idiot. If we'd known this on Saturday, we could have saved ourselves a nightmarish weekend and prevented the problems in school this week with Willie.

I look at my watch. It's 8 P.M. — too late for Dr. Miller to call the prescription for Dexedrine in to our pharmacy tonight. We agree that he will call them first thing in the morning, so we can try the new medicine before Willie goes to school — assuming they let him in the door tomorrow morning.

Peter comes into the bedroom to tell me that it's time to go to dinner with a group of Peter's friends from work. The get-together was planned over a month ago, but now I want to cancel. Given the situation with Peter's job, it will feel more like a wake than a party. This has been, without exception, the worst day in my life. Between the bad news about both Peter and Willie, I want to crawl into bed with a pint of Häagen-Dazs and never come out.

I read a story to Willie before we leave for dinner. I want to have some quiet, good time with him to offset all the upsetting things that have happened today. Peter can find another job, but Willie is our child, irreplaceably. Willie's buried himself under his Babar sheets and blanket. I wonder what he's understood these last few weeks about the situation with Peter, our nervousness and uncertainty. Every time the phone rang tonight, Willie got angry and hostile. I think he's scared because he understands that something is wrong and we don't know what to tell him.

He seems more cuddly than usual when I kiss him through his blanket, but he still has that dazed and slightly manic expression that he's had ever since he went on Ritalin. He's giggling as I tickle him with a shower of kisses. The Ritalin trial has lasted exactly seven days.

"What do you want me to read?" I ask, but Willie is silent.

"Are you going out?" he finally says, looking angry again.

I tell him we have to go out, though we'd much rather stay home with him and Nicholas. Willie shrugs at my flimsy apology. Why should he trust anything that grown-ups say, anymore? After all, aren't we the people who promised we'd find a way to help him?

I get *Runaway Bunny* off the bookshelf and start reading it to him as Willie pulls me close. The story's familiar, pastel drawings always remind me of my childhood, what it felt like to nestle in my own mother's lap and feel perfectly safe. In the story, a little bunny wants to run away from home by doing things like turning himself into a flower in a hidden garden or joining the circus, but his mother, because she loves him so much, won't let him go.

" 'If you become a sailboat, I will become the wind,' says the mother bunny, 'and blow you where I want you to go.' "

Willie stares hard at the picture of the mother in the sky, hovering and vigilant, in spite of the little bunny's anger.

I know that he's smart enough to understand the metaphor, even if he's too young to put it into words of his own.

"I love you, Willie," I whisper in his ear, blowing lightly to guide him, just in case Mother Bunny is right.

January 21, 1994

There's no medicine in Willie's system but he wakes up wild, as if he's still on the Ritalin. At breakfast, he flips his puffed-corn cereal onto the table like so many yellow tiddledywinks.

"Willie," I say, forcefully, "keep your cereal in the bowl."

He ignores me, crunching the cereal on the table. I mentally count the minutes until I can stuff the Dexedrine down his throat. Please, God, this behavior has got to stop. Willie rushes impulsively to the sink, turning the water on and off repeatedly.

"Stop your hands," I say, grabbing the faucet, giving Willie the words to tell himself what to do. He pushes past me, flipping the handles back and forth.

"This is your warning and then you're getting a time-out," I say.

Willie cackles maniacally, unable to even meet my eye let alone get it together enough to calm down and turn off the water.

"Okay . . ." I say slowly, still hoping he'll do it on his own. I take his hand away from the faucet to lead him into his room for a time-out. But before we can leave the kitchen, Nicholas—who's been sitting at the breakfast table eating his own cereal—suddenly bounds from his chair, thinking this is some exciting game from which Willie and I are excluding him.

"Pickah *me* up! Pickah *me* up!" he howls.

In the few seconds it takes me to spin around back to Willie, he's gone, leaving a trail of destruction in his wake. Water is gushing into the sink, splashing all over the drainboard. Cereal crumbs coat the tabletop near his seat. I don't even bother to clean up the breakfast dishes as Nicky clings to my leg and I rush after Willie, dragging Nicky as if in some strange dance. Willie is hiding under his trundle bed, still quivering. I pull him out, not even angry anymore.

"Come on," I tell him. "I'm getting your coat."

"Where are we going?" he says, suddenly compliant at the thought of an excursion.

"We're going to the drugstore. Right now. The medicine isn't working for you. It's not your fault. It's nobody's fault. We just need to try something else."

I leave Nicky with the baby-sitter, and he's not happy about it. I can hear his howls all the way downstairs in the elevator.

The Dexedrine, when we get it, is white, bigger than the Ritalin but easier to split in half for Willie's 2.5-milligram dose. Willie gulps it down with a cup of water supplied by the pharmacist. This time, I don't meet the pharmacist's eyes, not wanting to see even a sympathetic face. I don't want to get my hopes up if this medicine fails, too.

By the time we get to nursery school, I'm a nervous wreck. "How do you feel, sweetie?" I ask.

"Great," Willie beams, trying so hard to be better.

I spot the pregnant substitute teacher whom I haven't seen since I dragged Willie out from under the table before Martin Luther King Day.

"Willie seems in a good mood this morning," she observes.

I'm still shaken by the thought of Willie trying to kick her in the stomach. "I'm so sorry for what happened," I tell her. "Willie has Attention Deficit Disorder, which can make him overly defensive at times. He's on some new medication, which we hope will get it under control."

I'm not sure if this is news to the substitute teacher or not. I realize this is the first time I've told anyone outside of our immediate family or Willie's main teachers about his ADD. Though the school may have told the other instructors who work with him—like the librarian or science specialist—from the look of concern and surprise on the substitute's face, I have the feeling that Willie's situation is far from common knowledge around the school.

"I really hope the medicine helps," she says, graciously. "He's a sweet kid."

The head teacher heads over to ask me about the new medication. "Do you think it's going to work better than the Ritalin?" she asks, anxiously.

"I don't know what to prepare you for," I tell her, truthfully. He hasn't been on it long enough for me to notice any changes — for better or worse.

We agree that I'll wait outside the class for a little while just to make sure that we don't have a repeat of the under-the-table incident on the Dexedrine. I tell Willie that I'm going out in the hall to read the newspaper. This doesn't strike him as odd, though perhaps it should. All the other parents have left already. No one else is pulling up a nursery-size chair next to the water table in the hallway. I can see a wedge-sized chunk of the classroom from my little perch. On my right is the bathroom, with little step stools pulled up under the sinks and toilets so all the four-year-olds can reach. Everything looks so orderly and controlled on the surface. I feel so bad for Willie, I almost want to cry. He deserves to be happy in school, to learn and have friends just like the other children here.

The class gathers outside to go to the library next door. Willie is yawning, stretching wide with his arms. Why is my child exhausted? He's on amphetamines! Shouldn't they be perking him up? I glance at my watch. I gave him the pill half an hour ago. It should definitely be working by now.

I can't see what goes on in the library, but I don't *hear* anything unusual — no shouting or crying — which is obviously a good sign. I see the children march back into their classroom about half an hour later. Willie and three or four other boys retreat to their usual bunker in the block corner. A few minutes later, I hear one of Willie's friends saying, "No, Willie," loudly.

I move closer to the door but don't go inside because I want to give Willie a chance to solve the problem on his own. One child, John, is holding a block that Willie wants him to put down in a certain section of the structure they're building. Willie pulls on John's hand, trying to make him drop the block where he wants it. I'm wondering where the teachers are—why they're not intervening when something is obviously about to erupt.

Suddenly, John extracts his hand from Willie's grip. "*I'm* playing over here, now," he says in a dramatic voice. Willie doesn't follow him or try to force him back. John moves over and starts his own block building. I sit back down. The whole scene hasn't been ideal, but it's a vast improvement from Willie's behavior on Ritalin.

A few minutes later, I hear more rumblings of trouble when Willie tries to get two other boys to help him build a castle he's working on. "That's our castle over there," one of the boys tells Willie, pointing.

Willie grimaces but accepts the information without violence. This is good. I see him build a bridge from his building over to theirs. I'm so proud of him, I want to rush in and give him a hug. (*Where are the teachers?* They're the ones who should be recognizing his effort and praising it.) Willie looks toward the door and sees me beaming. I wink at him and give him a thumbs up. He waves back proudly.

I get up to go to work, buoyed by the thought that maybe the Dexedrine is helping. In half an hour of observing him, I saw two scenes that would have normally erupted into a total battle in the block corner, but Willie managed to stay in control.

The writer's studio is empty when I get in to work on my novel. Across the street, I see the grandiose marble balconies of a Beaux-Arts apartment building. Stone angels spread their wings over the wide strip of Broadway. Closing my eyes, I pray, "God, if you're up there, please let the Dexedrine work." I hear a car horn outside and open my eyes to see one of the trucks delivering produce to a gourmet supermarket across the street. I think about the millions of mothers around the world praying for their children—boys and girls who are starving in places like Somalia and Haiti. And here I am on the Upper West Side of Manhattan, desperately worried because my child can't fit into nursery school.

If I were God, would I listen to me?

Not a chance.

January 25, 1994
8:30 A.M.

I've met the headmaster of Willie's school exactly once before at a new-parents' meeting with approximately fifty other people, but now he's greeting me by my first name and leading me into his office as if he were taking me to a tea dance. The room is painted tan and has a threadbare oriental rug. Because the room is directly underneath the east staircase, we hear the thud, thud, thud of children running up and down to their classrooms every few minutes. The nursery school director is here. The head teacher is here. The psychologist whom I got so mad at for scheduling this meeting in the first place is here; along with Peter and me.

Though I'm convinced that this gathering was originally convened to expel Willie from school, his teachers and the psychologist are now convinced that—on the basis of two days' evidence—the Dexedrine is working wonders. While it seems to me to be too early to judge after just forty-eight hours, I keep my mouth shut. If Willie gets kicked out of another preschool, there's no chance of getting him into any private school for next year. And if he can't handle the noise and stimulation of having sixteen children with him in a private school class, how would he cope with the twenty or more in even the best-rated public school?

The nursery school director starts off the meeting. For once, she is smiling, looking upbeat and relaxed around us. "The change in Willie's behavior is just night and day," she says.

I nod, pleased at the news, though the change at home hasn't been *that* dramatic. Outside school, Willie has been more moody and disruptive than he was before Ritalin. But his teachers agree that they're very pleased. They say they feel the Dexedrine helps

Willie keep his cool, even in the block corner. He hasn't been shouting in class since he started the new drug, no tantrums at all.

I nod but I still have a tight, punctured feeling in my stomach. We haven't earned our smugness yet, I think. There's so much that can still go wrong. Willie's only been on Dexedrine at school for two days. And as much as I'd be the first person who'd like to believe the stuff is working, I think it's still too early to be jumping to conclusions.

"We're very grateful to everyone here for working so hard with Willie," Peter says. This is pure diplomacy speaking. Peter and I know that it's crucial to get the school back on our side. In the next few weeks, they will be filling out teachers' recommendations for Willie for next year. Given that his old school tripped us up so badly by their lukewarm recommendation of Willie, we are taking the process quite seriously this time. The headmaster looks at me as if he can read my mind.

"I see you've been applying to schools," he says.

"Our first choice for Willie is the Kenwood School," I say, naming an all-boys school on the Upper East Side.

"We want Willie at a school where his day is carefully structured," Peter adds.

The headmaster nods. "I think that's a fine idea. I'm actually friends with the lower school director. Do you want me to put in a good word for you."

"That would be very nice of you," Peter and I say simultaneously.

"Have you told them about the ADD?" the nursery school director asks.

I frown. "Should we? I don't want them to hold it against Willie."

The head teacher, nursery school director, psychologist, and headmaster all start nodding. "Schools don't like to be surprised by these things," the headmaster warns. "And they always find out, anyway."

The nursery school director leans forward. I wonder if she

thinks we surprised them by announcing Willie's ADD. Maybe some of the resentment we've been getting from the psychologist and the nursery school director is due to the fact that we presented Willie's ADD as a fait accompli without giving them an opportunity to participate in the diagnosis. But would *they* have admitted Willie if they'd known he had ADD?

"You can always present the situation in a positive light," the nursery school director says. "Explain that, since you applied to Kenwood, Willie's been diagnosed with ADD and that he's on medication, which is working great."

"It won't hurt his chances?" Peter repeats.

"If anything, they'll appreciate your honesty," the headmaster says.

I nod but I'm not so sure I share his faith in human nature. Besides, how do we know we're being so *honest* by saying Willie's been doing great on the Dexedrine. It's only been two days.

"They're bound to find out, anyway," the psychologist says. "They'll be the ones giving him his medication, after all."

It seems decided, so Peter and I say we think it's a good idea. I still have misgivings, though. At a recent CHADD meeting for parents of children with ADD, one mother reported being asked to withdraw her seventh-grader from the private school he'd been attending for six years after his ADD was finally diagnosed. A lot of private schools talk about being a "family" but, if our experience at Willie's first school and this other woman's tale are at all representative, these are families that seem to disinherit their black sheep with alarming regularity.

We leave the meeting, Peter to finish up his last week at the magazine. The new editor will be coming to take over in two weeks, and Peter will have to find a new job. Still, we can't help smiling at each other as we leave the headmaster's office. So this is what it feels like to have a normal meeting at our son's school, one where I don't break down in tears afterwards outside in the hallway.

I think I could get used to this.

3:30 P.M.

I pick up Willie after school to take him to his biweekly speech therapy appointment. Through Dr. Levine, we found a speech therapist on the East Side, only a few blocks away from the crosstown bus we take from Willie's school. The therapist is in her mid-thirties, with a roomful of toys that Willie gets to play with as a reward if he pronounces his words right. I love the speech therapist. Willie loves the speech therapist. The match is almost perfect except that our insurance company has refused to reimburse us for her services because she doesn't have the specific license they require, though she does have two others.

I buy Willie a hot dog from a cart near the bus stop as we walk to the speech therapist's. He takes a huge bite. "Fankth, Mom," he lisps.

When I stop in the bathroom at the speech therapist's office after dropping Willie off, I realize I haven't told her that we've switched Willie to Dexedrine. I wonder if she'll even notice the difference on her own. By the time I come out, the speech therapist is waiting for me in the hallway.

"What's going on with Willie?" she asks in an enthusiastic voice. Behind her, Willie is sitting at a table, totally absorbed in his language workbook. A car honks outside and Willie doesn't even look up. In the hall, we hear the voices of people coming off the elevator—all aural distractions that would have completely unnerved Willie before.

"We've switched Willie to Dexedrine," I tell her. "I guess it works."

"You can say that again," the speech therapist declares. "I can't believe the difference. It's like night and day."

Night and day: That's what all the mothers at CHADD and Dr. Miller said the medicine would be like when it worked. I don't want to let myself feel the thrill that is rising in my throat, a tightening like, if I let myself think the Dexedrine is helping him, I might scream and not stop until I shouted myself hoarse. Night and day, day and night. You'd think it wouldn't be so hard to tell the difference. The speech therapist closes the heavy door to her office behind me. I know, without seeing, that Willie hasn't looked up.

January 26, 1994

We get another good report from the assistant teacher in Willie's logbook:

> 9:00 A.M.–9:30 A.M. *Morning work time:* Willie worked with bristle blocks along with four other children.
> 9:30 A.M.–10 A.M. *Meeting:* Willie didn't want to be counted at attendance but saw us continue without him and quietly rejoined the group.
> 10:00 A.M.–10:50 A.M. *Work time:* Willie painted and worked in blocks. Toward the end of work time, he became upset when drawing at the blackboard with another child. He yelled and screamed but quickly calmed down when he needed to do his job (ringing bell for cleanup). Then he disappeared. He turned up five minutes later. He had been hiding behind the coats at the cubby. He told me that he wanted to be alone. That was fine, but he should let us know because we were worried. He came out on his own ten minutes later.

I'm not thrilled to hear that Willie is still acting up so much on Dexedrine—shouting when he gets frustrated and doing impulsive things like hiding in the cubbies—but it seems as though he's not quite so disruptive and can calm himself down better than when he was on Ritalin. But if the teachers aren't complaining, who am I to look for trouble?

January 27, 1994

So much for night and day. My beeper goes off while I'm at the writers' studio this morning attempting to get some work done.

Between Nicky's nursery school interview, meetings for Willie, and speech therapy, I've been working at my office only three half-days this week.

I'm not nervous when I press the black button to reveal the number of the person who's calling. It could be Peter trying to reach me about a four-day trip we're planning to the Caribbean — our first vacation without the children since Nicholas was born — a kind of consolation prize to ourselves for Peter's getting replaced at the magazine.

My heart rate goes up when I see it's Willie's nursery school that's beeping me. I haven't gotten beeped by them since he went off the Ritalin.

"Willie's having a hard morning," the assistant teacher tells me when I call from the pay phone outside. "I was going to write everything down in his logbook, but there were too many incidents."

"What happened?" I ask, alarmed.

"He's been fighting with Tim again," the assistant teacher reports. "He was chasing him so much we had to take Tim out of the room to protect him."

My stomach starts churning. Tim, I know, is a real provocateur: the kind of child who pushes other children on the stairs and, when they push back, tells the teacher on them.

"Did you see how it started?" I ask. I want to give Willie the benefit of the doubt but the teacher sounds so grim, it's hard to be hopeful. "No, but it's not only Tim," she explains. "Willie's been very talkative again the way he was on the Ritalin. During circle time, he was interrupting all the other children and pushing their hands down when they were trying to speak. Can you come in?"

I grudgingly agree. Apparently, the nursery school director and the psychologist are both away at a conference, and there's nobody else to come and help. I pack up my things, frustrated and upset. But as I leave my office, I know it could be worse. They could be sending Willie home, which, logistically, would be a nightmare today because we're supposed to be bringing one of his friends back to our house after school for a play date. The friend's parents are divorced and the little boy's mother is a surgeon and his father lives in Chicago. If Willie gets sent home early, I don't know how we'll rearrange getting Willie's friend home because it's nearly impossible to reach his mother at the hospital during the day.

I call Peter before I grab a cab to Willie's school. Though he's been asked by the magazine company to stay on awhile to work with his successor, he's eager to move on and will be leaving his job at the end of the week. With his severance and our savings, we have a few months before he needs to find another job, but it's not as much time as we'd like. Because there's no way my novel can bring in money until it's finished, I feel particularly alarmed that I'm not getting any time to work on it. I'd take on some short-term, freelance assignments to bring in extra cash but that's been hard to pursue, too, since I've been spending most of my day dealing with Willie.

"I don't understand," I moan. "Why is this happening on the Dexedrine? I can't deal with picking up Willie all the time. It's bad for him. It's bad for me. I've got to finish this book."

"But you're his mommy," Peter says, sharply.

I know it's because Peter's under so much stress that he's totally missed my point. "We've *got* to find some way for Willie to function in that classroom. I don't know how understanding the school is going to be if Willie starts to have problems on the Dexedrine, too."

At Willie's class, the children are doing a cooking project when I rush in, still clutching the change from my taxi ride. "What are you doing here, Mommy?" Willie asks, surprised. It's been exactly two and a half hours since I dropped him off this morning.

"Mmmm," I fib, looking at the English muffin pizzas they're making for snack. "I smelled your pizzas all the way at my office and they smelled so good, I just had to come back." Being four, Willie and his friends need a minute or so to figure out that this is a joke. But they're used to my being here, after all. Most of them already call me by my first name.

Willie seems perfectly calm as I watch him eat his pizza, not even getting giddy or out of control with hysteria when Tim the troublemaker makes a mustache on himself with a fingerful of tomato sauce.

I stay with the children until it's their rest time. "I'm sorry to have dragged you in," the head teacher says. "The nursery school director is now insisting that either you or your husband come in to shadow him when he's having a hard time."

I understand. The nursery school director and I had talked, at one point before we put Willie on Ritalin, about the possibility that Peter and I might want to hire a "shadow" for Willie—a graduate-school student who would come in every morning and help Willie navigate the block corner and the other activities that gave him so much trouble. (Of course, because the school had no budget for hiring this kind of extra staff, we would be responsible for paying the shadow—one more expense that would now be even harder to afford with Peter out of work.)

"It's okay," I say. "I'm cheaper than a shadow."

"They're going to call you in all the time now," the head teacher warns. She shakes her head as if she disapproves of the nursery school director and the psychologist.

"What else can we do?" I ask her.

"I honestly don't know."

January 28, 1994

Willie's logbook from the assistant teacher says:

> 9:45 A.M.–10 A.M., *Meeting:* Willie became upset during meeting when a child didn't speak loudly enough for him to hear. He began to yell and cry and then left the meeting. When he returned, he couldn't find a spot to sit. All of the children tried to help, but he was very upset. The head teacher tried to comfort him as the meeting continued. It took him about five minutes to calm down.
>
> 1:15 P.M.–2 P.M., *Rest:* Willie slept and woke up on his

own before the lights went on. He stayed on his mat quietly until the lights went on. He packed up his own blanket and mat. A first!

January 30, 1994

We've had a bad weekend on Dexedrine—I say "we" because I
feel as if our whole family is suffering the side effects. Willie was
hypertalkative again on the ride up to our family's weekend house
in western Massachusetts. Normally on a Friday night, especially
during the winter when it gets dark so early, Willie and Nicholas
will conk out in the car, falling asleep before we even get out of
the city.

This trip, Willie just babbled the whole time we were driving:
pointing out every car and truck we passed on the highway, spinning out his theories about the kinds of things he thought they
were carrying, asking us where we thought each car was going.

This was cute for about five minutes, but the charm and cre-
ativity of Willie's observations definitely started to wear after three
and a half hours of difficult driving through the thick fog of yet
another winter storm. (We've already had record-breaking snow
accumulation this year, and it's not even February; they're calling
this the worst winter in a hundred years.)

Willie's ranting was actually quite disturbing. As Nicky dozed
in his car seat, Willie was bolt upright. Every light, every noise,
every thick patch of fog seemed to set Willie off on another verbal
eruption.

"Willie, enough, sweetheart," I would say, trying to trick him
into silence with bribes and "quiet contests." But nothing worked
for long, and sleeping was obviously out of the question. His foot
was bobbing, kicking the back of my seat every few seconds.
Willie was wired: whether from the excitement of the storm or
the medication, I couldn't be sure.

The weather didn't improve much the rest of the weekend,
and Willie's temper raged as if the storm had moved from outside

the house to inside him. Eating pizza for lunch the next day, he was a blustery mess, as bad as on the Ritalin.

"I wanted Aladdin, not Jasmine," he whines, holding up the plastic princess that came with the kiddie-size pizza from Pizza Hut.

"I'm sorry, sweetheart, they're not giving out Aladdin this week. Maybe next week. Should we put it on the list?"

The "list" was Dr. Andersov's idea. Instead of just saying no to Willie, she suggested making a list of things he wanted as they came up. Instead of starting a temper tantrum every time we couldn't or didn't want to give him something, we'd have a list of desired items that he could earn with good behavior.

"I don't want it on the list," he growls. "*I want Aladdin!*" Willie repeats, his face turning red. His hands are balled into tight little fists. His whole body is rigid, a braid of anger and adrenaline.

Dr. Andersov and Dr. Miller, the psychiatrist who prescribed the Dexedrine, explained that we shouldn't engage Willie in these kinds of verbal tugs-of-war. If he got angry or hypertalkative, Dr. Miller suggested, we should give him some time to "cool down," on his own. Willie had been doing this at school and was theoretically used to it. The "cool-down time" was different from a punitive "time-out," where Willie had to leave the room. The idea with the cool-down time was to physically remove him from whatever it was that set him off in the first place.

"Come on, Willie," I say, "let's cool down."

"No, I don't want to," he says, getting up from the table. When I try to stroke his hand, he swings around and scratches me. Two red marks well up on my wrist. I'm so astonished, all I can do is grab him by the hand and pull him up the stairs to his room. So much for our cooldown. I'm white-hot and Willie is howling.

"No, no! I won't take a time-out, I won't do it," he's shouting, totally unrepentant.

"You *scratched* me," I shout. "That is *not* okay!"

I deposit him in his room, slamming the door behind me.

"You can come out when you're ready to follow the rules of the house," I hear myself saying. Somehow, my voice sounds more firm than angry. I'm mad—furious, really—but I don't want to raise the stakes by getting into a screaming contest with an out-of-control four-year-old.

"I won't stay here," Willie shouts from inside his room, "I'm going to escape. I'm going to get a match and set the house on fire. . . ."

He pulls at the door, which I'm holding closed. We don't have an outside lock on this door—had never thought we needed one. But I'm using all my strength to keep Willie from pulling the door open. How can I keep this kid in his room? After all these doctors and medicines and specialists, I feel as if we're no better off than we were a year ago—worse, maybe. I can't believe how awful the scene is: Willie butting against the door like a caged bull, me the grimacing monster making him a prisoner.

Willie hurls his body against the door for a few more minutes. I pull on the doorknob as hard as I can so he won't get it open. What's going to happen when he outweighs me? Already, it's hard to carry him up the stairs when he's wild like this.

The movement stops on Willie's side of the door, and I pray that he has just worn himself out. I'm about to let go of the door handle when I hear the huge crash of something slamming against the door. I can't tell what it is Willie's thrown against the door. Something solid and large—a chair, maybe, or a wooden block.

"*Willie!*" I scream. "*That is enough!*"

"I'll teach you," Willie howls from inside. "I'm going to kill myself. That'll teach you. I'm going to run away and never come back and then you'll be sad forever."

I know he's just threatening, but I make a mental inventory of what's in his room—if there's anything sharp or stringy he could hurt himself with. I can't believe this is my own sweet child in there. I still hold the door closed, wishing I would wake up in an instant to find this has all been a bad dream. How do I get out of this? And more important, how do I help Willie get out of this?

I don't know what to say or do, so I do and say nothing. Clutching the door handle as if it were a life raft, I stand at the door in a complete panic. *Don't engage him, don't enrage him,* I think.

I lean against the door, trying to hear Willie. My own breathing sounds deafening to me, huge waves of oxygen that seem to bring no air. A few minutes pass and I hear nothing from inside. After a few more, I finally release the doorknob. Willie has finally calmed himself down, though I'm a nervous wreck.

"Peter," I say, when I get back downstairs, "we've got to do something. I don't think this medicine is working, either."

We hear the skittering of little feet on the stairs, Willie making his escape. "Mom," he calls, in a soft voice, from the hall, "I'm ready to come out now."

His face is cool and clear, no trace of the tears from the tantrum before. I notice his hair is wet on the sides. He must have washed his own face upstairs, trying to pull himself together. "Can I come out?" he repeats.

He looks—and is acting—perfectly normal. It's as if he had been possessed up there. Willie's had tantrums before, but these new threats of violence to himself go way beyond the scratching and spitting he did to other children at nursery school.

"Are you ready to follow the rules of the house?"

"Yes, Mommy. I'm sorry I scratched you."

He moves over to where I'm standing, shell-shocked, next to Peter. He hugs me, and I pull him close. I can't take any more scenes like this. What's going to happen when Willie grows up? What if he ever did anything self-destructive on an impulse—hurt himself, or hurt somebody else? Peter and I stare at each other helplessly. All we know is we've got to do something.

February 1, 1994

I'm having serious second thoughts about going on vacation. Despite my misgivings about leaving while Willie is having so much trouble at home, Peter points out to me that the reports from school are overwhelmingly good. (It's just at home that we're having frightening scenes.)

"Honey," he says, looking anxious at the thought that I might cancel when we're supposed to leave in two days, "we really *need* this vacation."

I don't disagree. Dealing with Willie, his school, and the situation at Peter's job has left us both completely exhausted and dispirited. And the boys seem fine about our vacation. (At age two and a half, Nicky doesn't really seem to understand what it means that we're going away, and Willie reacts with his typical lack of separation anxiety.)

While Peter checks with friends for restaurant recommendations and sightseeing tips, I'm busy arranging schedule after schedule for my mother and mother-in-law, both of whom have generously offered to help Jolie for the four days we're gone.

"Are you going to bring me back any souvenirs?" Willie asks.

"Of course," I tell him. "Seashells and candy and lots of things you like."

We show Willie where the Caribbean is on his globe. He even seems to be looking forward to the idea of four days of Jolie and his grandmothers—all of whom are much easier marks for McDonald's and action figures at the local toy store.

Willie's teachers have asked who the contact person will be while we're away in case there's a problem and someone needs to come in and "shadow" him—as they've put it. My mother volunteers to be on call Monday, Tuesday, and Wednesday even though she works full-time and is planning a wedding for one of her best friends that will be taking place at her house on Friday. My mother-in-law will help after school and on weekends.

I'm worried about teaching Jolie to use the beeper while we're away. She's never been on the receiving end of a page even though she's paged me many times at my office. What happens if they beep her and she's forgotten to turn it on? Or what if she calls the school and they can't understand her heavy Haitian accent?

In the middle of all this, Mrs. Mielho, the lower school director at the Kenwood School, the school we're eager to get Willie into, calls to ask if we're going to get Willie retested on his ERBs, the standardized test administered by the Educational Records Bureau that preschoolers must take in New York City to get into private school.

When Willie was tested originally, his scores had ranged from the highest percentile in the vocabulary section to the lowest in "geometric design," in which he needed to reproduce drawn patterns like stars and diamonds—a difficult task given his poor handwriting. According to Dr. Levine and Dr. Andersov, this type of "picket fence" test results can indicate future learning problems like dyslexia and are always a red flag to admissions officers.

Though we were troubled by the thought that so much importance is placed on the standardized test scores of four-year-olds, we'd asked Dr. Levine to retest Willie in hopes of improving his chances of admission. (For the official test, parents must take their children to one of the ERB's testing centers; to retest Willie in an informal session, we were free to use our own private tester.)

When I hear Mrs. Mielho tell me Willie's scores are due today, I start to panic. We'd put a lot of time and effort into looking at schools—reading all the information we could find on six or seven of them; talking to friends with children in the schools; visiting them for parent tours; taking Willie to each for his own interviews—and I didn't want to blow his chances by being late with these test scores now.

"I thought we had two more weeks to get the results in," I tell her. "We had him retested, but the results haven't been written up yet."

"Can you get them faxed over here? The headmaster is going to a convention, and we need to do admissions before he leaves."

"Okay, I'll try," I say, determined not to let Willie's chance to attend Kenwood slip through our fingers.

Knowing that Willie had a hard time in noisy, crowded places, we were looking for a school that would make him feel as secure as possible with a calm, nurturing environment that wouldn't overwhelm him with stimulation. Specifically, we wanted a school with small classes—eight to ten children per teacher, if possible. We thought a relatively structured class would be best, given his problems during unstructured activities. If he was going to have gym, for example, we wanted him to be learning a sport—doing running drills or playing basketball—something on which he could focus. We didn't want a school that would just dump him in a gym with thirty or so other children and tell him to "play" for an hour.

We wanted to know that Willie would be sitting at a desk for his academic classes or working in small groups with a teacher. Willie was too distractible to sit on the floor or on a beanbag chair for English, as the kids do at some of the more "progressive" schools. I could just picture him feeling the carpet or picking a fight with his classmate whose beanbag might encroach on his space. He'd be so busy struggling to adapt to the environment that he'd never have the energy or composure to focus on his work. We wanted him to sit at a desk, where there'd be plenty of room for him to fidget without bothering anyone. We wanted a faculty that would tolerate Willie's mild hyperactivity and excitability (which would already be tempered by his environment); a staff that would also be committed to working with different learning styles.

We'd loved the Kenwood School the minute we'd seen it. The teachers all seemed to be in full command of their classes. It was a boys' school so, obviously, the only teachers there would be people who liked teaching boys. The kindergarteners worked in a large room that might be visually stimulating for Willie, but the class seemed to break up into small groups often enough to counterbalance the large overall enrollment. The school was "traditional" in the sense that the boys wore uniforms and the school enforced a strict code of behavior—not just for "problem" kids but for everyone.

This was not a place where Willie would be provoked as often by the teasing and rowdiness of his peers. The boys wouldn't be left to their own devices long enough to act that way in the first place. Last, but most important, it was a school that I thought we might get Willie into. The lower school director, Mrs. Mielho, was a college classmate of my mother's and I've known her my whole life. And while she'd never admit a child who she didn't think could succeed at the school, I knew she would try to give us every possible consideration.

The thought that things might get fouled up now for Willie at Kenwood because of some misunderstanding about the deadlines sets me in a panic. As I hang up with Mrs. Mielho, I dial Dr. Levine's office and leave a frantic message on her answering machine. I don't have her home number but remember it starts with 718, the area code for the Bronx, Brooklyn, and Queens. I try the operator, but Dr. Levine isn't listed. She might be in the phone book under her husband's name—but with at least a hundred other people with the same name in the New York City phone book, there's no way I can call them all. It's a needle in a haystack.

My adrenaline racing, I hang up the phone, staring into the empty suitcases lined up on our bed for our Caribbean trip. As I'm staring into the canvas bags, trying to figure out what to do, Dr. Levine calls back. "Don't worry," she stresses, typically encouraging. "We've got *plenty* of time."

"Oh, yeah," I say sarcastically. "At least forty-five minutes."

I glance at the clock. In two hours, the office at Kenwood and a dozen other private schools in New York will close for the day. Then, the admissions staff will retreat to some back room to decide the fate of my son and hundreds of other applicants. On the one hand, they've got a kid with ADD, a kid who needs medication and who's struggled with every classroom situation he's ever been in. On the other hand, there are all these other wonderful children, with normal neurons, test scores, and utterly normal prospects.

I remind myself of an essay by George Bernard Shaw in which he writes that, after an eye exam, he was depressed when the doctor told him his vision was "normal." What a devastating thing it was for a writer, Shaw recounted, to be told that his vision, his viewpoint, was unremarkable. Who wants that? he wrote.

Nonetheless, Peter and I could bear for Willie to be a little less "special" at the moment if it would help him get into that school we love so much.

"Willie's scores on the geometric design part of the test went from the sixteenth percentile to the thirty-seventh," Dr. Levine says.

She sounds happy about this but, to me, 37 percent still doesn't sound so great. She tells me that this score is well within "average" range and is impressive, considering that the Dexedrine has only been in effect for two weeks. "Imagine what he will be doing when he's been on it two years," she says. I see her point, but my stomach is churning with anxiety—a burning feeling that I just can't seem to shake.

"Don't worry about Willie; just have a relaxing vacation," Dr. Levine urges.

I think about the time sheet I'm making out for Willie's nursery school, the calls I still have to make to confirm things with my mother-in-law. A relaxing vacation? Not bloody likely.

February 7, 1994

The Caribbean island turns out to be everything we could have hoped for in terms of an indulgent, adults-only vacation: sandy beaches, lots of reading time, and romantic, candlelit dinners for two. And despite my continuing stomach troubles, we're enjoying ourselves thoroughly, almost guiltily, knowing that everyone else is back home in New York in the snow.

We called home our first night, and my mother answered the phone: Everything was fine, she said. She'd picked up Willie at nursery school and taken him for his appointment at Dr. Levine's. "He came out rubbing his eyes, though," she says. "Do you think he was crying?"

I thought of the sand table in the psychologist's office, how Willie liked to play "sandstorm." "I doubt it," I tell her, explaining to her about the sand table. Willie gets on the phone next, his little-boy voice sounding even more disembodied on the overseas wire. "Where are you, again?" he asks.

I repeat the name of our island.

"What kind of food are you eating?"

I tell him all the things he hates so he won't feel bad we've left him home with his brother, Jolie, and the grandmothers. "We're having shrimp with tomatoes and lots of chili peppers."

"*Yuk,*" Willie says, critically. "Are there any Ninjas with swords at your hotel?"

"No," I tell him, "but we'll bring you back some pirate's stuff." Willie seems satisfied with this and doesn't even ask when we're coming home.

The next evening, I call again. Peter chides me for being so nervous, but I'm concerned that Peter's mother was able to pick up Willie up from school and take him to speech therapy as she was supposed to. I was afraid she might have trouble finding the unmarked, side door from which Willie's class was dismissed. Jolie answers the phone and seems surprised that it's me. "Hello," she says. "Are you having a good time?"

I tell her we are but that I just wanted to know how things went after school. "How did you know about *that?*" Jolie asks, alarmed.

I have no idea what she's talking about and am suddenly getting frightening visions of my son stranded with his teachers at nursery school, my mother-in-law searching up and down the entire Upper West Side of Manhattan for the side door. "Didn't she find him?"

"Yes," Jolie says. "When the school called to take him home."

I grab the schedule I photocopied before we left for the Caribbean. Willie obviously had had some kind of problem in school but, instead of calling my mother to help, as we'd arranged, they'd just sent him home. Why had I spent so much time making the shadowing arrangements if they were only going to ignore them when they were needed?

Jolie puts my mother-in-law on the phone, and I ask her what had happened. "Did they send the logbook home, at least?"

"Logbook? What logbook? They didn't send home anything."

Great. Here we are a thousand miles away and the only information we need, the school forgets to send home.

"They seemed a little disorganized there," my mother-in-law observes.

Peter gets on the phone and tells Jolie to keep Willie home for the rest of the week. "Better he should play with his brother than get his self-esteem ruined."

I couldn't agree more, but I'm weeping in our hotel room. Poor Willie, getting sent home with us so far away. My stomach does another flip-flop—out of guilt or actual illness, I don't know. So much for a tropical escape. Even for four days, Willie's ADD will not take a vacation.

February 14, 1994

When we get home, we learn that Willie's school was closed for two days last week because of the snow. Because all the airports were closed, our flight back to New York that Friday was canceled and we had to spend the weekend in our hotel. Under any other circumstances, Peter and I would have been grateful to be stuck in a Caribbean paradise, but we were desperate to get back home. The airlines agent on the island was particularly unsympathetic to our plight.

"It's not our problem," she said, coldly.

Eventually, we stopped phoning home, afraid of what we'd find and being unable to do anything about it from the Caribbean. "Let Jolie and the mothers handle it," Peter said. "They've raised seven children between them. They can handle Willie and Nick."

On Monday morning at 1:30 A.M., we finally got home. The boys were sleeping peacefully, Willie looking like an angel in his rocket-print pajamas and Babar sheets. How can a good boy like this still be having so many problems?

At 8:30, while Peter and I are still bleary-eyed from lack of sleep, we get a call from Willie's nursery school director. Peter explains we're not planning on bringing Willie in that morning. Jolie is going home for a much-needed rest after three extra days on duty because of the snow. And we wanted to spend some time with the boys. Peter didn't have an office to rush off to as usual; his job at the magazine had ended before our vacation.

"That's fine," the director says, "but there's still a problem."

Based on last week's events, they didn't want Willie to come back to school without a permanent "shadow," someone to be his assistant on a full-time basis. Even with his suntan, Peter's face turns ashen. He covers the receiver and relays the conversation.

"Well, how are we supposed to know what happened last week if they forgot to send the logbook home?" I snap, still dazed from lack of sleep and the short notice of the director's decision.

"The director wants to have a meeting before school to discuss Willie," Peter says, his hand over the receiver.

I begin to protest. "But if the meeting's that early, we can't bring Willie to school, and he does so much better when *we* drop him off."

But then Peter reminds me. They don't want Willie at school tomorrow—or any other day until we can get his behavior under control. I want to call Dr. Andersov before we agree to anything. I tell Peter to tell the director we'll call her back. The phone rings continuously for the next forty minutes—all the telephone tag that I usually have to handle via beeper and pay phone at the writers' studio.

"See what I have to deal with every time this happens?" I ask Peter, who is on hold with the psychiatrist to talk about changing Willie's dosage of the Dexedrine (Dr. Andersov's idea) or stopping the medicine entirely.

Peter nods at me with new appreciation.

February 15, 1994

Our meeting is in the nursery school director's office, the same drafty, dark room where we met in September to discuss Willie's ADD. "Don't worry," I remember the director saying, at the time. "We'll be happy to work with you and help Willie have a great year." Some great year.

As the other parents pass us in the hall downstairs, we see Willie's classmates come in the door bundled in their snow boots and parkas.

"Where's Willie? Where's Willie?" the children (and parents) want to know. Why would we be at school without our son?

"Willie's not feeling well," I fib to Willie's friends, trying to read their parents' looks, to see if they're buying this. I have no idea how much the other families know about what's been going on in the classroom this year, whether they have any idea of the recent problems with Willie. Most of them look blank, or mildly concerned: "Well, tell him we hope he feels better," seems to be the generic adult response. It startles me how good I am at lying about what's going on. To me, it feels as if the pain and anger are written all over my face.

All the usual suspects are gathered in the director's office by the time we get there: the director, the psychologist, and the head teacher. The headmaster isn't coming, which I take as a good sign. They won't kick Willie out if the headmaster isn't there, right?

The director, school psychologist, and head teacher surround us seated in upholstered chairs while we sit on a low couch. Above the director's desk, I can see a handmade sign given to her by her two school-age daughters. The sign has their names written vertically down the page. Next to each letter of their names is a characteristic. "L: Loves Mommy. H: Horse-crazy. A: Always talking." Uncharitably, I stare at the crayoned sign and think that, when her kid yammers, she puts it on a sign on her wall. When our child's prescribed medication makes him overtalkative, they ban him from school.

The head teacher gives us the logbook they kept while Peter and I were away. Though they forgot to send it home, they kept making entries in it, after all.

Feb. 3:
9 A.M.–10:30 A.M., *Meeting and Work Time:* Willie worked in blocks with many other children. He had difficulty during cleanup when he pushed a child into the block shelves. He had trouble calming down, so we left the class and eventually made our way to the library. While in blocks, two children had trouble cooperating. Willie wanted to offer his help, so he whispered in the child's ear. That child tells us that he told her to hit the other child. 10:45 A.M.–12 noon, *Snack/Gym:* Ate all of his snack. Pill at 12 noon. At the end of gym time, Willie was jumping on another child. The head teacher stayed behind to help him calm down. *Lunch and Rest:* He ate very well and slept during rest time. He has been verbally threatening during different times during the day.

Feb. 8:
9 A.M.–9:45 A.M., *Work Time:* Willie came into the classroom and went over to the block corner and began yelling. He was alone in the block area and just standing and yelling. It lasted about two to three minutes and then he went to draw. When he went to get a piece of paper, he pushed another child who was drawing quietly. This erupted into an argument among the two children. Willie had a difficult time calming down. He eventually left the

drawing table and went to the computer area. Two children were already using the computer, but Willie had a hard time waiting. He would push the keys and disrupt their game. We involved him in another game but when the cleanup bell rang, Willie became very upset. When I told him he could continue his game, he held his hands over his ears and yelled. I tried to move the game to another area so he could play by himself, and he began to kick me. He then left the classroom and ran down the stairs. The head teacher called for someone to take him home.

Feb. 9:
NO SCHOOL—Snow Day

Feb. 10:
9 A.M.–10:30 A.M., *Work Time and Meeting:* Jolie brought Willie to school. He began his day by drawing four pictures, using only black marker instead of his usual green. Willie then went to the block area. During meeting time, Willie was *very* talkative, which seemed to continue. After block building he joined many of the other children who were cutting animal pictures from magazines. Still very talkative, he became upset when the other children would not look at his cutouts. He began yelling, "Hey, everybody! Look, look, look at this!" He eventually became so upset that he needed to change activities in order to calm down. He then asked me to read the words on a map but when I did, he began to scream and cry. He said that I didn't read it right. Still yelling, he threatened to break all the buildings and call the police. We called the office, and I brought Willie to the library to calm down. Dr. Andersov, who happened to be observing another child in the school, arrived a few minutes later and helped him calm down. 10:30 A.M.–11:30 A.M., *Cleanup, Sharing, and Snack:* Dr. Andersov stayed in the class. When Willie returned from the library, he began to help clean up but, five minutes later, he got upset again and started yelling, "I'm going to lose control again!" He then

went to the library by himself to calm down. Willie came back to the class. He was more calm but still very talkative and silly. 11:30 A.M.–12 noon, *Playtime:* Willie played a running game with the other children. At 12 noon, he took his pill. 12 noon–2 P.M., *Story, Lunch, and Rest:* During story time, Willie found a pushpin on the floor and stuck it into another child. At lunchtime, he ate but was still very talkative. Willie slept at rest time and woke up on his own. He ate a few crackers because he woke up hungry. 2 P.M.–2:45 P.M.: *More sharing and good-bye*— during sharing, Willie was unable to raise his hand to ask questions. He just kept talking and talking.

I can hardly take in the information in the logbook: It's all so awful. I stare blankly at the head teacher, amazed she didn't send Willie home every day. If any other child had been involved with just one of the episodes described in the logbook, it would have meant a time-out—if not a phone call home—for that child. Both the head teacher and the assistant teacher have been putting an enormous amount of energy into dealing with Willie. Writing in the logbook alone must be incredibly time-consuming. But Willie's pushing, kicking, sticking pushpins in other kids, yelling, and running away: this isn't supposed to be happening on the Dexedrine! Peter speaks because I'm unable to. I cannot erase the image of Willie's face that day under the table, tear-stained and full of fury that nobody could help him.

"From the logbook, last week was clearly hard for everyone," Peter is saying. "But we'll hire a shadow, do whatever we need to do to keep Willie in school." Peter mentions that he will talk to his cousin, who works at a graduate school for education, in order to find a student who would be available to shadow Willie.

The nursery school director looks relieved. "It's good you have a connection like that," she says. "This time of year, most of the students who are looking for work have already found jobs."

What do the families do without connections? I wonder.

We explain that, based on our conversations yesterday with Dr. Miller, the psychiatrist, we can increase Willie's Dexedrine slightly to see if that helps but, if not, this is the end of the road for medication. Contrary to what I heard from other families at CHADD and what I'd read on my own, Cylert, another amphetamine cousin that is used when Ritalin and Dexedrine fail, isn't an option for Willie. Dr. Miller says he won't prescribe it or any other medication at this point. (Cylert's safety and effectiveness haven't been proven in children under six, Dr. Miller explains.)

And, beyond that, if the two psychostimulants we've already tried haven't controlled his symptoms, it's unlikely that we'd have any better luck with this one. If Willie were older, another alternative would be an antidepressant like Prozac, Dr. Miller said. Apparently, the selective serotonin reuptake inhibitors (SSRIs) like Prozac or Serzone have worked well in controlling the mood swings of ADD. But Peter and I are not about to give Prozac to a four-year-old. In our opinion, it hasn't been studied enough in young children to warrant the risk of long-term side effects.

"What about changing the dose of Dexedrine?" the school psychologist asks. I smile in spite of myself. Suddenly, we've all become psychopharmacologists.

"Peter or I will shadow Willie at school until we can hire someone full-time," I offer. "So we'll be here if he has a bad reaction on the higher dose."

"But even if we change the dosage," Peter announces, "we're only going to give it three more days. Next week is school vacation. We want Willie to start the spring with the Dexedrine working or nothing."

"You'd take him off the medication entirely?" the school psychologist asks.

"Yes," Peter and I say, in unison.

I expect a battle but the nursery school director, the school psychologist, and the head teacher all look pleased. "Good," Willie's teacher says. "We were going to suggest that."

How could we have gone from thinking about drugs as our savior to regarding them as the enemy in such a short time? Willie's teacher points out that Willie's most disruptive behavior occurred since December, when he started the Ritalin. Before the medication, Willie's teacher says, when he was upset, they could comfort him. He was reachable. The worst day, she recalls, was when she was out sick, the day he went under the table. But we know those kind of disruptions are hard for him, she observes. "Maybe it's also why all the extended family last week was disruptive and confusing rather than one person dropping him off and picking him up every day."

"I thought it would be fun for him," I sputter, remembering Dr. Andersov's observation that most children with ADD crave excitement and novelty.

"Well, Willie's been very upset lately," Peter says. "He's been having these terrible nightmares."

The psychologist leans forward, intrigued. "Such as?"

"Ninjas and robbers breaking into our apartment, killing the doormen with swords, chopping down doors with karate and using their swords to break through our locks," Peter says.

"We always thought it was because he watched *Home Alone* once too often," I explain. "It's his brother's favorite movie."

"Have you talked to Dr. Andersov about this?" the school psychologist asks.

"We thought every kid has nightmares," I say.

The school psychologist explains that these kinds of fears are just the kind of thing that traditional play therapy (versus social skills work) can alleviate. She repeats that Willie's "anxieties" were one of the reasons why, at the beginning of the year, she thought Willie's problems were more emotional than physical.

I tense at the word *anxiety*, remembering what the first psychologist said two years ago: that she wanted to use family therapy to get at the root of Willie's problems. Could it be that she was, at least, partially right about our son? Suddenly, the school psychologist and the nursery school director don't seem so foolish. I remember a line from a book I read on vacation written by a nursery school teacher about the children in her class, that some of the parents were paying more attention to their children's behavior than they were to the emotions underlying that behavior.

Have we been guilty of this because the idea that Willie has

ADD let me and Peter off the hook? Was it easier to blame it on his neurons than on our own failure to make him feel secure and safe on some basic level?

Dr. Andersov has suggested raising the dosage tomorrow, and we agree that we will experiment until Friday. But, in my heart, I know the higher dose will not work. I'm expecting uncontrollable talking and rage like on the Ritalin. I almost wish I were going into school with Willie tomorrow instead of Peter (who has agreed to spend mornings at Willie's school observing and helping out). I want to see for myself what happens—not that I don't trust Peter to tell me. But I'm the one who's been handling Willie at school all these months, and I know I'll be too nervous thinking about him to get any work done anyway.

My stomach churns painfully in a way that's all too familiar. Though I'm not a hypochondriac, my mother (who is hypochondriacal on my behalf) has been urging me to get myself examined for an ulcer. I wouldn't be surprised if I had one, given all the stress at Willie's school and with Peter's job. I can't believe I was in the sunny Caribbean thirty-six hours ago. Last night Peter said to me, "What happened? You were so happy and light a day ago."

New York is gray and so am I.

February 16, 1994

Willie was up *four* times last night—the worst he's slept in many months. Peter tells me he came into our room at 1:30 A.M., but I didn't even hear him. Peter thinks it's the Dexedrine that's making Willie so wakeful, but I'm not so sure. Theoretically, last night's dose would have worn off already, but Peter wonders if it's not building up in his system. Overall, Willie's sleep at night has been improved since the Dexedrine because he's too restless to settle down for his long nap during the day.

Willie is cranky at breakfast, back to his old tricks pulverizing his breakfast cereal. The little crumbs cling to the table like flakes of fresh snow. "Put it on a plate, Will," I say, handing him one to catch the crumbs. It's not worth the battle to get him to stop picking at the cereal entirely. He's doing a fairly good job keeping the crumbs on the plate and my main concern, at this point, is to keep the mess under control.

Nicky is dancing around the kitchen to *Sesame Street*, which is blasting from the television. My head is throbbing from interrupted sleep. (Though I didn't get up at 1:30 A.M., I did get up at 4 and 6, the other times Willie awoke.) Nicky slept well—thank goodness—despite Willie's being up so much. Willie looks exhausted with big bags under his eyes. Peter rushes in, late to take Willie to school for his first day of shadowing. He takes one look at Willie's puffy, sleep-deprived face and shakes his head.

"I want him off that stuff," he says, referring to the Dexedrine. He gulps his tea, exhausted from getting up last night with Willie. "I'm not giving him that higher dose. We *know* it's not working."

I'm not surprised at Peter's 180-degree turn about the Dexedrine, only concerned about whether the school is going to give us a hard time for making such an important decision without consulting them first. Not as if we need their permission, though. He's our child, not theirs. Since Peter is the one who'll be shadowing Willie this morning at nursery school, I don't argue. I can't force him to give Willie the medication—not that I'm such a Dexedrine fan myself anymore. Still, when I watch them go off to school, Willie's small hand in Peter's, I'm frustrated and anxious. We're working without a net, now. The drugs didn't provide any feeling of safety or concrete help for Willie but it was a sustaining idea for me that, somewhere out there, was a magic pill to make Willie "all better." I know this was a dream, but it was a comforting dream, at least.

When Jolie arrives, I leave to go to my internist, who examines me for gastroenteritis and a number of other stomach ailments I cannot pronounce let alone explain. My doctor says I probably just have irritable bowel syndrome, for which I can get medication. But, just to rule out ulcers and parasites, he suggests I go to a gastroenterologist, who will do a series of tests that all sound incredibly invasive and expensive.

The nurse writes down the GNT's name and number and the name of the parasite lab on a piece of paper. I take it and thank her but, even as I fold it into a neat square in my pocket, I know that I'm not going to call either of them if I can possibly avoid it. All these specialists and medicines remind me too much of what we did with Willie and how it got us absolutely nowhere.

Before going back to my office, I get paged from home. Jolie is off at an art class with Nicky—taught by the same teachers who were so wonderful with Willie the year before. Peter is supposed to be at school with Willie, so I'm surprised when he answers the phone. "What's going on?" I ask, trying not to jump to the obvious conclusion that Willie's behavior was just as dreadful off the Dexedrine as on it and that Peter was asked to take him home early again.

"Everything's fine," he says. "We're back here because Willie got tired and wanted to go home to go to sleep. I just wanted to let you know so you'd pick him up here for speech therapy instead of going to school."

"What do you mean everything's fine?"

I hear an energy in Peter's voice, a happiness that hasn't been there in months. "There were two small incidents that did not get out of hand and, both times, Willie did *not* provoke them."

"Great," I say, letting a little of my own excitement break through. Though one voice in my head is telling me not to get my hopes up about Willie's behavior off medication—after all, it was Willie's ADD-influenced excitability, impulsivity, and low frustration tolerance before medication that got us started trying drugs for him in the first place.

When I pick up Willie for speech therapy, he seems more impulsive and distractible than when he was on the Dexedrine, though he's happy and cheerful enough—already a big improvement over the angry mood swings on medication. The snow is piled high from last week's storms, wedged between uncollected garbage bags that the city hasn't had time to pick up. (There's been so much snow that all the sanitation workers have been enlisted to remove it instead of the trash.)

The garbage sits frozen in its green bags and blue recycling containers like stage props from a particularly gritty piece of urban performance art. Willie scampers up the snowbanks and garbage bags though I tell him repeatedly not to. The salted sidewalk is slippery but safer, all in all, than a ten-foot-high jungle gym of Manhattan trash and dirty snow. At the bus stop, Willie becomes fascinated by a group of teenage boys.

"Look at the fat one," Willie says, in a low, careful voice.

"I like the way you're whispering," I tell him. Willie is still very physically suggestible, mimicking the boys' posture and the way they wear their baseball caps backwards, but it's a whole lot better than last year, when Willie undoubtedly would have been all over the boys, trying to get them to pay attention to him.

The language therapist looks exactly the way I felt this morning when I tell her that we've taken Willie off the Dexedrine: not exactly pleased but not very surprised about it, either. "Maybe it's for the best, with his mood swings on the drugs," she says, philosophically. She tells me what happened at Willie's appointment yesterday while Willie was still on Dexedrine. The therapist was playing a game with Willie that worked on category skills and word retrieval—two of his problem areas.

In the game, the player picks a category and has to name a word in that category starting with a letter picked at random. Yesterday, instead of easy, age-appropriate choices like Flowers or Food, Willie kept picking the ones that were much too hard for him, like Football Teams and Biblical Figures, and then becoming furious when he couldn't think of an answer.

"The Dexedrine increased his focus," the therapist explains, "but instead of letting him think of more words more easily, it was as if all he could focus on was what he wanted to pick in the game and how frustrated he was that he didn't know the answer."

To test how Willie would cope off medication, the therapist suggests that they play the same game today. Would Willie be able to handle the frustration better or would he be too distracted by the other noises in the office? The therapist gives him two game pieces and tells him that they would save those for last: He could pick the hard categories at the end of the game. Willie complains but eventually agrees to her rules. As I suspected, he's much more distractible off the drugs: fiddling with the game pieces and biting his clothing. From time to time during the game, he gets really silly, hiding his chips under the table and rolling around on the floor like a baby. It's much harder for Willie to wait than when he was on Dexedrine. A few times, I see him take his turn, then immediately grab another card to go again.

The therapist is pretty patient with him, but I can see how problematic Willie's behavior would be for him in a regular nursery school. What four-year-old would be able to tolerate Willie playing like this? I could see and hear the whole school scene in my mind: Willie takes a turn and insists on a hard category nobody understands or likes; the other children say he's trying to cheat when he forgets and takes two turns in a row; Willie gets angry at being called a cheater and starts yelling at them or hitting.

Clearly, there's a huge trade-off in terms of Willie's attention span without medication. Still, if all Willie could focus on while taking Dexedrine was his own anger—as the language therapist observed—maybe we're still better off in starting again from scratch. At least his mood is improved. And that's something.

March 7, 1994

For the past few weeks, since we got back from the Caribbean, Peter and I have been shadowing Willie in school. Peter is doing it mostly because he's not working now, which is fine with me because I can finally get some work done. At first, we stay with him all day, Peter from 8:45 to noon and then me from noon until his dismissal at 2:45.

The way it works is this: Peter takes Willie to school each morning and stays there, trying not to get involved when Willie has a problem; trying to let Willie and the other children work things out for themselves first. If something comes up where Willie gets flustered or, if it looks like he's getting angry and might hit someone, Peter talks Willie through the right way to handle the situation, be it taking turns or remembering to play other people's way.

The shadowing has worked well so far, and Peter says Willie has been learning. By the time I come in the afternoon, Willie is in the play yard or starting lunch, parts of the day that are not particularly challenging for him. The more structured activities like science and art tend to come after rest. It's mostly the mornings— free play and gym—that Willie finds so difficult.

For me, Peter's shadowing Willie has been a sanity saver. For the first time in three months, I go entire days without my beeper going off, and I don't even look at my watch worrying when Willie has gym. On March 2, Willie's birthday—can he really be five already?—I bring cupcakes in at snack time. I can already see the difference in the way the other children and the teachers are treating him. The children stand closer to him; they involve him more in their games. Even the teachers seem much more relaxed.

Though I still notice the same tendency in the assistant

teacher to point out the negative versus the positive (how many times Willie has hit a child while Peter's been shadowing, for example, as opposed to how many crises have been averted), even she's thrilled at Willie's progress.

When they put the special birthday crown on Willie, he looks so proud of himself I start to cry. As he blows out the candles, I make a wish—for him, for all of us. "Please, let this be a better year. Let this be the year Willie feels good."

A few days later, there is more excitement when a thick envelope comes in the mail from Kenwood, the school we want Willie to go to next year. As with college admissions, a thick envelope is good—it means there are registration forms and return envelopes inside. I hold in my hand the creamy package that represents months of hard work on everyone's part, especially Willie, who tried so hard to do well on his many interviews and tests. Peter and I literally jump for joy and hug each other when we read the letter of acceptance.

What's more, we know that the school really wants our child, ADD and all. In January, after our meeting with the headmaster of Willie's school, I called Mrs. Mielho to explain that Willie had been diagnosed with ADD (we wanted to tell her before Willie's school did, especially since I've known Mrs. Mielho for so long). At the time, we told her the Dexedrine seemed to be working. "Not to worry," Mrs. Mielho said. "A number of the boys here are on that or Ritalin."

Willie's been doing well with us shadowing him, but we know that situation can't last forever. (We've already contacted a graduate student about the possibility of her taking over the job as Willie's shadow. It's not good for Willie to have his parents in school with him every day—he's got to learn to handle himself properly without us. And eventually Peter and I will need to go back to work.) But I know that Willie can learn and can do it on his own; he's just got to find the right setting. At least now, with his admission to Kenwood, we know he has the best chance at success.

March 9, 1994

This afternoon is Willie's birthday party, and I'm going crazy putting up decorations in the living room and getting the food ready before it's time to pick him up for speech therapy. In the middle of all this, I have a meeting with Lisa, the graduate student whom we're interviewing for the job as Willie's shadow.

I'm up on a ladder, hanging a huge "Happy Birthday" sign over the dining-room door, when Lisa rings the front bell. She is tall and slender in her baggy minidress and Doc Martens. She has a scar in the center of her neck that looks exactly like a tracheotomy scar a friend of mine has. Lisa's face and hands are tan, which strikes me as odd for New York in March, but then I remember that Peter's cousin said she'd been living in California, recuperating from an illness.

I was just wondering if the illness has anything to do with the scar when Lisa startles me by joking that her short hair is not a fashion statement but the result of chemotherapy she received in California as part of her treatment for Hodgkin's disease. "That's why I'm available to shadow," she explains. "I was supposed to be an assistant teacher at a private school this year, but then I got sick."

I'm still shocked, but I don't want to make Lisa feel uncomfortable by asking too many questions. Obviously, she must feel healthy enough if she's applying for the job. I try not to stare at the scar on her neck or look at her hair too much, which, I can't help noticing on second glance, *is* quite short.

We sit down in the dining room underneath the sagging birthday sign. When I ask Lisa if I can get her anything, she asks for a glass of water but then insists on helping me get it—which I like because it shows initiative and energy. Lisa seems fairly knowledgeable about ADD, and I wonder if they teach about it in graduate school now or whether Peter's cousin explained it all to her.

Back in the dining room, she sips her water while I explain

the situation with Willie in school, the whole awful background with his first school and the medication, how our main goals with him now are to be more flexible about playing other people's way and not always trying to be the boss.

"It sounds like a buddy will really help him," Lisa says.

"Yes," I agree, wondering why no one at the school ever put it that way before. I've never liked the word *shadow*. It always had the ring to me of someone lurking or slightly menacing. A buddy, or advocate, is exactly what Willie needs, someone who understands him and can help him negotiate his problems.

"Well, I'd love to meet him," Lisa says, enthusiastically. "From what I've heard, he sounds like a great kid."

I take out my date book and Lisa fishes for hers in a large leather backpack in which I can't help but notice two or three large bottles of pills. Lisa explains that she's about to leave for a two-week trip to Florida to visit her grandparents, so the date with Willie would have to be after that.

I stare at the birthday sign hanging above us, a lump rising in my throat at the thought of Lisa's grandparents and family: their sorrow and fear when they found out she had cancer. I haven't asked Lisa's age, but she can't be more than twenty-five. I imagine no more birthday parties, no more candles to blow out. I've never been grateful that Willie has ADD, but at least it's not life-threatening.

We agree that she'll come back for a visit after Florida. If things work out—as I'm almost 100 percent convinced they will—she can start as Willie's buddy at school after that. Though I'm a little worried about Lisa's strength in dealing with Willie if he ever got into another kicking and screaming temper tantrum, I'm thrilled at the thought of her working with him. As soon as she leaves, I rush to the phone to call Peter to tell him about Lisa. Maybe this is the best present Willie could get for his birthday: a guardian angel. After all he's been through at school, he certainly deserves one.

March 10, 1994

Although we've already sent in our deposit for Kenwood, the all-boys school for Willie next year, we made an appointment for a tour at a "special" (in other words, special ed.) school on the Upper East Side. I want to cancel. "We've already found a school for Willie," I say. But Peter insists that we take the tour, "just in case."

I grumble something to him about not being so negative. "Why do you assume things won't work out next year?" I argue. "I don't like the thought of Willie in a special school."

"How do you know you don't if you've never seen one before?"

It's true. I've been prejudiced against these special schools ever since the director at Willie's old nursery school showed us that brochure when they were kicking Willie out. I think, unconsciously, I've been linking special schools to all my negative feelings about that day, when the director suggested Willie had brain damage. In fighting the idea of a special school, maybe I am still trying to battle that director and Willie's old threes teacher, to prove somehow that Willie's just fine.

But it's important to be realistic, Peter says. What if Willie's behavior doesn't improve with Lisa shadowing him? What if his symptoms inexplicably worsen as they did in December, before the Ritalin? Or what if Willie is one of the large percentage of children who have learning disabilities like dyslexia in addition to his attention problems?

"Look, honey," Peter says, sensibly, "let's just look at some of the special schools. If we don't like it more than Kenwood, we'll just forget all about it."

What Peter says makes sense, but it still doesn't make me feel any better. Why are we looking at a special school for a child who seems to be—at least in the biased eyes of his parents—quite intelligent? Why does a child who likes to act out the soliloquies from his videotaped version of *Romeo and Juliet* need help any more than a "normal" kid whose brain is glued to the Power Rangers? I tell myself to stop thinking about what's wrong with my child—that his abilities aren't what's at issue here. If anyone or anything is to "blame" in the situation, it's the fact that even well-intentioned mainstream schools aren't equipped to handle kids like Willie.

The special school is located on a handsome, tree-lined street near million-dollar brownstones and fancy gift shops selling brocade tassels and China pug dogs. The school is imposing though somewhat down-at-the-heels, compared to its wealthy neighbors. Inside, the waiting room has been painted a dark shade of gray, an unfortunate color scheme that extends to the hallway and meeting room, which, we're told, doubles as a gymnasium for the students. The hallway twists and turns—impenetrable to outsiders. "I think we're lost, honey," I hear a woman behind us say to her husband.

When we finally make it to the meeting room, we're surprised by the turnout. Although it is March and most schools already closed their admissions process weeks ago, about fifteen parents are here for the tour. We recognize a man we rented a vacation home from three years ago. He says hello, and we ask him about his house. He and his wife have two boys, and I'm sure it's the younger one he's here for. When we met his family at their vacation home, his son was five and, in retrospect, had all the symptoms of ADD, with severe hyperactivity. The boy couldn't sit still, was constantly interrupting the adults as we tried to speak. On our first visit, he jumped off the kitchen table while he was holding a knife that nearly put out his eye. The father seems tired, now, much older than I remembered him looking.

"My son is seven years old and still struggling to read at a first-grade level," the woman next to me volunteers by way of a conversation starter.

"Ours has ADD," I tell her.

I hear Peter and our friend talking about New York politics and the effect of certain legislation on the man's weekend community upstate. Maybe it's because they're men, but I'm astounded that neither one has asked the obvious question about why they're here.

The school director comes in and sits in the middle of the semicircle of parents' chairs. The director is blond and friendly with the sort of perky insistence that reminds me of Tipper Gore. She explains the philosophy of the school, that its emphasis is on "mainstreaming" children as quickly as possible back to regular school.

The classes here are small—eight to ten children with two teachers and usually a graduate student as a third adult in the room. The classes are not grouped by traditional grades. Rather, each child is placed in a mixed-age class according to skill level. There are on-site specialists for reading, speech, even physical therapy for those who need it. There are social skills groups after school, which many students attend.

"What's great about a program like this is that your child is never singled out for special help, like in a mainstream school," the director says. There's no stigma attached to going to tutors or therapists—all the children use them. "And what's nice for parents," she continues, "is that you don't need to fill up your child's schedule after school with a lot of remediation. Your child will have time to be a kid, do sports after school or other extracurriculars."

"What about medication?" the woman next to me asks.

"Well, we're not doctors, so we wouldn't ever tell you that we think your child should or shouldn't be medicated if that's what you want to try. Many of the children here take medication but not all, by a long shot."

Peter and I look at each other. We like her and what we've heard so far. The parents split up according to the age of their children. Our group, the one that's looking at the kindergarten, is larger, I'm interested to see. Does that mean that more kids are getting diagnosed earlier, or that those of us in this category have fewer mainstream school options?

Our tour leader, a volunteer who is the parent of a child at the school, shows us the library and science room first. This means a trip down the labyrinthine hallway in which, after two minutes, I have already lost all sense of orientation. I don't know whether we're in the new or old building anymore. Everything looks the same shade of gray. The tour guide is encouraging about the difference the school has made for her child and diligently answers all of our questions about the library and science program. Still, the rooms feel chaotic and cramped. Because so many children use the buildings, space is at a premium. Computers have been set on two tables in the library, and the noise from the computer class going on while we visit is clearly distracting to the children trying to read in the library.

Upstairs, the homerooms don't seem any better. Though the teachers all seem friendly enough and take the time to answer our questions about the academic program, the rooms seem crowded, even messy—with unfinished art projects, collage paper, and glue left out on tables, and children running around doing many different free-play activities at once. This is clearly not the calm, structured environment we pictured for Willie. While I like the idea of Willie being in a school where they understand his problems and don't single him out, I still don't see him in this gray, hectic building.

"Well, it's not my *first* choice," Peter says, drily, as we leave the school. "But maybe we should think about it if Kenwood doesn't work out."

"But we shouldn't send him to Kenwood if we don't think it's going to work out," I say. "It's not worth it, even if we've already sent in our deposit."

"Did you like it here more?" Peter asks, surprised.

"No, but I liked the people."

"Maybe we should look into that other special school. Do we still have the brochure?"

"I'll schedule a tour," I say. "If it's not too late in the year."

Peter and I look at each other. Why has it been so hard to find the right school for Willie? When we signed him up at his first preschool, it seemed as though things for him would be so easy. He would go there through nursery school and then probably to the same school I went to from kindergarten through twelfth grade. Of course, we assumed that college would follow. Maybe, we even hoped, a school in the Ivy League. How could we have been so naive? It's as if we were living in some parallel universe—a place where children were always born gifted and behavioral problems didn't exist. But ADD wasn't our first choice, nor is it anyone else's.

March 15, 1994

I go to the gastroenterologist for an ulcer scan and full workup (upper and lower GI, to be exact). Talk about feeling as if the cure is worse than the disease. The good news? It's not a full-blown ulcer. "I'm going to prescribe you some Zantac," the doctor tells me.

"Xanax?" I ask, thinking he meant the tranquilizer. "Shouldn't I go to a psychiatrist for that?"

"No," the doctor says, smiling in spite of himself. "Zantac—it's a stomach medication. But maybe we should talk about your stress level. Have you been worried a lot, lately?"

Now it's my turn to laugh. I tell him about Willie's ADD—the horrible year we've been having with the medicine trials, how he's almost been kicked out of his second nursery school. I tell the doctor about all the stress we've been under from Peter's career. I consider throwing in the saga of my unfinished novel, but I figure the doctor probably doesn't have that much time.

"You've got to try to take it easy," the doctor says.

As trite as this advice seems, I know he's right. I can't spend next year worrying the way I have about Willie. Peter's job situation will take care of itself—he's already started to do consulting for a new women's magazine. But we've got to get Willie into a school where he's getting the right kind of help. Another year like this one and I'll have an ulcer for sure.

March 21, 1994

It's my watch at school for the early shift. Peter is at his consulting job, so the shadow business is falling on me until Lisa gets back from visiting her grandparents in Florida. Willie had a rough morning from the minute Nicky woke him up at 5:45 A.M. — and everyone else in the house, too — due to a wheezy cold and ear infection poor Nicky is suffering from. By the time Willie and I get to school, Willie's cranky and miserable, scratching and fighting about stupid things he's usually able to ignore, like not getting the exact seat he wanted on the bus.

At school, a play fight turns into a real fight with a little girl during music class. When the teacher and I intervene, Willie turns his anger on us: shouting and batting at us wildly with his fists. Although we manage to calm him down, more problems erupt later in gym. When Tim refuses to let Willie give him a hug, Willie gets mad and throws a plastic jug of toys at him. This time, Tim has done nothing to provoke Willie, and the teacher and I decide that Willie must be sent home.

Our big issue now is teaching Willie the difference between what he means to do or say, and what he actually does. Even though Willie's howling, "It was an accident!" I know it wasn't. Willie has got to learn that there are consequences to his actions.

Clearly exhausted, Willie takes a three-hour nap when we get home. I know he woke up early but I still don't understand why he sleeps so much during the day, how he can sleep for so long even when he's had eight or nine hours' sleep at night. Most five-year-olds have given up their naps by now.

At Dr. Andersov's we talk about what happened at school, how Willie felt tired and angry, and what he could have done instead of shouting and fighting. After quickly reassuring me that these kinds of setbacks are normal, Dr. Andersov tells Willie that he should use his words to say "I'm tired and angry" when he feels that way. "Then Mommy could have found you a place to rest for an early nap," she says.

I'm embarrassed by the fact that, even though I knew he was exhausted, it never occurred to me to ask Willie's teachers if he could lie down before the regular rest time. Willie and I agree that if he ever feels so tired again in school, he can tell me or his teachers and we'll make sure he gets a rest when he needs it.

The rest of our visit is taken up by playing Candyland, Willie's choice. The game takes a long time to play because each of us gets sent back to the starting line when we're nearly at the end. Willie is bored and getting frustrated with the slow pace of the game.

"This was a bad choice," Willie says, reflectively. Next time, Willie says he wants to play a board game named Trouble, or what he calls "Getting into Trouble." I have to laugh at the Freudian association because Trouble is the game that Tim gave Willie for his birthday. Getting into trouble is what happens to Willie every time the two boys play together. All in all, the day has been like a card from the Candyland game board: two steps forward, one step back.

March 23, 1994

Lisa is meeting Willie for the first time this afternoon, though it's not the best time for a visit, as I have just rushed home from the writers' studio where I was desperately trying to get some work done, and Jolie and the boys have just come back from Willie's language therapy. Willie seems jumpy and distracted, not making eye contact when I introduce him to Lisa. Nicky is racing around the hallway and the phone rings after that, making things feel even more frenzied and boisterous.

"Willie, I want you to look at me," I say, trying to get Willie to focus. "Lisa is going to be helping you at school." I still can't get Willie to pay attention for more than a few seconds. It's the end of a long day, and he needs some playtime to vent his energies. Willie seems thoroughly uninterested in talking to Lisa. When she begins to tell him something about how excited she is to see his classroom next week, he impulsively puts his hand over her mouth to try to get her to stop talking.

"Willie," Lisa says, in a firm, authoritative voice. "It is *not* okay for you to do that. That might give me a cold and it's bad for me to get sick."

I think about her Hodgkin's disease, how her resistance is still low. It didn't occur to me to ask Lisa if she'd have any physical limitations because of her illness and, now that we've made a commitment to hire her, I feel we should at least give her the benefit of the doubt. (In some ways, I think we were just so thrilled to find anyone who'd be willing to work with Willie that we didn't want to look for trouble more than we had to.) But how useful is Lisa going to be if she's constantly worried about germs? Willie asks Lisa if she wants to play hide-and-seek, but she says no. Too tiring, I wonder, or is it just that Lisa doesn't think she'll be able to get to know Willie if he's running away from her?

We all agree that Willie should show Lisa our family's new computer. This is the perfect activity because it allows Lisa to observe Willie without his getting self-conscious or wriggly. And Willie can see Lisa with me and understand that she's someone I like and trust, which will be important to him when she steps in as my replacement at school.

We set up a schedule for the transition. At first, Lisa will come to class a few hours at a time while I'm still there. Once Willie becomes accustomed to her, she'll start her regular schedule: 8:45 A.M. to lunchtime. After lunch, I'll be on call through my beeper with the understanding that, if anything happens, I have to make myself available to come in and help out, or possibly take Willie home.

While I'm glad to know that, finally, I'll be able to get some work done, I still worry about what's going to happen with Willie when I'm not at school. Is Lisa going to be able to handle his mood swings? And if problems erupt, will the school feel that they can expel him more easily, because they now feel that they've tried everything? Why does everything have to be so hard?

March 28, 1994

Though Nicky's been getting up early for the last week with an ear infection, I manage to keep him from waking Willie this morning, which is good, because Willie needs his sleep. I've scheduled a play date today with Cody, a boy who will also be attending Kenwood next fall. I'm trying to introduce Willie to as many boys who will be going there as possible; that way, he'll feel comfortable by September and—ideally—will feel as though he already has friends in his new school.

Cody's house is around the corner from our building. Though Cody's mother is a business acquaintance of mine, I've avoided getting Willie and Cody together before now. The few times we've run into them in the playground or supermarket, Cody struck me as a bad match for Willie: a little competitive and quick to tease. But last week, we saw them at a newsstand, and the boys seemed to hit it off right away—yakking it up as much as we mothers. Children change, I figure. Willie had grown up a lot, too.

To get things off to a good start on the play date, I picked up some Power Ranger stickers for Willie to give Cody as a gift. "Great!" Cody says, smiling broadly. But as soon as Willie picks up one of Cody's toys, he grabs it away. "Not *that* one," Cody says, hiding it behind his back.

"Hey," Willie says. "No fair!"

Cody's baby-sitter is staring idly at the blaring television, oblivious to what is going on with the boys. I'm annoyed at Cody's behavior. "Cody," I say, firmly, "Willie needs something to play with. What are you ready to share?" After about fifteen minutes of back-and-forth, he settles on showing Willie a skateboard, which the boys take turns using in Cody's room. Against my better judgment, I go to the kitchen with the baby-sitter for a drink of water. "Let them play," she encourages me. "They'll be fine."

I drink my water, crushing the ice with my teeth nervously. I feel that I have to explain about Willie and why I'm so nervous about leaving him and Cody alone together without scaring her into thinking that Willie might hurt Cody. "Willie can be hard to understand," I say. "Sometimes kids tease him about his lisp, and he gets angry."

A little later, we hear shouts from Cody's room and rush in to find them arguing over a clay castle. I look at my watch. We've been here nearly an hour already—plenty of time for a play date, especially with a child Willie doesn't know that well.

"Don't leave yet," the baby-sitter urges, as if eager for the company. But before I can respond, Willie marches into the hallway. "I don't like him," he says, pointing at Cody. "I want to go home."

The baby-sitter grabs Cody's arm. "*What* did you do?!" she shouts, assuming Cody's provoked Willie.

Great, I think. Now Cody is going to blame Willie for getting him into trouble. I'm desperately trying to end things on a good note, suggesting quietly to Willie that he shake hands with Cody and we'll try again another time.

"I want to go," Willie shouts, getting red-faced and furious.

I don't know what to do. I'm still alarmed at the way the baby-sitter is treating Cody, and I don't want to leave with everyone angry.

Suddenly Willie is squirming and kicking, lashing out at us all and kicking Cody's baby-sitter, who is standing closest to Willie.

"*I want to go!*" Willie shouts, totally out of control.

"I know you're upset, but it's not okay to kick and fight," I tell him calmly. "We're leaving right now. Please try to say you're sorry."

The baby-sitter stares at us in shock—still rubbing her leg where Willie has kicked her. Cody is backing up, as if he's scared to be in the same room with Willie. My hands are shaking, and I feel a lump rising in my throat. What is going to happen next year if Willie can't handle kids like Cody at his new school? I have visions of next year, of his nearly getting kicked out or needing a shadow, boys going around school saying what a freak Willie is and his never getting invited anywhere. I feel totally alone, as if I've betrayed Willie, somehow, not preventing this situation. But I'm furious, too. Why did he have to start kicking? And why can't he just say he's sorry?

Tears of anger and confusion are streaming down my face as I stare at my defiant son. I've got absolutely no idea what's going through his head. He knows it's wrong to kick. I don't care if he's got ADD, I'm not going to allow him to attack someone for no reason.

"Willie, I'm really ashamed of you," I say, trying to goad him into an apology by making him feel guilty. This totally backfires. Willie runs down the hall and out the door to the elevator. "Willie!" I shout, grabbing his arm. Now I know I must seem as crazy as the baby-sitter did to me when she grabbed Cody's arm. But I'm so angry at Willie and frustrated that, after all our hard work at Dr. Andersov's, this is happening again and I don't know how to get out of the situation.

I'm yelling and pulling Willie down the street going home, saying stern, useless things like, "When we get home, you're going straight to your room, young man, and don't try to get out of it," as if I'm stuck on the audio track of a *Father Knows Best* rerun.

Irrationally, I feel that Willie's somehow done this on purpose, that he could have behaved better if he'd only wanted to. Willie is so angry when we get home that he runs into his room, slamming the door behind him. Nicky is napping, though I'm sure the noise Willie's making will wake him up soon. Jolie comes out of the kitchen, takes one look at my face, and then crosses herself.

"It was *that* bad?" she asks.

"You don't want to know."

What I feel worst about is that I had an opportunity to stay calm and I blew it. If I hadn't freaked out when Willie kicked

Cody's baby-sitter, no one else would have, either. I still don't understand Willie's explosive anger. It seems far beyond simple ADD. Maybe he *does* have some grave neurological disease or oppositional behavior disorder, after all. I call Peter and Dr. Andersov right away. Something is seriously wrong with Willie, I say. We know other kids with ADD, and they never act so violent. Maybe we've missed something. Maybe we just wanted to believe Willie has ADD because it was nicer than thinking he might have something much worse.

I insist that we meet with Dr. Andersov later that afternoon. Willie has fallen asleep again after he stopped screaming during his time-out. He's still sleeping when I leave: another three-hour nap. Maybe he's got narcolepsy or a brain tumor, I think. Maybe the school psychologist was right that we didn't rule out enough other medical or psychological problems before deciding he had ADD.

For the first time since we've started working with her, Dr. Andersov looks drawn and tense when we sit down on her black leather couch. She knows how upset Peter and I are and says she can imagine too well the type of problem I'm describing. She reminds us that she saw Willie in school when Peter and I were on vacation: how he was so volatile and impulsive, running out of his class to hide in the library.

"I just don't understand what's wrong with him," I say, wringing my hands. "Why does this keep happening? Why can't he get better?"

"Well, we've just started our work with Willie," Dr. Andersov says, patiently. She insists she's still confident of the ADD diagnosis. As far as the sleeping goes, she says that researchers are still looking into why some ADD children like Willie—particularly those without a lot of hyperactivity—sometimes get what she calls "catastrophic exhaustion."

"It's not uncommon," she assures us. "And it's definitely not narcolepsy. We did tests to rule out other behavioral disorders. Dr. Levine, Dr. Miller, and I all agree that he's not emotionally disturbed."

"I still don't understand why he acts this way. You two weren't there. He just started shrieking and writhing around on the floor. He kicked Cody's baby-sitter. She didn't do *anything* to provoke it."

Dr. Andersov says she's spoken to Dr. Miller since I talked to her after the play date. Apparently, antidepressants aren't out of the question, after all, but Peter and I cut her off almost as soon as she gets the words out of her mouth. "I don't think we want to get into drugs again with him," Peter says, echoing my thoughts exactly.

Dr. Andersov goes over the play date with us, pointing out all the places where I could have done things differently. I should have prepared Cody's baby-sitter before we got there, not waited until we were there to alert her to issues that were sensitive for Willie — it didn't give her any time to get Cody on board with a plan. And I shouldn't have waited to leave until things got difficult between Cody and Willie. It's much harder to make a negative situation into a positive one, she notes, than to just leave the play date while everyone is still having fun. ("Forty-five minutes is plenty of time for two five-year-olds," Dr. Andersov says.)

"Well, what do I say to Willie?" I ask. "I've apologized to him already for losing my cool, but that doesn't really solve things. We can't have these scenes anymore. I can't take it, Willie can't take it, and his school next year is not going to tolerate it, either. I haven't seen him that wild since he was on Ritalin."

"Tell him that you're sorry the play date didn't work out," Dr. Andersov says, "but that some kids just aren't going to be good friends for him and maybe Cody is one of them. Tell him you can always try again, that kids do change, but that next time you're going to make a plan so he can tell you when he's ready to leave."

Willie loves secrets and spy stuff, Dr. Andersov reminds us, so she suggests making it into a game, like it's our secret code. We can have a word or a sentence, she says, like "I want to go to the sandbox" or something he makes up that will be our cue to leave.

She doesn't mean to pin blame, but it's all too clear that Peter and Dr. Andersov both think my own emotionality and ego about trying to save face got us into trouble at Cody's. Peter joins in: "You've got to stay calm with him, honey. Put his needs in front of yours."

Peter and I leave Dr. Andersov's office and walk home in the rain. I feel as bad as the day we left that first psychologist's office when she told us she thought Willie might have brain damage, only this time, I agree with the professional diagnosis: bad parenting. I should have stayed calm. Willie needed my help, not my embarrassment and anger.

"Have you filled out the application for that second special school?" Peter asks.

"I didn't realize we were in such a hurry," I say. "Aren't we still going to send him to Kenwood next year?" I stare at the wet pavement, the puddles accumulating there. Peter and I have stopped in the middle of the sidewalk as everyone else pushes by with their umbrellas. I feel that we'll be worrying about Willie in school until the day he graduates from college. I try to picture him in Kenwood's kindergarten class and gym, in the line the boys make to go to the park. I envision Willie pushing and struggling, the boy who's always having some problem.

"Willie has to get on a good track now," Peter says.

I agree but feel helpless, as though I'm going to have to accompany him to every classroom and play date until he's twenty-seven years old. I know I have to stop thinking about what it all means to me but I can't help but think about my unfinished novel, the work I haven't even begun flying away from me like a kite with a broken string.

Willie is awake and relaxed when we get home, playing a game with stuffed animals with Nicky. Willie has made a noose out of the cord for his Venetian blinds and has hung two of his teddy bears by the neck.

"What are they doing?" I ask.

"They were bad so I hanged them," Willie tells me earnestly.

"You know, you don't have to kill someone when he's bad," I say. "Mommy was kind of bad this morning, and I don't want to be killed. I'm sorry I yelled at you. That boy, Cody, wasn't so nice.

He didn't make you feel happy. Let's work out a password so you can always leave play dates before you get upset."

"Ooh," Willie says, delighted with the game. "What about 'Let's go to a toy store'?"

"And then we'll leave?"

"And then you buy me a toy," Willie says.

"Okay," I say, laughing. If ice cream worked to build good associations with Dr. Andersov's office, maybe the promise of toys can help Willie remember to enlist my help if he needs it on play dates. "If we have a bad play date that you want to leave, you tell me, 'We have to go to the toy store now,' and then we'll go get you a present for being such a good sport."

Willie winks at me and gives me a thumbs-up. "You have to wink, so you know it's a secret," he says.

Peter, who has been playing with Nicky the whole time, finally looks at me in relief. "Do you feel better now?" he asks.

"No," I say, truthfully. "I think I'm going to feel guilty for the rest of my life."

April 11, 1994

Dr. Andersov and I have been developing a strategy for Willie in his therapy—her strategy, really, I just kind of watch and learn. She's isolated a few specific social skills that we want Willie to improve: tolerating teasing and not always being the one who sets the rules during games.

The idea is to desensitize him, alternating things that are hard for him to handle with what she calls "sugar time." Dr. Andersov thinks if we can stretch his tolerance of frustration in these sessions in her office, he'll be able to tolerate more at school. This is the theory, of course. Seeing how it all works in practice is like being an archaeologist, uncovering the layers of Willie's behavior. As much as we try to program things beforehand, we never know when we're going to reach a dead end or when something we do will lead to buried treasure.

We work out a plan in presession phone calls of what we'll do and what activities we'll choose during the session. The way it works is that each visit is divided into three "turns," one for Willie, one for me, and one for Dr. Andersov. Willie's turn is first today and, as usual, he heads over to the sand table to play with his plastic soldiers. He sits in the "boss" chair, the rolling chair in the middle that he, Dr. Andersov, or I get to sit in depending on whose turn it is. The rules are that the person in the boss chair gets to have total control over what happens in the game. Willie's legs dangle off the boss chair, swinging excitedly as he dumps about two dozen green plastic soldiers out of a plastic bag onto the sand. He starts lining them up, making two armies in a face-off.

"*Bam, bam-bam,*" he says, pretending that they're shooting at each other.

"What team are your mom and I on?" Dr. Andersov asks. Willie can get so absorbed in what he's doing, he can easily forget that we're even in the room.

"Mom's on the good-guy team and you're on the bad-guy team," he tells Dr. Andersov.

Dr. Andersov smiles, having just pointed out to me this afternoon in our presession phone call that one of our goals for today should be to try to get Willie to put me on a different team than his soldiers. Emotionally, it will be harder for Willie — Dr. Andersov thinks Willie likes to have me on his team because he feels more secure than if I were fighting him. (Even play-fighting with soldiers is threatening to Willie, she says. At his age, he doesn't see much of a difference between my soldier wanting to kill his soldier and my wanting to kill *him.*)

"I want to be on the bad-guy team," I say, arching my eyebrows like a cartoon villain.

Willie looks up at me, trying to figure out if I'm joking. "But, Mommy," he says seriously, "you have to be on *my* team."

"Can't your mom be on a different team than you, Willie?" Dr. Andersov asks, providing a scripted reality check.

"Yeah, sweetie," I say. "My soldier's feeling like a terrible guy today, really stinky." Willie's opposition melts from his face as he sees we're starting to get silly. *"Eew,"* Dr. Andersov joins in. "Are you feeling stinky?" I make a face at Willie as if I've just smelled something awful. "Yuck," I say. "I'm stinky like a dirty diaper."

"Yeah," Willie says, getting excited, "You're stinky like a dirty diaper!"

"Should I be worried about being stinky like a dirty diaper?" I ask Dr. Andersov.

"No, it's just a game," she says, pointedly. "It's just funny teasing. It doesn't hurt you."

"That's true," I say, acting this all out for Willie. "Being stinky is just a game. It's okay to call me stinky. It's not mean teasing. It's just funny."

"But your mom can't be on the clean team if she's stinky like a dirty diaper," Dr. Andersov says to Willie.

"I'll be on the dirty diaper team," I say.

Willie's eyes are wide with delight and shock at the toilet language Dr. Andersov and I are using. He must think we've gone completely mad.

"Okay, I'm on the clean team, Mom, and you're on the stinky, dirty diaper team."

"What team are you on?" I ask Dr. Andersov.

"Smell my hand," she tells Willie, seriously. "Do I smell stinky or clean?"

Willie sniffs at her sleeve and then scrunches up his face. *"Eew,* stinky," he tells her, joyfully. "You smell like a dirty diaper."

"Bam, bam-bam," I say, picking up a soldier to fight.

"Uhhh," says Willie, knocking over one of his men dramatically. "You killed me with your stinky smell."

I beam at Dr. Andersov, never so happy to have been insulted in all of my life.

April 18, 1994

In keeping with our plan to pursue the special schools just in case Kenwood doesn't work out for Willie next year, I'm visiting the last one on our list. The school is tiny, off the beaten track in the ADD circles in which I now find myself traveling. It is half the size of the first one, which Peter and I visited last month. The brochure itself was brief: stating that the school was founded in the late sixties by parents of children with special needs. What I did particularly notice was the price tag—almost double that of most mainstream Manhattan private schools, which are expensive enough already. A year at this school costs more than two semesters at Harvard.

Willie and I are buzzed into the lobby through a series of locked doors. The building was once a private home, and a grand one at that. A marble staircase winds up more than four floors. In what must have originally been a formal reception area, children's artwork is framed above a small bronze dedication plaque. A serenely beautiful woman in her mid-twenties greets us at the door to the administrative offices.

"Hi," the woman says brightly, introducing herself. She is the head of the lower school and will be evaluating Willie while I get a tour. Willie can't stop staring at her and neither can I. If Sharon Stone were a kindergarten teacher, this is what she'd look like. Willie takes her hand and sidles up to her immediately.

"Are you ready to play some games, Willie?" she asks, smiling.

Willie nods, too lovestruck to utter a word. They head for the elevator hand in hand while I stand in the lobby, feeling like one of Cinderella's ugly stepsisters at the ball. Yet I'm glad Willie went with her so easily. I've seen children cry at school interviews, clutching their mothers' skirts for dear life.

I wait a few minutes more in the lobby for someone to get me for the parent's tour. Officially, the admissions season is long over. Most mainstream schools wouldn't even let us in the door at this point. I duck my head into the office near the front door. Two women are typing in a cramped but sun-filled room. "Excuse me," I say. "Is there anyone available to give me a tour while my son is upstairs?"

"Didn't anyone come get you?" the receptionist asks, surprised.

After a few minutes, they find the director, a dark-haired woman in her late sixties who resembles my late grandmother, a vibrant woman who loved to sculpt and go to museums until the day she had a stroke at age ninety-one. The director tells me about the school and their rigorous academics; how, although all the children have specific learning problems—everything from cerebral palsy to dyslexia and ADD—they expect them to achieve up to grade level if not higher. The more she talks, the more she reminds me of my grandmother, who, despite her casual bohemianism, could strike fear into anyone who challenged her family.

The director and I discuss Willie's unsuccessful trials on medication, his experiences in mainstream preschools, and his therapy sessions with Dr. Andersov.

"He sounds so bright," the director says. "It's really a shame these other schools can't tap into that with you."

"I agree. Sometimes I feel that all he does all day is play with blocks. If they actually tried to teach him something, maybe he'd do better."

"These children need structure and classes small enough so they can get individual attention," she says.

"Don't all kids?" I respond. What child wouldn't benefit from being in a class of eight children and two teachers?

After speaking with the director, the registrar, a petite woman with large glasses, comes to give me a tour. Unlike the first school, the classes here are all neat and well organized. Upstairs, the library looks as if it came out of a Merchant-Ivory movie: rows of leather-bound books, beautiful furniture, and a fireplace. The gym is small but they're expanding it next year, the registrar says. She shows me the kindergarten, the room where Willie would be if he were coming here next year instead of Kenwood. The classroom is bright with large windows and two sets of tables with four youngsters at each. The children are all age five or six, but I notice they are all doing work that is much harder than in the kindergarten at Kenwood: addition and subtraction with two-digit numbers; reading and spelling. And not just words, either—whole sentences, paragraphs, little books.

I do what I do on every school tour: I find a child who reminds me of Willie. Here, it's a boy who is obviously very distracted by my presence (another kid with ADD maybe?) and keeps looking up from his work to stare at me. The assistant teacher working with the group spots the problem immediately and moves his chair slightly so I'm out of his line of vision. The boy gradually goes back to work without any distraction. It is such a small accommodation on the part of the teacher, but it impresses me immensely. The other thing I notice is how quiet it is here compared to a mainstream class. None of the children are talking or pestering one another. The class is too small for any of the kids to tease. They couldn't possibly get away with it.

Although to someone who didn't know anything about children with special needs the approach of the school might seem a little strict, the kids don't seem unhappy. It's just a busy class, hard at work. The teachers are making each child follow the steps of his or her assignments in the proper order, seeing that each part gets done, such as coloring in or circling groups of items the right way. The children all wait their turns and work with the correct materials—no pens when it says pencils only, for example.

This is the most wonderful school I've ever seen in my life, clearly much better for Willie right now than Kenwood. When the registrar leads me out to pick up Willie, I look her in the eye. "I don't suppose there are places still open here for next year?"

"Let's see what comes up on the evaluation and we can talk about it," the registrar says, encouragingly.

Willie comes down with the beautiful lower school director, and we take a cab back to Willie's school. It is 12:15 P.M., much later than I expected to be back with him. As soon as we get out of the cab, we see Willie's class coming back from Central Park. "You missed the trip, Willie," one of the boys says, tauntingly.

"Hi, silly Willie," Tim says. My stomach tenses nervously. This is exactly the kind of teasing Willie normally can't handle. "Hi, silly Willie," the first boy repeats.

"Hi, stupid," Willie says, not missing a beat.

I'm so thrilled to hear Willie give it right back to Tim that I hug him and make a mental note to tell Dr. Andersov about how well Willie did with teasing. Score one for the dirty diaper team, I guess.

As we walk back to the school, the head teacher pulls me aside. "We didn't expect you today," she says, confused. "You should really let us know when you're going to be this late."

"Didn't you get my message?" I ask, explaining that I left a message with the nursery school office that morning specifically asking them to tell Willie's teachers we'd be in around lunchtime.

"Oh, well," the head teacher says. "I guess they got busy or something."

"Or something," I repeat. Lisa helps Willie find a place in line and gets ready to go upstairs with them, although she has to leave soon to get to her afternoon class.

I give Willie a kiss before he goes upstairs, and then I head back home. I'm there for literally fifteen minutes when the nursery school director calls in a panic.

"We want you to come pick up Willie," she tells me.

I try to keep a calm tone. "What's he done?"

"He hasn't done anything yet," she says. "But we're afraid he might have a problem because he came in so late and now Lisa has to go."

"Let me get this straight," I tell her, my fury slowly rising. "You want to send Willie home because you *think* he might do something? Have you considered that might send the wrong message? If you're going to send him home, at least make it for something he's done, not something you *think* he's going to do."

"But the teachers need to take their breaks and I don't want to have just one adult in the class with him."

I don't even ask why she can't send in one of the substitute teachers to cover during the teachers' breaks (there are usually three or four available for this purpose). Have there been so many staff absences today that *all* the "floaters" are busy? But I'm not going to get into this with the nursery director now. "I'll come in," I tell her, not as a question but an announcement.

I slam down the phone. In that instant, I know I've made my decision about next year. I want Willie with teachers who are experienced with behavioral issues. I want an administrative staff that's supportive, not antagonistic. Whatever we've got to do, I want Willie at the special school we saw today. I never want to get another phone call like this again.

April 20, 1994

When I tell Peter about the school I saw with Willie, he's just as excited as I am to think Willie could go there next year. The registrar called yesterday saying they have one space open in a class for next year, and Peter and I can't believe our luck. While the school doesn't say Willie definitely has learning disabilities, they do indicate that, with his impulsivity and poor attention, he's at risk for doing poorly in a mainstream school.

Peter and I no longer need any convincing. We'd love Willie to go to that special school next year. There's just one hitch. This week, a company has approached Peter about an editing job in Boston.

"I can't believe this is happening now," I tell him, after congratulating him on the offer.

"I know," Peter says, looking equally glum.

"If this had only happened a month ago, *before* we saw that school . . ."

There's nothing worth talking about, though Peter feels the exact same way I do. We need the income and medical benefits of a full-time job, especially for Willie. Since Peter left his old position, we've paid to have our medical coverage extended. However, even under that plan, we were only covered for 50 percent of Dr. Andersov's sessions (not including a $1,000 deductible). Additionally, we're not getting reimbursed *at all* for Willie's speech therapy because that's simply not covered by our insurance. And though that can be deducted in April from our taxes as a medical expense, we still need to cover out-of-pocket his twice-weekly sessions at a cost of $80 each.

There's another issue at stake, too, which is nearly as important as the money. This job in Boston is a chance for Peter to run his own magazine. The consulting work he's been doing since March, though it pays well and is fun for him, is still not the same as being in charge of and creating his own publication. Besides, consulting is not steady work and we can't count on it forever.

I try to be optimistic about the idea of moving to Boston. Peter and I both know the city well, and it's not so far from New York that we won't be able see our families regularly. And as far as my work goes: Have computer, will travel. I could be in Bora Bora and still be productive—assuming I ever get out of Willie's nursery school.

"Let's go visit, at least," I suggest. "If we don't like it, we don't have to move."

Peter looks pained, as if it's his fault for going after this job in the first place. "But what about a school for Willie?"

"If there's a perfect school for Willie in New York, maybe there's a perfect school for Willie in Boston."

This morning, when Peter goes off to his consulting job, I take out my directory of ADD support groups in the Boston area and start making phone calls. I track down a school in a nearby suburb that sounds exactly like the one we love for Willie in New York, but they don't start until first grade and Willie is too young by one year.

"Any suggestions?" I ask the admissions director of the school in Boston. He names a few other schools and gives me the number of the administrative office of an association of New England private schools. The group faxes me a list of members in the Boston area, but it's hard to know where to begin. There are about twenty schools listed in central Boston and that's not even counting the dozens of suburbs that are within half an hour's driving distance. I buy a map to get myself oriented and circle some suburbs that I know are supposed to have good public schools with relatively small classes. If worse comes to worse, I figure, we could just try a public school for Willie and get a shadow for him if we need to—it couldn't be any worse than what we did this year, and it's what might have happened if we'd sent him to Kenwood in New York anyway.

Being that it's already April, most of the schools I call are all filled for next year. A very helpful man in the admissions office of one of the schools suggests I look into local nursery and kindergarten programs. As in New York, the schools that offer a kindergarten/age-five year tend to have openings since many of the students leave after nursery school to go to ongoing schools.

"How do I find out about private kindergartens?" I ask. "There's no listing of them in the New England Independent Schools Association directory."

"Wait a minute," the admissions director says as I hear him type into his computer. "I'm calling up the files of some of the students we've admitted for next year. Most of them come from area preschools. Here are a couple."

For the next twenty minutes, he rattles off names. Lexington, Milton, Cambridge, Concord. I feel as if I'm back in seventh grade, memorizing the sites of Revolutionary War battles.

"That should be enough," he says. "Please say that I referred you personally."

I look down at my list. There are at least fifteen schools, complete with the names of many of the admissions heads at each: an invaluable resource. The admission director just saved me hours and hours of research.

"I don't know how to thank you," I tell him.

"Just find a nice school for your son," he says.

Dozens of phone calls later, I find three schools that still have places for next year: a Montessori school in Cambridge; a Jewish day school in Newton; and a nursery school–kindergarten in Boston proper. I explain to everyone I talk to that Willie has ADD. No one at these schools seems particularly scared off by this, which I take as a good sign. I tell them that we're coming to Boston soon. I don't tell them that this visit is so Peter can size up the magazine offices there and have a final meeting with the publisher. After that, if all goes well, I'll set up an appointment for us to visit the schools. (At this point, I'm not even worried about finding a class for Nicky. It's a lot easier to find places that want a "normal" three-year-old than a kindergartener with Attention

Deficit. At least I can take Nicky to art classes or swimming at a local YMCA or someplace next year and then apply to kindergarten for him the following year.)

Peter comes home with a stack of Boston Sunday newspapers that were FedExed from friends at the *Boston Globe* so we can check out the real estate listings. I start fantasizing about what life would be like in the suburbs. I picture a porch, a basement rec room, and a big backyard where the boys could play. Perhaps things would be easier for Willie if he had lots of room to run around outside, instead of being cooped up in a Manhattan apartment.

Maybe it's just a fresh start I'm after, a place where nobody knows us or will prejudge Willie. Or I still could be in some kind of denial, as if living in a new place would give us all new, perfect lives. Peter and I stay up all night wondering what's going to happen. I tell him I want flowered wallpaper in the living room of our new house if we move. It would be just like living in the middle of a garden.

April 23, 1994

Jolie arrives early this morning, and Peter and I rush off to the airport to get the shuttle to Boston. We're going to meet the publisher of the magazine that's courting Peter and see some houses with a real estate agent. It's a postcard-perfect day when we land at Logan Airport: blue skies and a light breeze blowing straight off the Charles. We have the taxi let us out at Boston Commons and walk through the park, watching the swan boats in the lake.

The publisher meets us at his magazine's offices, which are a lot smaller than we expected. I see Peter wrinkle his face the way he does when he's concerned, but no one else seems to notice. If Peter accepted this job, he'd need to expand the staff and make some big changes in the art department, which is seriously outdated. Peter mentions the amount of money he thinks the publisher would need to invest in terms of equipment and a larger staff. The publisher shakes his head. "We can do more with less;

we always have." Then they get into a discussion about freelance budgets and promotions. From the look on Peter's face, I can tell he isn't pleased. "Well, I suppose your wife is in a hurry to look at those houses," the publisher says.

"Oh, no," I say, brightly. "This is all very interesting."

"Actually," Peter says. "We probably should go; we're meeting the broker in half an hour."

Over sandwiches in a coffee shop in Belmont, we talk about the meeting with the publisher, whether it went as badly as I think it did. "I don't know," Peter keeps saying, between bites of his sandwich. "I really don't know what to think."

The real estate tour isn't much more inspiring. Everything seems just as expensive as in New York, and I can't get used to the way the houses are so close together. At least in apartments, there are whole streets dividing you from your neighbors. We have the real estate agent drop us off in Harvard Square, where we pick up some souvenirs for the boys. I look around at the dorms where I used to live as a college student. For dinner, we meet up with one of my former roommates who is now in graduate school in the area.

"Is it strange," I ask, "living back here again?"

"You get into the mode pretty fast, if you're a student," my friend says, waving her hand at the roomful of people who all look as if they're not old enough to legally drink. My friend explains she can't stay for dessert. She's got to leave to go to a party. I can almost smell the beer kegs as we exit the restaurant. It's Saturday night in Harvard Square. My knees suddenly feel shaky, as if I've been walking in a circle for seven years since graduation. I know immediately that I can't live in Boston. China, maybe, but not Boston. It all seems impossible. Peter had been decidedly lukewarm about the job at the magazine, anyway, so what would be the point of uprooting everyone?

"It'll be okay," Peter says, squeezing my hand as we get in the cab to the airport. He's pretty sure he'll take another job in New York—not running his own magazine, but a good editing job at a good salary. I've also talked to my mother, who's an investment advisor, about how we might be able to pay for the wonderful school we want Willie to go to.

Though we don't qualify for financial aid, the school's registrar has explained that the tuition is considered by the federal government to be a medical expense and is tax deductible. Additionally, under the Americans with Disabilities Act that ensured the physically and mentally handicapped the right to a "free and appropriate education," we may be entitled to tuition reimbursement from the city if we can prove that Willie could not have obtained the class size or learning specialists he needed in our local public schools (ADD is considered a "handicap" under this definition). The trick, of course, is to get the money together to pay the tuition up front in the first place. Generously, my mother offered to help. ("He's my *grandchild*," she said, understanding how embarrassed we were about taking the money. "Pay me back by doing it for yours someday if he needs it.")

"At least Willie can go to that wonderful school now," I say to Peter in the airport.

That wonderful school. I feel that we can't get Willie there fast enough.

May 2, 1994

Dr. Andersov has two goals for Willie this session. It's her turn first and she wants Willie to play on the dirty diaper team at the sand table and, when his soldiers get shot, for them to die and stay dead. This is hard for Willie. Not only does he always like to play on the "good guy" side, but—like any good general—he hates to lose a man. "No, no," he usually argues as he resurrects each one of his plastic soldiers after we shoot them in our pretend battles. "You missed me, you didn't get me." It's important for Willie to understand that he's sometimes going to lose games and that he'll often have to play according to someone else's rules.

Willie puts up a bit of a fight when Dr. Andersov tells him what she wants him to do.

"But I don't *want* my soldiers to die," he says plaintively.

"Willie, are they real soldiers?" Dr. Andersov asks, gently. "Does it hurt them when we pretend to shoot them?"

"N-o-o-o . . . ," Willie says, slowly.

"So when they die, it's just pretend, right? They're not really hurt, and you're not really hurt. It's just a game."

"See, sweetie?" I say. "It doesn't hurt to have the soldiers die. It's just a game."

I hold up my soldier from the dirty diaper team. "*Pow, pow,*" I say, pretending to shoot him. "*Aaaaugghhh.*" I let the soldier flop out of my hand and do a long, spiraling death drop onto the sand table. Willie doesn't seem too convinced that this is as joyous an experience as I'm trying to make it appear.

"Do you think he smells when he's dead?" Dr. Andersov asks, still trying to stir Willie's interest.

"Yeah," I say. "I think he smells like an old, dirty diaper. What do you think, Willie?"

"*Auugghhh,*" Willie says, with a little smile, finally getting into the spirit of things. "Help, I smell! I'm dying! I'm a dead, poopy diaper . . ."

We finish Dr. Andersov's turn at the sand table and, as we arranged in our phone call before the session, I go next and pick an add-on game with clay that is supposed to help Willie with transitions and playing by other people's rules.

The way it works is that I take a piece of clay and make it into something—a flower, for example. Then Dr. Andersov takes it and adds on something, like a ladybug on the flower. Although the first time we played this back in the fall, Willie had a hard time with Dr. Andersov's and my changing what he'd made—getting angry or even destroying a sculpture once we'd altered his design—as the months have gone by, he's been able to give up his rigid ideas of control and cope with, even enjoy, the sculptures' transformations.

This time, we go from Dr. Andersov making a boat to me adding a pirate to the boat. Then Willie adds a whale eating the boat with the pirate on it—a typically violent image. When it's

Dr. Andersov's turn, she turns it into something more peaceful—adding on a fish playing with Willie's whale.

"That's dumb," Willie says, when he looks at the fish. But he stays in his seat without yelling or breaking the clay apart. He doesn't have to like what other people do when they play with him, Dr. Andersov's explained. He just needs to find a strategy to cope with it, which he's doing by verbally criticizing. So what if it's not exactly a shower of praise for the fish? His behavior is certainly within the bounds of reason for a five-year-old.

Everything has been going so well this session that I'm a little surprised when Willie argues about being the last to have his turn. "But you went second last time and you were first the time before that," Dr. Andersov reminds him.

Willie's face is red, and he's clenching his fists by his sides—a telltale sign that he's getting frustrated. "It's not fair," Willie says, loudly.

"It's exactly fair, Willie," I tell him. "You know the rules here. We all take turns being first, second, and third." We don't have that much time for Willie's turn, and he's wasting the time he does have by arguing so much.

"Come on, honey," I say. "Just pick what you want."

"Monopoly, Jr.," Willie says, going to the games closet.

"Okay," Dr. Andersov says, checking her watch. "We can start Monopoly, Jr., but there's not going to be time to finish it."

"No!" Willie says, suddenly shouting.

I glance at Dr. Andersov, trying to get a reading from her as to what's going on. Willie's been so cooperative this session that I don't understand why he'd be getting so frustrated now. Dr. Andersov either doesn't see me or can't explain to me in front of Willie what she thinks I should do, so I just follow her cues and try to ignore Willie's outburst.

We start the game: Willie quickly buys a few places on the boardwalk. Dr. Andersov gets a good roll and wins some money.

"Okay," Dr. Andersov says, "one more turn for everybody."

"No," Willie cries. "Not one more turn. It isn't fair!"

"But, Willie, we're out of time," I say.

"No, no, no!" Willie jumps up, knocking the board over. Dr. Andersov and I are completely shocked. We've got no idea what set him off, so I don't know how we're supposed to get him out of it.

"No!" Willie shouts again, tears streaming down his face. "It's *not* over! It's not fair. You're cheating!"

"Willie, it's time to end the game," Dr. Andersov repeats more firmly.

Her face is blank. She looks neither sympathetic nor angry. I don't know if this is a technique she's trying to use to calm Willie down, but it doesn't seem to be working. I'm not sure if I'm supposed to ask her what I should do. We've never talked about what should happen if Willie got wild in her office.

If we were at home, I'd be cuddling him, trying to help him feel better. But I get the sense that Dr. Andersov wants Willie to deal with this himself. That's one of the reasons we're here, after all—so Willie can learn to calm himself down instead of me or some other grown-up always intervening. I feel totally panic-stricken watching Willie spin out of control when I know I could fix this whole mess in a matter of minutes. Dr. Andersov is silent, and I get the feeling that, as part of his therapy, I'm supposed to ignore Willie's shouting, too. But how can a mother not react when her child is *this* distressed?

Willie sticks his face right up close to mine. "I hate you!" he screams, again and again, trying to get a reaction out of me, but, like Dr. Andersov, I'm trying to remain expressionless because I think it's what she wants me to do. Of course, this only frustrates Willie more because he can't get a rise out of me. His eyes are bloodshot and his nose is running. I desperately want to get him a tissue, to kiss him and hold him.

Willie is shouting, banging the door to the office open and shut.

"I'm going to run away," he yells again. "I'm going to run away where you'll never find me! Don't you care that I'm crying?"

I can't take it anymore. "Of course I do," I tell him, near tears myself. "But you *have* to calm down."

At that moment, the other therapist who shares the office with Dr. Andersov comes storming into the room. I have seen adult patients go into her office before, but I've never actually seen her face-to-face. She's in her mid-fifties and wearing a dark dress. Next to her, Willie looks tiny and scared.

"This is *not* all right," the other therapist says, sternly. "I've got a patient next door." She's addressing her remarks to the whole room, but I'm not really sure if she's talking to Dr. Andersov, to Willie, or to all of us at once. Willie is startled into silence.

"Okay," Dr. Andersov says, taking advantage of the distraction. "Let's say good-bye for today."

I look at her, surprised. First she gets Willie all riled up by not reacting to his anger and seeming to encourage me to do the same and then, when he gets all upset, dumps him back in my lap. What am I supposed to do now? As usual, after a big fight, Willie regresses into babyish behavior almost immediately. He's yawning and docile, slumped in my lap like a rag doll. Why did we go through all this if I'm now going to cuddle and baby him, anyway—which is exactly what I could have done to avoid this whole blowup in the first place?

Walking home from Dr. Andersov's office, Willie says he's hungry. I let him get a chocolate-chip cookie from a nearby deli even though I know it will spoil his dinner. I'm disturbed and confused by Dr. Andersov's behavior. "Do you feel better?" I ask Willie.

He nods. Since we left Dr. Andersov's he's been perfectly obedient and calm. We walk along in the light, spring breeze, a pink twilight unfolding as we head west. Willie's face no longer looks tear-stained or furious. His shirtwaist flops out from his baggy jeans. Because he's been growing so much lately, I've been buying him a size too big and just rolling everything up. Clutching my hand with his baggy shirt cuffed at the sleeve, Willie seems so young to me all of a sudden, like a little boy dressed up in

Daddy's clothes. I wonder if this kind of therapy is asking too much of him; if despite all our work, he's still just too young.

"This is my in-control cookie," he says, chewing thoughtfully. "It helps fight my anger."

I nod, but I don't think this is what Dr. Andersov meant by "sugar time."

May 9, 1994

In our conversation before Willie's therapy, Dr. Andersov apologizes for last week's session. "Generally, I think it works best to ignore that kind of behavior and not to feed into it by paying the child a lot of attention, but I think you're right about Willie. When he's in a rage, he needs our help—at least for now—to get back in control. What I'd like to do is talk to him about it and ask him what *he* thinks we should do to help when he gets out of control."

"But I hate to see him get upset at all when he's so easy to manage if you get it *before* he gets frustrated. . . ."

"You're not always going to be there to joke him out of everything," she tells me firmly. "What we're trying to do is give him a way to feel permanently better on his own."

Dr. Andersov suggests a game that we could play at the sand table that might ease Willie's anxieties about playing with other children. In our presession phone calls, she's explained that she thinks one of the reasons Willie is so intent on being "the boss" when with his peers is that he fears they won't accept him or allow him into their games if he's not in charge of the activity and that this might relate back to his early experiences in his first preschool, where he had the stigma of being the "bad boy." She believes Willie still feels "bad" on some level. And, since he knows that bad behavior gets punished, he feels overly worried and self-defensive. It becomes a self-fulfilling prophecy: because he thinks that the other children won't like him or want to play with him, he can't deal with even the mildest forms of social rejection. Simply put, he's got too much at stake.

In order to help him navigate his emotions and concerns, Dr. Andersov says we need to give Willie little reality checks during our sessions, saying things like "You're okay, even though you lost the game" or "You're okay, you just feel upset right now—you'll feel better soon." We need to reassure him that, just because he feels angry or upset, it doesn't mean things are going to spiral out of control and everyone will wind up being angry at him.

My turn is first. Dr. Andersov wants me to set up a fence at the sand table, keeping some plastic figures in the shapes of children and soldiers on the inside of the fence and plastic tigers and other wild animals on the other side. "I want to be the soldiers on the clean team—you be a dirty diaper," Willie says, handing me some soldiers.

"No, Willie," Dr. Andersov reminds him. "It's your mom's turn to pick."

According to Dr. Andersov's instructions, I'm going to be the Mommies and Daddies, who are represented by the soldiers; Dr. Andersov will play the boys and girls who play inside the fence; and Willie's going to be the wild animals prowling outside.

Willie gets into the part, typically dramatic. With his chubby, little-boy fingers he pushes the animals recklessly toward the fence, growling and roaring ferociously. Every once in a while, Willie forgets the rules, rushing his plastic beasts—lions, tigers, and a King Kong doll—through the flimsy, plastic fence.

"No!" I say, my Mommies and Daddies rushing to bolster the fence. "We're the parents and we're going to keep our children safe!"

Willie's eyes grow wide. Though he tries a few more times to make the animals break through, I stop him each time and he eventually pulls back. Dr. Andersov, meanwhile, is doing her own Academy Award–winning performance. Every time the animals get near the fence, she makes the children jump up and down nervously.

"But we've been naughty!" the boys and girls say. "Maybe the animals will hurt us!"

Then, according to the prearranged script, my Mommies and

Daddies say, "No, you're all good kids, even if you sometimes misbehave. We'll keep you safe." I keep my eyes squarely on Willie the entire time, expecting him to shake his head any minute and say something like "Come on, guys, don't you think you're being awfully obvious?" But he's listening hard, blinking first at Dr. Andersov, then at me. I keep looking at Dr. Andersov, too. When she thinks Willie's had enough, she's going to give me a sign: All the children will lie down and then I'll say, "Okay, kids, time for bed." But Willie's doing so well, she just nods to keep going.

It's Dr. Andersov's turn now, and she tells Willie she's going to change the rules. This time, we're going to put some larger wild animals outside the fence and the smaller animal "babies" and children inside the fence together. I play the children now and Dr. Andersov is the "wild animal Mommies and Daddies." We all shift positions and Willie seems a little confused at first, not knowing exactly how to shift gears from being a wild animal to being a calm animal inside the fence. He gives little, halfhearted growls, ignoring my children dolls who are inside the fence with him.

Dr. Andersov is roaring and growling outside the fence. For a minute, Willie looks scared. He doesn't understand what he's supposed to do. Before, he was trying to attack the other children, now he's inside the fence with them, trying to protect himself from the wild animals outside. I'm starting to wonder about what message is getting through in this game—the wild animals causing all the problems are the *parents*.

Dr. Andersov addresses Willie: "Parents can be scary sometimes, can't they? But they still protect their children."

"Ouch," I say, pretending one of the children is hurt.

"Don't worry," Dr. Andersov's tiger says, suddenly calm. "I'll get your Mommy and Daddy. They'll make sure you stay safe."

"*Oww*," Willie says, after a beat. "My lion broked his tail."

"There, there," the big lion says. "Let me give you a hug."

"Are the grown-up animals mad at us because we got hurt while we were playing?" I say.

"No," Dr. Andersov says, being King Kong this time. "Kids sometimes get hurt. The Mommies and Daddies love their children anyway."

"Come over the fence," Willie's lion says to its mother.

"No, I can't," Dr. Andersov says. "It's just for kids. You're okay in there on your own. We'll be out here if you need us."

"We'll be okay in here," I have my children dolls say to Willie's baby animals. "Want to play?"

Willie offers my children dolls a ride on his animal's back. A tiger is tamed both literally and figuratively. Dr. Andersov and I are beaming.

May 16, 1994

As I'm in a drugstore doing some errands, I see a dark-haired woman come in with her three daughters. From where I'm standing in the cashier's line, I can't see the woman's face, but her prickly voice sounds familiar as she tells her girls to pick out only one candy each for their trip to the movies. As she gets closer, I can't believe who it is—Willie's threes teacher, the woman who was so awful to him that fall: putting him out of class to stand in the hallway when he'd yelled or gotten angry; constantly phoning me at all hours of the day and night with her litany of complaints about him; the way she'd smirked after the director asked us to withdraw Willie, as if he was somehow getting what he "deserved"—as if he wanted to behave that way.

My stomach tenses, and I have to consciously tell myself to try to relax. But just seeing her has brought back the fear and concern we experienced during those awful three months—the sense of impending disaster I had to face every time I dropped Willie off in the morning.

I'm too stunned by the chance encounter to think about subterfuge—slipping out of the store unnoticed, or hiding in a distant aisle, for example. Besides, there's really nowhere to hide. Her daughters are standing so close to me as they lean over the candy rack that I can read the name tags in their sweatshirts. "Hello," I say to the teacher as she steps beside me in the line for the cashier.

Her eyes widen as she recognizes me and then narrow again quickly. I reflexively think back to those three months Willie was in her class and tell myself to try to be charitable. It was her first year teaching, after all, and even experienced educators often misdiagnose ADD. Still, I can't help but feel that she could have tried harder to see Willie's good side, to work with me and Peter instead of constantly trying to pin blame. I like to think that if I had been in her shoes, I would have been a little more tolerant— or at least had more of a sense of humor about being called an "old wallpaper" by a three-year-old boy. In our therapy sessions, Dr. Andersov and I are still trying to undo some of the lasting effects we feel those three months had. I doubt that this woman has any idea of how disastrous it was for my child that he wound up in her class that year. I have to assume that she went into teaching because she cares deeply about children. Maybe in her mind, she thinks she did Willie a favor by kicking him out of nursery school. At least we were forced to get him help early.

"How's Willie?" she asks.

I pretend not to have heard her. I'm afraid of what I might do or say if I start talking to her about Willie. I don't want to make a scene or have a confrontation with her in front of her daughters. I'm still too angry about everything that happened at that school for her to think she deserves to have any kind of stake in his progress. Instead of being treated as though we had a child worth saving, we were sent out into the cold.

My throat feels shaky, but I force myself to talk. "What movie are you seeing?" I ask mildly.

She says the name of a film but I instantly forget it. My heart is racing, but in some weird way I'm also determined to draw the conversation out as long as possible.

I can see by her face that she's just as uncomfortable as I am and, unflattering as it is to admit it, I'm enjoying her unease as my one shred of revenge. After all those phone calls and meetings, the lukewarm letter she wrote about Willie—recommending him, but so grudgingly, to the other schools—it's so hard just to turn the other cheek and forget about it.

As I continue to speak with Willie's former teacher about the movie they're going to see and make chitchat about her daughters' school, I notice she's started taking baby steps in the opposite direction, as if she can't get away from me fast enough. It's funny, in the past year and a half, I've thought long and hard about what I'd do if I ever ran into her but, the way I imagined it, I'd have had some pithy remark ready that would have reduced her to tears. But now I feel too bad about what happened to Willie to be nasty to her in front of her own children.

"Well, we've really got to run or we'll miss the movie," she says.

We leave on a smile because I really don't have the heart to be vicious. How would it change things, anyway? What's done is done and no matter what I do or say to her now, it won't change what happened to Willie in her classroom.

May 23, 1994

Peter and I have a lunchtime appointment to talk to Mrs. Mielho, the lower school director at Kenwood, to tell her in person we've decided not to send Willie there next year. Mrs. Mielho has been a friend of the family for years. Out of respect for her and the fact that she must have personally extended herself for us at Kenwood, Peter and I feel she deserves to be told face-to-face.

Kenwood is on a quiet, tree-lined street on the Upper East Side. When we arrive outside at noon, the school looks as though it hasn't changed in the seventy-odd years since its first class graduated. There are uniformed nannies pushing baby strollers toward Park Avenue, well-dressed women in hats walking to the fashionable restaurants nearby for lunch. It's absolutely quiet in the entrance foyer of the stately Georgian building when the school receptionist buzzes us in.

The more I look around, the less I can imagine Willie here

next year and am so grateful we found a place for him at the special school instead. I'm listening to the silence, to the well-mannered order of this place and the neighborhood, knowing that I still wish for Willie some of their polite, controlled demeanor. Maybe this is another reason we wanted Willie here so badly. Besides the wonderful academics, the sports facilities, and all the male teachers, it was this silence that was so alluring, how we wanted Willie to be able to be.

A row of boys in their navy blazers walks by in a tight line on the way to art class. I try to imagine Willie walking in one of these lines, but I can't. He would be pushing, too hemmed-in by the bodies around him to remember even where he was going. A teacher would single him out of the group and he'd start to cry or scream. All the boys would think he was different. He *is* different. It's a beautiful school and the people here seem truly kind, but Willie's not ready for this yet and, realistically, I have to admit to myself that he might never be.

Mrs. Mielho comes down herself to get us. We follow her through the circuitous halls to her office—a windowless room nonetheless made colorful by students' drawings on the wall and a handmade quilt sewn by a recent graduating class. Peter and I sit facing her. I feel my face heating up, unsure how to begin. In my wildest dreams, I couldn't have imagined how awkward this would be.

"There's a problem with Willie coming here next year," Peter says. "When you accepted him, he was on Dexedrine, which didn't work for him. It's much harder for Willie to pay attention again. He's in behavioral therapy, but we're just not sure he'll be ready for such a big class by the fall."

"Is he on any medication at *all?*" Mrs. Mielho asks, hopefully.

"We didn't feel it was effective," I explain. "He's only five. Our doctor didn't want to try any of the other drugs on a child that young."

"I see," Mrs. Mielho says. "Where have you decided to send him instead?"

We tell her the name of the school, and she nods encouragingly. "I think that's the best one, academically. You're fortunate to have gotten him a place there."

"We were impressed by it," I agree, noticing she isn't arguing with us to reconsider. I don't know whether I should feel insulted or not.

"I have to say," Mrs. Mielho tells us, "most parents wouldn't have made the choice you're making once they'd gotten a child admitted to a school like this."

"We're not picking a school for Willie so we can brag about it to our friends," Peter says. "We want the school that's best for him right now."

Mrs. Mielho smiles. "That's my point. You're very brave."

"I don't feel it," I tell her. "We're just thinking of him."

Outside, Peter gets a cab to go back to work. "It's okay," he says, kissing me before he gets in.

"I know," I say, feeling like my stomach is sinking.

I decide to walk across the park to my office. The day is beautiful, with a beneficent, light breeze and the scent of cherry blossoms. In Central Park, I see a group of boys from Kenwood—I can tell by their matching blue sweatsuits and the way they all walk in a line. The gym teacher is joking with one of the boys, who tilts his head back and laughs, happy for the joke, the hale perfection of the moment. I think about Willie and what might have been. The cherry blossoms cascade to the ground, blowing in soft flurries stirred up by wind. I don't let myself cry. It already seems as if the trees are doing it for me.

May 26, 1994

As expected, Willie's school has lost interest in us now that we've got Lisa, his shadow, in place. There have been no follow-up meetings with the director or the psychologist since we hired Lisa. And though the director had to sign all the forms when we applied for Willie to the special school, she's never even asked whether we're still sending Willie to Kenwood or not next year. When I see her in the hall, she rushes by without stopping. In the past, I couldn't come within ten feet of her office without being pulled aside to hear the latest litany of Willie's misbehavior. Everyone loves a crisis. Now that we're not a "hot" topic, I guess she's lost interest.

June 15, 1994

Willie's class is having a picnic to celebrate the last week of school. All the families gather in Central Park as the class parents dispense pizza, juice, and cookies. It's a steamy afternoon—over ninety degrees in the shade. Although siblings are invited, I've decided Nicky should stay at home with Jolie. It's been a big year, and I want to see Willie enjoy his friends and his teachers without being distracted.

At the picnic, many of the parents draw me aside to say that Lisa has worked wonders. "Willie is so calm now," the assistant teacher says, when we get a moment to speak privately. "He's made so much progress."

I nod, knowing that Willie has thrived this spring with Lisa. As a thank-you gift, we gave her a silk scarf with angels on it because she's truly been Willie's guardian angel. Yet I still can't help but wonder: What if someone as sophisticated as Lisa had been his teacher this year instead of just his shadow? Maybe he wouldn't have even needed extra help.

I watch Willie as he plays baseball with some of his friends. None of the boys can throw or catch very well but they're having fun anyway. One of the rowdier kids in his class throws Willie the ball—a wild, loose pitch, which, of course, Willie misses. Everyone runs off the bases to look for the ball, which is now rolling madly toward a large thicket of bushes. In the past, this is exactly the kind of thing that would get Willie furious: the missed catch, the chaos of the other children interrupting the game. But now, he's just one of the crowd, happily looking for the lost ball.

The class gathers to sing "Happy Birthday" to the two children who will turn five over the summer. One of the birthday kids does a funny dance that involves turning back to the class and wiggling his rear end in time to our singing. His mother turns bright red, and Willie and I both laugh loudly—this kind of mischief is so typical of Willie's friend.

It's strange to think of Willie leaving this class—much as I couldn't wait to get him out of it this winter. Finally, he feels close to these children, and they like and trust him. Next year, we'll all have to get used to a new arrangement: Willie in a new school and me rarely in his class at all. I've seen these children almost every day for six months, spending more time with some of them than their parents. I'll probably never have another chance to know Willie's friends this closely, or to see him so often in school.

"I'll miss my class this year," Willie says plaintively, as they cut the birthday cake.

I'm amazed to realize that, despite it all, I will, too.

June 27, 1994

"Where are all the kids?" Willie asks, sounding anxious.

"I don't know, honey. The letter they sent said to come to this entrance."

Willie fidgets from side to side, pulling on my free hand. It's Willie's first day of summer camp—a program run by the nursery school where he went this year. Given the problems we had with the school, we considered sending him elsewhere but figured it would be better for Willie to be in a camp with some children he already knew. We didn't want him to have to adjust to a new day camp and then make another transition to a new school in the fall. I peer into the deserted school lobby through the locked glass doors, as if I might see Lisa coming down to meet me and explain where everyone else is. But that's impossible, because Lisa isn't shadowing Willie in camp this summer. With three counselors for ten children, we didn't think he would need her.

"Let's go home," Willie says, sounding even more miserable than before. I know he's nervous—and why wouldn't he be? Poor Willie. These transitions are so hard for him. I squeeze his hand hard, hoping the small act will bolster him in some way.

"Maybe everyone is at the other building," I suggest, trying to sound calm. "Maybe Mommy made a mistake about the meeting place."

"Maybe it's the wrong day," Willie says, sounding hopeful.

"Could be," I say, as we head back downstairs. "Maybe camp starts tomorrow. Wouldn't that be silly if it was the wrong day?"

Willie still looks nervous, despite my best efforts to keep things lighthearted. If I show how nervous I am, it will just make him feel worse. As we head around the corner to the other building, we start to see clusters of kids and parents with camp T-shirts and lunch boxes, and Willie starts to look relieved. Inside, the school guard explains that the other entrance will be closed all summer. They don't use that building for camp anyway, he says, and it's too expensive to hire a guard for just one door. Fine, I think, but they could have let us know. This is exactly the kind of thing that drove me crazy about this school during the year.

With the confusion about the entrances, we are now running late. Upstairs, we discover glitch number two. A young woman named Debbie introduces herself as Willie's head counselor instead of the counselor we'd been told to expect.

"What happened to Jenna?" I ask.

"I don't know," Debbie says. "Some last-minute switch, I guess."

"This is so typical," I mutter. I've already spent half an hour talking to Jenna about Willie, explaining about his ADD and the best way to handle his behavior in a large group.

Debbie explains she's one of the school's kindergarten teachers—trying, I suppose, to establish her credibility. She seems very nice, and I feel bad if I've appeared unhappy with her. It's more the situation that's annoying. Why did the camp change all these things without informing us first? I'm especially surprised because Willie's former teacher, who runs the camp, should have known how important predictability is for Willie. How would any of these teachers have felt if they showed up for work one day and the school entrance changed and the director changed without anyone letting *them* know?

Debbie bends down to introduce herself to Willie, but I can tell he's not really paying attention. He's twisting his head to see behind her, eager to go over to his friends from during the year. Debbie says something about how she knows they're going to have a wonderful summer. At least his old friends are in the same group, as promised.

The room is quiet. Except for some pictures of frogs that list the children's names, the bulletin boards and display cases are bare. There's no posted list of activities or daily schedule, so it's hard to brief Willie on what to expect. I don't know what to say—

how or if I can prepare him. I miss the familiar bustle and noise of his friends from his old class and wonder if Willie is thinking about this, too. Debbie goes off to greet some of the other families who've just arrived. Willie races to his friends, and they all start building a tower of blocks. The new kids, who don't go to this school during the year, look at the happy cluster wistfully. I feel sorry for them, having to be the new ones.

Most of the other parents have gone but, as usual, I am lagging behind, reluctant to leave until I know Willie is settled. He seems unusually quiet, moving a plastic tiger in and out of a block building. I wonder if the fact that he's picked a wild animal has anything to do with the games we've been playing with Dr. Andersov, but it doesn't seem like the right time to ask him about it.

"Okay, sweetheart," I say, stroking his cheek. He seems so little to me as I look at the downy, blond hairs along his jawline that will take ten years before they need to be shaved. "Let's go over the names of your counselors again."

He gets two of the three right, and I remind him of the third.

I whisper in his ear, so I won't embarrass him in front of his friends: "And what do you do if one of the kids bothers you in camp?"

"Just ignore him, or walk away, or tell the teacher," Willie says fast, his little mantra. He *should* know it by heart, I realize. It's the fourth time we've gone over it today.

"Good," I say, rubbing his back. "I know you're going to have a great summer with your new friends. You've done such good work staying in control in school. I'm really proud of you, Willie. Daddy and I love you so much."

"Okay, Mom," Willie says, hardly looking up. I don't want to leave him, but I force myself to get up and go. It's my problem with separation today, not his. I feel guilty for all of the confusion this morning, as if there were something I could have or should have done to prepare better. I march off to work, reminding myself of all the good reasons why we wanted to send him to day camp in the first place: that he does better when he has some structure in his day; that he'd get bored hanging out with Nicky and Jolie with no play dates of his own because all his friends are in camp; that Willie still needs the practice of being in a social group with his peers.

In my presession phone call with Dr. Andersov I ask whether Willie shouldn't have a lot of "sugar time" today because he might be feeling anxious about starting camp.

"Let's take our cues from Willie," she suggests. "We'll start with pickup sticks and see how he does. Don't let him get away with too much. Play the way his friends might. If something dynamic happens, stick with it as long as you think Willie can handle it."

Willie settles right down to the game when we get to Dr. Andersov's. He's patient with the pickup sticks—a game where each player has to extract a long, toothpick-thin wood stick from a pile without touching any of the others in the pile. He shows good attention today, watching for mistakes when Dr. Andersov and I take our turns.

When it's time for Willie to pick a game, he goes over to the sand table, as usual. He puts the wild animals and soldiers on the same team. Dr. Andersov leans over, sniffing loudly to see if she can provoke Willie. "*Eeww,*" she says, pretending Willie smells like a dirty diaper. "You stink!"

Willie shrugs, barely glancing at Dr. Andersov. "No, I really don't."

Dr. Andersov and I nod to each other. Willie is tolerating our teasing extremely well, despite the pressures of having started camp this morning.

Casually, as if she's just thought of the subject, Dr. Andersov asks Willie, "So, how did everything go today."

"Fine," Willie says, still staring at the soldiers. Getting information out of Willie sometimes can be like pulling teeth.

"What'd you do?" I ask.

"Play in the gym."

"What'd you play?"

"Just a boat game."

I have no idea what he means, but it's not important *what* he played as much as *how* he played.

"Was it fun?" I ask.

"Yeah," he says, offhandedly. "Until my head got stuck."

"Excuse me?" Dr. Andersov asks.

"My head got stuck in the boat, but the counselors didn't help me."

"That must have been very scary," Dr. Andersov says.

"I was trying to get out," Willie says, getting more excited, "but I couldn't and I was stuck and I tried to get out but I couldn't. . . ."

"I'm glad you weren't hurt, Willie," Dr. Andersov says in a gentle voice. "Why didn't your counselors come and help you?"

"I was thinking I needed help, but no one comed," Willie says.

"Wait a minute, Willie," I interrupt. "Did you call out for them or just think in your head that you needed help?"

Willie looks blank for a minute, as if he doesn't understand the difference. "I just thought and thought about my head bein' stuck, but no one heard me so I got out mysef."

Poor Willie! I could just see him in the gym with the kids running all around and he with his head stuck, not knowing what to do. "Willie, if you need help you have to ask for it," I remind him.

"Everyone likes you at camp and wants to help keep you safe," Dr. Andersov adds. This is still the important issue for Willie, I realize—being scared and not knowing how to get help from the grown-ups. To him, most adults have been pretty useless, at best, and mean-spirited and vindictive toward him at worst, so why should his camp counselors be any different?

"Do you understand, sweetheart?"

"I do, Mommy." Willie nods.

I stare at the game Willie's made at the sand table. The wild animals and soldiers are all mixed up together. Attackers, defenders. I know just how he feels. In a new situation, it can be hard to tell who's going to be on Willie's side.

June 30, 1994

I've been taking Nicky to a toddler gym class, and it's fascinating to see the difference in the way Nicky plays compared with Willie at the same age. The class has about twelve children ranging in age from eighteen months to three years, although the group is really supposed to be for two- and three-year-olds. The teachers set up the equipment—trampolines, uneven bars, balance beams, and cushioned climbing towers—in different ways each time. Nicky races through the tunnels, ladders, and slides with ease. He loves coming here and seems to be the voluntary guinea pig, always happy to try some new hair-raising stunt on the trampoline, or swing upside down on the uneven bars.

When Willie took classes like these, they would always end in tears—either mine, his, or another child's. He physically couldn't calm himself down to follow the rules to do half the activities even when he wanted to. Nicky, on the other hand, doesn't *like* to stop playing and listen to the teachers but he *can*, with relative ease. Most of the time, I just follow him around, watching in amazement at his sheer normality. To me, it seems extraordinary that he can compose himself so quickly—even after something as physical and exciting as jumping on a trampoline. Nicky is a wonderful athlete, lean and well coordinated—built perfectly for sports where speed and agility are important. Willie, on the other hand, is huskier—a slower runner than Nicky though, at this age, he'd rather push his younger brother out of the way in a race and get in trouble than lose to him.

Willie's ADD seems to work in interesting ways in sports. Though he might storm off a field in a frustrated rage if he fails to hit or catch a ball, his impulsivity often works in his favor in games where he needs quick reflexes. Nicky makes a great running forward in soccer, for example, but Willie is an equally talented goalie—diving to block the ball the instant it is kicked.

"Mommy, look at me!" Nicky says, doing a split-jump on the trampoline. I see his small body, his unconscious grace and skill. To me, Olga Korbut couldn't look better.

July 5, 1994

Willie seems to be adjusting well to camp. Each morning when I drop him off, he goes right over to his group of friends from his class last year. I am particularly glad he's doing so well with Tim, the boy who always used to tease Willie and whom Willie would constantly hug-wrestle and poke. Tim gives Willie a high-five each morning. Even the new kids seem to have found friends in the group. By the time I leave each day, Willie is usually playing happily in a small group of five or six children.

This group of kids likes board games—a welcome change from the ubiquitous building blocks in last year's class. Candyland and a memory game where you have to match game cards to the pictures printed on the board are the most popular. I'm glad Willie's had a chance to practice most of these games at Dr. Andersov's. By now he can patiently wait his turn, take one card at a time, and follow the rules. It's also interesting to see how well he copes with the way the kids team up, yelling for him to turn over one card or another—or rooting for his opponent. I haven't seen Willie get angry or storm away from a game once this summer.

I wonder what the difference is between camp and school— why Willie seems to be doing so well in camp but struggled so much during the school year. Maybe it's the mix of kids in his camp group. Except for Willie and Tim, there aren't really any other children I would call particularly "difficult."

Or perhaps the improvement in Willie's behavior comes from having three counselors instead of just two teachers. More important, one of the counselors is male: Joe, a high-school senior who's a counselor-in-training. Joe plays with the boys in a way the female counselors never do. He doesn't seem to mind their teasing him or using toilet language. He's more playful, getting in the games with them and chasing them around in the play yard (of course, Joe is also seventeen, which gives him a teenager's energy that most full-time teachers don't have).

Or could it be that Debbie is just better organized and more inventive in the classroom than Willie's teachers were last year?

Debbie brought in a tape player, and a few families lent tapes—
so there's always cheerful music playing when the children come
in each morning. I know all kids like music, but it especially
seems to help Willie get in the right mood each day. Tim lent his
Lion King tape and, by now, all the parents and kids know all the
words to "The Circle of Life" and "Hakuna Matata," a song that
has a particularly appropriate message for Willie: Don't worry, be
happy.

Since camp started, we haven't had to take Willie home early
or come in once to deal with one of his white-hot rages. After all
the time that Peter and I spent agonizing about how he would
manage without Lisa, it seems that Willie's doing just fine.
Hakuna Matata, as the song says: No worries, for the rest of our
days. Wouldn't it be nice?

July 11, 1994

In our pretherapy phone call, Dr. Andersov outlines some new
goals for Willie. We've pretty much gotten him to give up his
habit of always wanting to be the boss. She says what we should
aim for now is more flexibility in general: Willie being able to
change the rules of a game without our telling him about it in advance. "The idea is to help him with transitions from doing things
his way to being open to do all kinds of new things."

When we get into her office, Willie takes his turn first. As expected, he goes to the sand table with his usual army of green
plastic soldiers. He swirls them around in the sand for a while, in-
structing Dr. Andersov and me to dig trenches in the sand.
There's no "good guy" team, and no dirty diapers are on the
scene. I think that Willie's world has gotten a lot more subjec-
tive—no one's at war anymore, which I take to be a good sign.

It's my turn, and I want to stay at the sand table so I can
change Willie's game in a way that he will clearly recognize but
(I hope) tolerate. I grab the Tupperware container of plastic
fences and "wild animals" that Dr. Andersov keeps under the
sand table. "Okay," I say, setting up the fences quickly. "Willie,

you be the turtles inside the fence and Dr. Andersov, you be the alligator outside."

"*Hih-ya!*" Willie karate-chops, with his turtles in the fence. "We're *Ninja* turtles."

Dr. Andersov smiles at me. This is clearly a coping trick on Willie's part: as if it's all right for his characters to be locked up, as long as they're really superheroes about to outsmart their captors.

Willie is perched happily on the chair, his legs dangling off the seat. He's not supposed to be having fun in this game: he's supposed to be trying to get out of the cage. I notice his left knee is dirty and scraped, but I stifle the impulse to interrupt the game in order to ask him how he hurt his knee and why nobody at camp cleaned it up or got him a Band-Aid.

Willie sees me staring at him and mistakes the concerned look on my face for a scowl.

"*Hih-ya!*" He chops angrily in my direction, thinking I am frowning at him.

"*Grrrr, grrrr,*" Dr. Andersov roars, having the alligator charge at the fence. "I'm going to eat you turtles up for dinner."

"No!" Willie suddenly shouts, burying the toy alligator under a fistful of sand. Unable to handle the sudden shift in mood from merry to threatening, Willie is destroying the game rather than dealing with the aggravation of things not going his way.

"Time out," Dr. Andersov says, stopping Willie's hands in midair. "Willie, this is just a game. It's not real—the alligators can't really hurt the turtles. They can't really hurt you."

Willie starts to twist and writhe, trying to pull his hands away from Dr. Andersov.

"Okay, doo-doo," Willie says, immediately regressing. He pulls the turtles out from under the sand where he buried them and starts spinning on Dr. Andersov's chair and making farting sounds. His eyes have that wild look they get when he's starting to lose control. He's not gone yet, but I have that tight feeling in my stomach as if I'm about to witness a scene like the one when Willie stormed out during the Monopoly, Jr., game. Dr. Andersov blocks the chair with her foot.

"Willie, enough," she says in a voice that is gentle but un-yielding. "It's my turn now, and we're going to play a game called Unhappy Endings."

"Is it a *farting* game?" Willie asks, and then bursts out laughing in a high-pitched squeal. He's still very excited, but he has finally stopped swiveling. His body movements are slowing down. Dr. Andersov has captured his attention—for a moment, anyway.

Dr. Andersov gets Willie to agree to leave his turtles in the trap. The "unhappy ending" in the story is that they don't get to karate-chop their way out of prison.

"That's okay," Willie says, bouncing the turtles up and down in a little dance. "They're going to have a party all by themselves."

He smiles as he acts out a whole rock 'n' roll routine with the turtles, his concentration effortless when it's applied to something he's in charge of or creating. Despite the rules that the turtles stay in jail, Willie has found a way to make a happy ending out of the situation anyway.

After our appointment, I hold his hand as we walk home together. The street is full of happy shouts from children playing in a nearby basketball court. Willie is looking thoughtful as we pass the moving figures on the court. It's near dusk and he's unusually quiet—not worn-out the way he can sometimes be after having had a hard session.

"Willie," I say, "you know that all of the games we play with Dr. Andersov are safe. Nothing can hurt you in there."

"I know, but I didn't like the alligators to eat my turtles up." The way he says it, the word comes out more like "tortles." I have to remind myself what he's talking about. The idea of "tortles" sounds so fanciful—like little cakes floating in the air or those flying toasters from the screen-saver on our computer.

"What do you think you could have done instead of wrecking the fence when you got upset?" I ask.

Willie looks serious a minute, staring down at his sneakers. His face lights up suddenly. "I got it! Hakuna Matata—don't worry, be happy."

"Hakuna Matata. Exactly!" I say, amazed by how Willie

could distill exactly what he needed from such a seemingly non-sensical song as the warthog's aria from *The Lion King*. Giving him one, comforting line to say to himself when he gets upset is a brilliant idea. And, most importantly, Willie thought of it by himself.

Later that night, we get a chance to try our new strategy. At bedtime, Willie starts to whimper after I read him his bedtime story.

"What's wrong, sweetheart?" I ask.

"I'm hungry," he moans, pathetically. "I'm goin' to be starvin' all night and I already brushed my teeth and they'll fall out if I get cavities."

He doesn't have the dental knowledge or grammar necessary for such a complex sentence, but I know what he means. He wants a snack but is worried because he brushed his teeth already.

"Hakuna Matata," I say, stroking his hair. "I'll get you some crackers. Then you'll brush your teeth again."

Willie brightens. "Fank you. You're the bestest momma in the whole, wide world."

"Hakuna Matata," I tell him. No worries.

July 26, 1994

I drop Willie off at day camp this morning and Debbie approaches me while I'm in the hall. She has a nervous look on her face that I recognize immediately.

"Hi," I say, tentatively, knowing from experience that she's about to tell me something awful about Willie.

"We had a little problem yesterday," she says, drawing me over to the cubbies. "Willie scratched a child in the pool. We made him take a time-out but when he got back in the water, he did it again to someone else."

"What happened?" I ask, trying to make sense of what she's telling me. "Was Willie upset before the first incident? Was somebody teasing him or was there some fight with another kid?"

"He *scratched* the child," Debbie repeats, as if that should explain it all. "It's not the first time that something like this has happened. When I took him to the office after the second time, though, they told me you like to be kept informed of these things."

"I do," I say, nodding, though *like* is not exactly the word I might have used.

I don't know exactly what to think. It seems to me that, despite our strategy of Hakuna Matata—Willie's telling himself not to worry and get stressed—he's still been having a hard time lately. I've noticed that he's been getting impulsive and aggressive with some of the younger boys at his day camp. All the children take a big elevator up to the fifth floor of the nursery school building to get to the camp area. If a younger boy is dancing or acting out karate moves with another friend in the lobby, Willie tries to get in the middle and do bigger, tougher moves. The other kids always seem startled and frightened by his behavior. Then Willie winds up in a staring match—or worse, he'll start growling at them during the elevator ride. It's always younger boys this happens with—they're usually around three and a half. Is this behavior, as well as the scratching incident in the pool, part of a larger problem for Willie—some kind of turf-consciousness where he's trying to mark out and defend his territory?

Debbie is waiting for an answer, but I don't know what to tell her. I don't understand why he does these things, either. "Willie has ADD," I say finally. "It's why he lashes out sometimes—he just gets overstimulated. It's more self-protective than aggressive. In his mind, he's provoked." I suggest that she try to find out why Willie started scratching in the first place. If it happens once, I say, it's more than likely it will happen again that same day. If they see Willie having a hard time, they should send a counselor over right away—maybe Joe, because he seems so good at working with Willie.

"That's what we've been doing anyway," she tells me.

I feel guilty for not having told her about Willie's ADD

sooner. I would have told Debbie at the beginning of the summer, but then there was the confusion when they switched counselors and I didn't really get a chance to talk to her privately on the first day. And up until now, I hadn't heard anything was wrong, so I didn't want to get Debbie alarmed if Willie wasn't posing a behavioral problem. (Maybe it was also a good deal of wishful thinking on my part that, in the more casual setting of camp versus school, Willie's symptoms would be less disruptive.)

"I'm sorry," I tell Debbie. "I guess I was hoping this sort of thing wouldn't happen with him this summer."

"That's okay," she says. "It really wasn't a big deal."

I appreciate her graciousness, but I still feel bad. Debbie goes back inside to help the other campers get settled. Though Debbie is certainly a lot easier to deal with than the nursery school director and her psychologist sidekick, I sure miss having Lisa around. It was awfully nice when she was there to help Willie avoid these situations in the first place.

August 15, 1994

For the past week, I've been scouring the papers, looking for part-time or full-time writing or editing jobs. Even though Peter has landed on his feet at a magazine in New York, given all the expenses we have with Willie's therapy, I'm still worried about our finances. For now, I've given up on my novel. I don't have the energy or inclination to finish it. The realities of our family—what's happening outside my imagination—seem much more important. Nicky is starting a half-day nursery program next fall and, with Willie going to a special school, I won't have to worry about the constant phone calls to pick him up because of his ADD-related outbursts. At his new school, the teachers are trained to deal with defensive outbursts if they happen—but with only seven other children in the class, it's unlikely that Willie will feel overwhelmed.

As usual, Peter supports my decision. He thinks it's a great idea for me to go back to work if I want to, but we both know the economy is pretty tight right now, especially for someone like me who has been out of the job market for a few years. Still, my résumé is in good shape, and I've done freelance work at enough respectable magazines to hope for a few callbacks.

There's a features editor position open at a Manhattan weekly newspaper, and the editor in chief seemed to like me a lot when I went in for the interview. The staff is quite young—most of the writers are in their early twenties. As the second-in-command, I'd have a lot of freedom to assign stories and write on a variety of topics that interest me, everything from local politics to the arts and entertainment. I'm hoping the job works out, but it's still a long shot. Peter and I are taking the kids to the country for a two-week vacation, and the editor promised me she'd be ready to let me know before Labor Day. I'm keeping my fingers crossed.

August 24, 1994

We're on our vacation at our family's house in Massachusetts. There's a brook nearby, and our neighbors raise sheep and horses. The boys are in heaven, catching frogs all day and eating ice-cream sandwiches on the porch after dinner. Jolie has come up with us to baby-sit for the first week. Peter and I have never taken this much time off before—the longest trip we've had together was ten days when we went on our honeymoon six years ago.

Though it was rainy and cold the first weekend of our visit, the weather cleared up—sunny and bright—by Monday. Peter and I are off doing our own things while Jolie looks after the boys. Peter has pretty much parked himself on the porch with a book and his guitar. I, on the other hand, have been taking advantage of the fact that I can go on long runs or bike rides without the asthma-inducing smog of Manhattan.

By today, though, the boys are getting restless for our attention.

"Please, Mom," Willie begs. "I'm dyin' to go swimmin'."

I ask Jolie to bring Nicky with us so I can sunbathe or swim while she watches the boys, but Jolie tells me Nicky has the sniffles and we both agree that it would probably be best for him to stay home where he won't be tempted to go in the water.

Willie's already sitting in the front seat with his seat belt on by the time I come back, smiling eagerly, his legs bobbing up and down excitedly in small, jerky motions. He looks so happy to be coming with me, I feel like Scrooge for even thinking of leaving him behind.

"The beach, the beach, we're going to the beach," he chants over and over.

It's a ten-minute ride to the closest lake, a still, black jewel flanked by rolling hills on both sides. I park and Willie pops out of the car, running to the beach with his little pail and shovel. He should be holding my hand, but there are no other cars in sight. It's late, and only a few kids are left on the beach. They range in age from about four to eight or nine and are digging what looks like a long canal winding from the top of a hill down to the water. The oldest boy, who is heavyset and darkly tanned, seems to be the leader of this mysterious project. Every few seconds, he cries out, "More water, more water!" and the other kids rush down to the shore with their buckets.

At first, Willie plays on his own in the sand with his pail and a red plastic boat. He digs a hole, fills it with water, and I watch him as he capsizes the boat over and over. Eventually, he looks up, bored. I watch from my beach chair at the top of the hill as he inches over to where the other kids are playing. He crouches down, watching them, trying to figure out their game and how he can be a part of it. I'm surprised and impressed by his behavior. In the past, when Willie was three or four, if he saw a group of kids he wanted to play with, he'd try to get their attention by doing something mischievous like knocking down their tunnels and running away giggling. The fact that Willie now understands he needs to negotiate an invitation is a big developmental step for him. I'm even prouder when he runs up to me on the hill and says, "Mom, I want those kids to play with me." Asking for help instead of acting impulsively is what we've aimed for all year at school and with Dr. Andersov in therapy.

"Okay," I tell Willie. "Which kid do you like the most?"

Of course, he points to the big kid, the group's leader.

"So, go up to him and wait for him to notice you, then say, 'Hey, your game looks cool. Can I play, too?' "

Willie rehearses with me for a minute, repeating it twice. He runs back down the hill in the tiptoeing, hopping run he does when he's excited. I lean forward in my beach chair, waiting to see how things go. Willie marches bravely up to the big kid who is punctuating his digging by loud commands for more sand and water. The other kids buzz around like dutiful soldiers, carrying their buckets. Willie says his speech but the big kid doesn't even look up. Willie looks at me and mugs for help.

"He's not sayin' anything, Mom," Willie shouts from the beach.

"Maybe he didn't hear you," I call back. "Ask him again."

The other adults turn and stare, but their looks are benign — not the accusatory glances I usually expect in these situations. Willie's doing nothing wrong. He just wants to play.

Willie asks the kid again, but he still doesn't look up. This time, Willie comes running back. "I did what you said, but it's not working," he says, frustrated.

"Try tapping his arm until he pays attention to you."

Willie has tried so hard, I am determined this child will notice and like him. Willie runs downhill tippy-toe again, endearingly obliging.

"Excuse me," Willie says loudly but politely, tapping the beefy kid's arm. "Your game looks cool. Can I play with ya?"

Finally, the boy turns and shrugs, as if it's the most natural thing in the world that Willie would join them. "Okay, get water," he tells Willie.

Willie grabs his bucket and is about to run to the lake when he wheels around and beams at me, giving me a giant thumbs-up. I smile hugely at Willie, then slump down in my chair, exhausted.

For the next two hours, Willie plays beautifully with this boy, not even rising to the bait when, completely unprovoked, the other kid says something Willie did was "stupid."

"I'm *not* stupid," Willie says, calmly insistent.

"Stupid is as stupid does," I mutter, thinking of the commercials for *Forrest Gump*, which are ubiquitous this summer. Why is this kid suddenly acting so mean? I wonder. Willie holds himself together waiting for the older boy to apologize, which he eventually does. Willie doesn't yell or scream, or lash out physically at him. The boy shrugs and they go back to playing until the other child's mother says it's time for him to go. Willie gives him a high-five, and the kid even lets Willie hug him.

"Okay, Willie," the kid says. "So will you be here tomorrow?"

"Sure!" Willie says, waving good-bye.

I wade into the water with him once everyone else has gone. The air is cool with a dampness that makes me think we're in for more rain. Over the hills, I can see gray clouds floating above the pines and bushes. I hug Willie in the water, feeling his strong back and waist; his smooth, sweet skin that is warm against mine. He's looking at the clouds, his tranquil face turned upward and silent. Sometimes I feel as though the whole world is reflected in those big, blue eyes.

August 26, 1994

The editor at the weekly newspaper in New York finally calls me back: I got the job! Peter and I celebrate by popping open a bottle of champagne after the kids go to sleep. We toast each other, this summer, and the new beginning we'll all have once we go back home to New York.

The champagne is crisp and cold, and I'm feeling a little giddy because of it and the excitement of my good news. As I let it sink in, I realize how much I wanted the job. I almost wouldn't let myself feel it before now because I didn't want to be disappointed if I didn't get it. I feel grateful that the editor is giving me a chance. I explained that I needed to leave a little early one day a week to go to a regular doctor's appointment with Willie but that I'd come in early the other days to make up the lost time. My boss seemed great about it over the phone. She's young and single and, I suppose, reacted in the way she'd like to be treated when she might find herself in the same situation.

I can't believe the changes that have taken place in only one year: Willie's school, Peter's job, and now me, going back to work full-time.

"I'm really proud of you, honey," Peter says, refilling my glass. We go out on the porch to look at the stars. I know having a full-time job is going to be really hectic—already I'm thinking about how we'll cope with our new schedules.

Willie will have to take a yellow bus to his new school because I've got to take Nicky to his all-day threes class, which is in the opposite direction. Peter would help out if he could but his job starts early, too. Getting dinner for everyone will be a production; I can see that already. Maybe we can switch Jolie to later hours so she can start work when she picks Nicky up and then stay to make the boys' dinner. I don't want to extend her hours too much, though, because the overtime alone would eat up more than I'm going to make at the newspaper.

It's a peaceful, quiet scene around me but my mind is racing: my welcome to the world of being a working mom, I suppose.

August 29, 1994

Small victories continue for Willie on this vacation. Today, we had a play date with the four-year-old daughter of friends from the city who are renting a house in the Berkshires for August. The last time the kids got together, Willie went into a rage when the little girl, who's petite and fairly tenacious herself, didn't want to play hide-and-seek or catch frogs in the brook.

I'm prepared for a little friction so I stick close to the boys, politely refusing my friend's offer to relax on the sun deck *sans* kiddies. The bedroom the daughter is staying in looks like a shrine to Barbie. The whole room is painted pink with a loft bed on top of what looks like a pink gazebo. The only toys in the room are— what else?—colored pink: Polly Pockets, makeup sets, pink telephones, and what feels like more Barbies than I have ever seen in a hundred visits to FAO Schwarz. I feel as if I'm in a pink paint factory that exploded. I have no idea what Willie and Nicky are going to do in such a feminine stronghold.

My friend and I sit cross-legged near the gazebo play loft.

"It's grotesque, isn't it?" she says wryly, gesturing at the little girl's bedroom in the rented house.

Willie, Nicky, and my friend's daughter are up in the loft playing with Barbies. Willie clambers down the ladder, shaking his fists. His eyes are red-rimmed and about to spill over.

"You *have* to give me one of the girls," he growls, shaking a fist toward my friend's daughter in the loft. "She's not sharing," he complains.

"What's the matter?" I ask, glad I'm up here and not downstairs on the sun deck. This is exactly the kind of situation that, left unchecked, could turn into a disaster for Willie.

"I want a doll," he whines. "*Make* her give me one."

"Sweetheart, you have to ask her yourself."

My friend makes her daughter, who's looking shamefaced, climb down from the loft. "Are you sharing with Willie?" she asks her child.

Willie's looking around the room uncomfortably, unable to focus on one person or thing, but then his face clears suddenly. "Oh, never mind," he says to us as he picks up a pink Polly Pockets. "I'll use something else."

My friend looks surprised. Though she knows all about Willie's ADD, she's never seen him change moods so quickly. "Are you sure?" she asks him. "Oh, yeah," Willie says, waving away her offer. "I'm gonna use this now."

I look at my watch, thinking of the rule I learned on that disastrous play date with Cody not to overstay a visit. Though my friend asks if we'd like to have lunch together, I decline and say we'll do it another time. We've been here two hours already, longer than I'd intended to stay.

"I think my daughter's tired, anyway," my friend confesses. "She's usually not this territorial."

On the way back to our house, Nicky falls asleep in the car. Willie and I sing along to the radio—a Beatles song that Willie likes. With all the stress and strain of our schedule in the city, I'd forgotten how much fun it is to just hang out with Willie and Nicky—how sweet and uncomplicated life can be. All in all, it's been a wonderful morning. Willie and I listen as the Beatles play "In My Life," and I wonder if the song makes as much of an impression on Willie as it does on me. These are places and moments I'll remember all my life. This feeling with Willie I know will be one of them.

September 2, 1994

The rain came as expected. Our second week here has been cloudy and cool with not much for the kids to do without their usual escape to the yard and beach. The big event of our vacation, however, is saved for the end of the day—a large fair that is held every Labor Day weekend. It's a big deal around here, with lots of rides and game booths. We drive to the fairgrounds and park in a huge lot. There must be over five hundred people in a space the size of a football field. And that's not counting the room taken up by the concession stands and Portosans.

Nicky and Willie seem insulted when I suggest we go on one of the tamer rides in the kiddie park. We agree to try the super-slide, which, though it's at least three stories high, seems like the safest of the grown-up rides. After the slide, we buy cotton candy and Peter takes Willie to the Ferris wheel. Willie makes a friend waiting in line, another boy around his age. The two boys ride up in the Ferris wheel together, Willie's delighted face silhouetted against the cool, black sky.

Willie and his new friend shake their heads in tune to the loud music blaring from the speakers. It's getting colder—near fall—

and Willie looks so big to me, bobbing up above us, not afraid of the height or dark. There are four more days to our vacation, and then we go back to the city to my new job and our family's new schedule. Willie's done so well this summer, at camp and on vacation. The season, all our preparations, are almost behind us. It makes me sad. In some ways, I wish we could float a little while longer together, like Willie on the top of the Ferris wheel.

September 6, 1994

I started my new job as features editor of a Manhattan community paper at 10 A.M. this morning. By noon, I've forgotten everyone's name. For now, I share an office with the person I'm replacing, a cheery, redheaded twenty-five-year-old, who's leaving the paper to work at a travel magazine. He seems nice enough — helping me learn how to navigate the company's archaic computers and filling me with enough "inside tips" to make my head spin. The only problem is that he keeps a boom box on his file cabinet, which he plays all day long. His musical taste ranges from Irish traditional music to disco — all of which I like, but the incessant noise is hard to take for eight hours straight.

I have new appreciation for what the world must feel like to Willie. I can't write or read an article, or even talk on the phone without being distracted by my office mate's music. Beyond the noise, my first day started somewhat chaotically. Late last night, my mother called to say her house had been broken into while she was away for the weekend, and she came to sleep over shortly after midnight. The police needed to dust the place for fingerprints, and she couldn't sleep there while they were scouring the house for evidence. At around 5:30 A.M., Nicky woke us up to announce that he'd discovered Grandma sleeping in the back bedroom.

My head is throbbing from lack of sleep and my office mate's music when my boss calls me in for a short meeting. Because of some unexpected cutbacks in her budget, she says, she isn't going to be able to hire a news editor as she originally expected, so she'd like me to be the features *and* news editor. It is a testimony to her faith in me that she thinks I can handle both positions. However, I'm not pleased about what feels like the bait and switch: I was hired to do one job only to find, on my first day, I'm expected to do double the work at no extra pay. I try to act professional about it but I decide that, if the situation doesn't get resolved in some way by the end of the month, I'm going to ask for a raise, or at least a title change, from my new boss.

The time goes fast at work, but it feels like forever until I can go home to Peter and the boys. It's a strange transition to go from two weeks of intense family time on vacation to a whole new life of being away from them for most of the day. Just from my schedule this first day, I can tell life is definitely going to change for me and not necessarily for the better. I feel slightly selfish for wanting to work. We can certainly use the money, but I know I'm not only doing it for that. If I didn't want to pursue my own interests, I could be a full-time mom, thus saving on Jolie's salary, though not necessarily my sanity.

On the subway, I feel an uncontrollable wave of sadness as I look around and see all the other working people. I think about what I'd be doing if I were at home: making dinner, probably, or playing some game with the boys. I race out of the subway, fighting back tears. By the time I get home, though, I'm practically weeping. I walk inside crying and I can't seem to stop.

Jolie looks at me as if I've gone crazy. "What's the matter? Are you okay?" Jolie has three grown sons whom she raised by herself—even giving birth to one of them in her kitchen in Haiti during the Duvalier regime because it wasn't safe to go out on the streets at night, even to a hospital. Compared with Jolie, I feel like an overpampered wimp, but I can't stop crying.

"I'm just so happy to be home," I say, wiping my eyes. "Isn't it silly?"

I try to pull myself together a little bit so I won't scare the children, but, of course, I lose it as soon as I see them. Willie and Nicky hug me, staring at each other in confusion, trying to understand why Mommy's laughing at herself while she's crying. I'm starting to tear up more because of the ridiculousness of the situation: me in my silk suit sitting cross-legged on the floor with the boys wrapped around me, four arms and legs wriggling; the expression on Jolie's face—as if she could live with Americans for the rest of her life but never understand them.

My mother arrives a half hour later. She still can't go back to her house because of the damage done in the burglary. The first thing she notices is my tear-stained face. "Is everything all right, sweetheart? Was your first day okay?" I start to smile, knowing I look like a wreck.

"I'm fine," I say, not really wanting to get into it with her. "It's just allergies. The air quality was very bad today."

I can tell she doesn't buy it, but she's respectful enough of my privacy not to press it. It's only later I realize she must know exactly how I feel. When my sister and I were out of kindergarten, my mother, too, went back to work—even though her parents were against it. (They told her she was taking a job away from a man who might need it!) My mother was the only woman in her office back then. And though I grew up expecting I'd be a working mother, I still feel guilty even though everyone in my family supports my decision—not laying a guilt trip on me about it the way hers did on her. She had it much worse than I do.

"You're probably just exhausted," my mother says, tactfully. "Maybe I shouldn't have called you last night after the robbery. I could have stayed at your sister's."

"No, Mom," I insist. "It's not a problem that you're here. I'm just really emotional about missing the boys."

"I think that's normal," she says. "But you're probably tired, too."

Peter is working late tonight, so he won't be home for dinner. We've ordered in Chinese food so no one has to rush to cook. My mother sets the table and we eat with the boys, chatting about everything except the fact that every half hour or so, I look at the boys and burst into tears.

When Peter gets home later, I tell him about the crying and another flood of tears starts. My eyes feel swollen, huge and ugly. Maybe I'm really starting to crack up. I'm starting to remind myself of Holly Hunter in the movie *Broadcast News*, where she cries for fifteen minutes before work each morning.

Peter tells me not to worry about worrying. "It's natural to feel anxious about all this stuff. Men just repress it." This is why I love my husband. Nonetheless, when Nicky wakes up early again the next morning, chanting that he wants to watch Grandma sleep, it prompts a new set of tears on my part because now I'm going to be an exhausted and emotional wreck for the second day in a row. How has Peter dealt with the children and gotten any work done the past five years?

September 9, 1994

I dash out of my office at 1:45 P.M. to meet Jolie and Willie at Willie's new school. I've worked it out with the people at the school office that I will bring him by to see his new classroom as Dr. Andersov suggested. Willie has been asking me for two weeks when he'd be able to visit and was so excited when I told him today was finally the big day.

Dr. Andersov said I should try to find out what Willie's feelings are about switching schools, but, honestly, he's seemed so blasé about it, it's hard to figure out if he's even worried. Some anxiety is emerging, however. When I meet him outside the school, he peers apprehensively at the door. "But what if I don't like it?" he says.

"Well, it might feel strange at first. It's going to be different from your old class, and it's natural to feel nervous when you're starting something new." Willie smiles and nods, and I know he's really thinking about what I'm saying.

Inside the school, there are five or six teachers milling around in the lobby. Classes haven't started yet, which is why this was a good time to bring him. Willie immediately becomes shy when we see the teachers. He hides behind my back, trying not to make eye contact. Normally, I think of Willie as such a big boy but, in his new collared shirt and short haircut for school, he looks tiny and scared.

The beautiful director of the lower school is there and bends down to say hi to Willie. He peeks his head out from under my jacket to look at her. When she extends her hand slowly, he comes out a little more, eventually allowing her to hold his hand while he smiles bashfully and clutches some baseball cards that he's brought in his other hand.

"Do you want to see your classroom?" she asks gently.

Willie nods and, as he did on our first visit here, eagerly follows her up the spiral staircase. I follow them, noticing how, with their sandy blond hair and gorgeous blue eyes, the two of them could easily be mistaken for mother and son. The connection is more than skin-deep, too. From the minute we first stepped through the door, they've treated us like family here. The school is genuinely concerned about his well-being, not just how high he scores on an IQ test or how long he can sit in a chair without fidgeting.

Upstairs, we get introduced to Willie's teacher, Mrs. Rose, the same head teacher I observed last spring. The room seems small, but I remind myself that only eight children will be using it, not sixteen. There are colorful pictures on the wall, and a sign that shows each student's name in gold letters.

"Hey, there's my name!" Willie says, sounding surprised.

"Yes, sweetie, this is your class. This is where you belong." As I say it, I'm conscious of how much I really mean it. No one here has acted as if we have problems or are different. They know why I want to bring Willie in early, and they support it.

"Do you want to leave some of your baseball cards in your cubby?" Mrs. Rose asks. "That way, when you come in on Monday, you'll already have some toys waiting here."

It's such a thoughtful suggestion, and I know that having some of his treasured belongings here will make Willie feel more at home on his first day. Willie nods and gingerly picks out a few cards for his cubby. After the visit, as Dr. Andersov suggested, I take Willie out for ice cream (Pavlov again). We order vanilla cones with rainbow sprinkles—Willie's favorite. Though I should be getting back to work, this "sugar time" is just as rewarding for me as it is for him.

"So do you like your new classroom, Willie?"

"Yeah," he says, taking a huge bite of ice cream. "It's going to be great."

I kiss the back of his neck, the fuzz of his freshly cut hair tickling my nose. "Yeah," I agree. "*You're* going to be great."

September 10, 1994

Peter and I dash out the door before work to get to a parents' orientation meeting at Willie's new school. I'm a little nervous about what Peter will think of the place. He's never actually been there before, only read the brochure and heard me say how much I love it. I'm sure he will like it, but what if he doesn't?

Even though I've only been there twice myself (the first time last spring and then yesterday when I took Willie to visit), I try to play tour guide as we go inside with the other parents. Two people greet us by name as we walk in the door—the lower-school director and the receptionist. Peter looks impressed, not only by their greeting but by the building itself. Even though classes don't start until next week, they've left up artwork from last spring so the lobby will feel familiar to the old students.

We're among the last to arrive in Willie's classroom and therefore get the chairs the other parents have rejected: two kiddie-size seats at the side of the room. I point out Willie's cubby to Peter and tell him about the baseball cards. Peter and I keep pretty much to ourselves as we wait for the meeting to begin. Some of the other parents are chatting with one another—the moms and dads of "old" kids from last year. I can tell the other new parents who, like us, look nervous and have brought notebooks in which to write everything down.

Mrs. Rose, the head teacher, starts the meeting by introducing herself and her new assistant teacher, a pretty, curly-haired woman in her early twenties who, all the old parents agree, looks remarkably like Mrs. Rose's assistant from last year. Mrs. Rose describes how the class will run, and how the children will be evaluated for speech therapy and occupational therapy (O.T., as she calls it). Peter and I expect that, given Willie's articulation problems and possible expressive problems (being able to "find" the right word as opposed to being able to actually pronounce it), he will need considerable speech therapy. We're not sure if he'll require physical therapy, or how it might benefit him, but we assume the school will let us know what they think.

"What's the age range in the class?" one of the new parents asks.

Mrs. Rose says the youngest child is five and a half and the oldest children are seven and a half. Peter and I look at each other, surprised. Willie is going to be the youngest child in this group. When he was admitted, we thought he was going to be placed with other kids his age. At first, I'm flattered that he's been skipped but then I start to worry: Can he fit in socially with the older kids? Will he be the smallest? Will they like him, or think he's too babyish because he's only five? Mrs. Rose hands out a list of things we need to buy Willie for school: notebooks, file cards, and a folder for homework.

"Homework?" I ask. "What kind of homework?"

Mrs. Rose explains that the students in her class get twenty minutes or so of homework each night. If they don't do it at home, they have to give up free time in school to finish their work. "We don't want you battling with each other at home," she says. "If your child gives you a hard time at night or if your family is doing something special and your child doesn't have time, just write me a note and your child will finish that homework at school."

All the old parents are nodding as the new ones scribble all this information down in our notes. This is real school, I realize, not like last year where most of the time was unstructured free play. Already I'm worrying about Willie doing his homework. Now that I've started working full-time, I find it hard enough to arrive home and fix dinner for myself and Peter, spend time with Willie and Nicky, and get them ready for bed. Where will homework fit in? Between Dr. Andersov, religious school on Wednesdays, and speech therapy, he's going to be pretty busy already after school.

Peter sees me frowning. "Don't worry," he whispers. "We'll work it all out."

At the end of the meeting, Mrs. Rose asks if we have questions. One of the new parents asks about bus schedules. Like us, she's concerned about how her child will adjust. One of the other parents suggests riding the bus with the child the first day to help him get used to it. One of the veteran parents raises her hand, a slim, attractive woman in her forties.

"I just wanted to say something to the new parents," she starts out. "As those of us who've been with Mrs. Rose for a few years already know, your child is very lucky to be in her class. You don't want to know what my seven-year-old was like before he came to this school, but you'd be happy to meet him now. He's flourished here socially and academically." She says that so much of what he's been able to accomplish is due to the people at this school and Mrs. Rose, particularly. She says she's sure we all went through difficult circumstances at our children's former schools—that they certainly did with their son. "But," she concludes, "I know all your children are going to have a wonderful year, especially with Mrs. Rose as their teacher."

This testimony has half the parents in the room wiping their eyes. Peter and I are dabbing under our glasses with Kleenex. Outside, after the meeting, Peter hugs me hard. I can tell he's still feeling emotional about what the mother said upstairs. "I'm so glad Willie's going to be here," he tells me.

On my way to the subway, I see the woman who spoke in Willie's class. I introduce myself and tell her how moved we all were by her comments. She seems embarrassed by the compliment.

"This school saved our lives," she says. "When my son was in preschool two years ago, the staff was just dreadful—they didn't care about his ADD at all. It got so bad there that the class parent called all the other mothers to tell them not to invite my son over for play dates."

"That's unbelievable," I say, unnerved. "How could a school let something like that go on? Where *was* this awful place?"

"Oh, ——, right up the block," she says, telling me the name of her son's former school.

I stop in front of the subway stop as the other commuters sweep by. She's just named the place Willie came from last year.

September 13, 1994

Today is Willie's first day of school, and we're all so excited that we're ten minutes early for the school bus. Willie's got his lunch box and a knapsack full of notebooks and pens and the other things on his teacher's list. Peter is riding the bus with Willie for the first day, and I wave and smile at them both as they get on the bus—Peter struggling to tuck his adult-sized legs under the low seat in front of him. Willie looks brave and scared at the same time. We're all downstairs to give him a big send-off.

" 'Bye, Willie. I love you," Nicky says, waving at the bus as it pulls away. I have a good feeling about this year, that this school is finally the right one for Willie. I twist the Kleenex in my pocket and watch as the bright yellow bus turns around the corner and out of sight as Nicky still waves.

Nicky's own program started yesterday, his first day of nursery school in the same building where Willie had summer camp. Nicky's class has sixteen children in all—an even mix of boys and girls. And as it turns out, Nicky knows one of the boys from his old play group last year. The two immediately recognized each other and seemed happy playing together—that is, until I tried to leave.

"No!" Nicky howled, when I tried to kiss him good-bye.

"But you're having so much fun; you don't need me here, honey."

Nicky latched onto my jacket and would not let me move. His teacher, a young woman in jeans with her hair in a ponytail, immediately came over to help with the separation. I didn't have a clue as to what I should do to ease Nicky's transition. Willie never even seemed to notice when I was gone.

"Do you want to see a great game we're playing over there?" Nicky's teacher asked, making it sound as alluring as possible.

Nicky's fists were balled into tight knots around the lapels of my dressed-for-work suit. His brown bangs swung firmly as he shook his head "no."

"Come on, sweetheart," she urged, flirtatiously, getting Nicky to at least emerge from where his face was buried in my chest.

"Oh, *look* at what they're doing over there!" I said in my most enthusiastic tone, having picked up the cue from his teacher.

Suddenly, Nicky had a small, pleased expression on his face—his little Mona Lisa grin. "Let's all go together," the teacher said, nodding at me significantly. I could tell she wanted me to accompany Nicholas over to the arts-and-crafts table, so I carried him over. Sure enough, Nicky was fooled by this subterfuge and slipped easily into a chair at the art table once we got there and started to work with a pile of pastel-colored cotton balls to glue for a collage. "Say 'bye to Mommy," the teacher told Nicky, winking at me slyly.

"'Bye, Mom. I love you," Nicky said, as I leaned down to kiss him. His teacher stayed at his side while I headed for the door. On my way out, I looked back and saw her give him a big hug. What a wonderful teacher Nicky has compared to the awful woman who led Willie's threes class.

Willie's school bus is gone now and I take Nicky's hand to walk him to his school. But as I think about Willie and all that's happened, I can't help but wonder whether it would have made a difference if Willie's threes class had been led by someone like Nicky's teacher. Would Willie even have needed a special school now if he'd gotten off to the right start when he was three? Maybe. Maybe not. As Nicky and I cross the street, his small hand in mine, I tell myself it's too late for that kind of thinking anyway. I have to stop punishing myself for Willie's threes class. It wasn't our fault.

September 16, 1994

I can tell that getting uptown to Willie's appointment at 4:15 is going to be a lot harder than I originally thought. The work just doesn't end when I need to walk out the door—especially on Mondays, when we send one of the papers we produce to the printer ("close" it, in newspaper-speak). At least my boss has been true to her word about letting me leave at 3:30. I haven't gotten one dirty look from anyone in the office. Of course, to compensate, I'm in earlier than everyone else and eat lunch at my desk every day. Still, the whole thing is a logistical nightmare, with me dragging myself back to work to stay late after Willie's session.

Today, I'm running later than usual. The cabbie makes a wrong turn as we get out of Central Park and, of course, winds up getting caught in traffic and can't back up to fix his mistake. Rather than wait in the traffic, I pay and jump out—running the rest of the way to Dr. Andersov's office. Jolie and Nicky are waiting for me outside—Nicky in his stroller clutching a bag of Gummi Bears.

"Hi, Mommy!" he says, reaching up for a hug. Bits of red and yellow candies are stuck to his soft cheeks.

"Willie is inside," Jolie says, glancing at her watch. I'm five minutes late for the appointment and, because I told her to get there a little early, she and Nicky have been waiting for fifteen minutes already. She's not acting annoyed, but it makes me wonder what's going to happen in January when it's freezing. She can't exactly wait with Nicky outside in the driving snow, and Dr. Andersov's waiting area is too small to keep a fidgety three-year-old entertained for fifty minutes. I don't have time to think of alternatives right now. I'm already late, and Dr. Andersov and Willie can't really start without me.

"Mommy's got to go inside," I say gently to Nicholas. "I'll see you a little bit later."

"No!" Nicky cries, his face turning red with frustration. He's having enough trouble with separation from me without having to do it twice in one day. He's still hugging my neck and, when I try to stand up, he doesn't let go. The stroller drags along with me as I try to make my getaway. Nicky's crying in earnest now because he knows I've got to leave. I kiss his hot face, which is sticky from the Gummi Bears.

"Okay, say bye-bye to Mommy," Jolie tells Nicky, trying to sound firm but cheerful. "We're going to the playground."

When I finally get inside Dr. Andersov's office, Willie is sitting in a big, black leather swivel chair, turning from side to side. He's wearing a black Power Ranger sticker that he got either at school or from Dr. Andersov.

"Willie was telling me about his first day at his new school," Dr. Andersov says.

"Really?" I say. "How did it go?"

"Really good," Willie beams. "There are seven-year-olds in my class!"

During his turn at the sand table, Willie builds a pyramid and a lake. From a psychological standpoint, his selection seems pretty uninteresting. My turn is next, and I take out some plastic people and have them try to climb to the top of Willie's pyramid.

"Is there quicksand in your game?" Willie asks, sounding hopeful.

I can tell he might like a little excitement, so I try to think up something dramatic. "Yeah," I tell him. "It *is* quicksand and the bad guy is sinking to the bottom!"

Willie's face flushes angrily. "No!" he shouts, suddenly furious.

I don't know what's happened to get him so mad. Since the idea is to have a nice, positive session for the first week of school, I try to think of a way to appease him. "Okay," I offer, pulling the "bad guy" out of the sand. "It's not really quicksand and he's not really a bad guy. It's a good guy and he got free."

"*That's it!*" Willie shouts, enraged, his fists and mouth clenched. He jumps up from his chair and storms out of the room so fast that Dr. Andersov and I hardly have time to react.

"He's been volatile like this lately," I explain to Dr. Andersov. "But I don't know what just happened that set him off."

"It was probably too close to home: the bad guy being punished," she says. So Willie still thinks of himself as a bad guy, even after all our work trying to boost his self-esteem. This can't just be because of that old play school, where they made him feel like an outcast.

Willie sticks his head in again, still looking furious. "I'm leaving this place, Mommy. I want you to take me home."

"But we're not finished yet," I say, stupidly. Since I have no idea what's wrong, I have no sense of how to make him feel better.

"No, I'm leaving!" He storms out again, banging the door to Dr. Andersov's waiting room two times after himself to make his point. The last time Willie walked out of Dr. Andersov's office, we agreed that we wouldn't just ignore these outbursts because Willie needed our help to calm himself down. In the past, when we'd try to get Willie to do something that he didn't want to do (like sit down for dinner or put away toys), Dr. Andersov told us to ask him "Can you do it yourself, or should I help you?" I decide to try a version of that on Willie now.

I open the door a crack so he can hear me. "Okay," I tell him. "Should I come out and get you or will you come back in when you're ready?"

"I'll never come back in," he shouts loudly in my face. "I don't love you anymore."

I've kept amazingly calm until now—probably because his anger came on so unexpectedly, I didn't have a chance to get my guard up. The frustration is rising in my voice, however. All I said was a stupid, plastic man was sinking in quicksand. Why does this make my child scream and run out of his doctor's office?

"I thought this was supposed to be a nice session today," I say out loud to nobody in particular but myself.

We hear the door bang again outside in the waiting room, and I'm afraid that Willie's gone out to the street. Dr. Andersov looks through her window, and I check the security camera she has at the office door. Willie is standing in the hallway between the waiting room and the front door.

"Let's give him a few minutes to calm down," Dr. Andersov suggests. In some ways, she says, it's not bad that he's gone off on his own to compose himself. Maybe when he comes back, he'll be able to tell us more about what set him off in the first place.

We wait a minute, cleaning up the sand table. By now, it is almost the end of the session. Jolie will be waiting with Nicky outside to pick Willie up, and I'm supposed to be going back to work. Willie finally meanders in, pouting and looking cross.

"Okay," Dr. Andersov says. "We're out of time for today."

Willie's mouth opens into a wide, surprised O. "But I didn't get to play."

"That's right," Dr. Andersov says. "You didn't get to play because you were outside in the hall. If you want to play in my office, you have to be inside taking turns."

"Not fair!" Willie shouts, balling up his fists again.

"Okay," Dr. Andersov says to me, purposely ignoring Willie. "See you next week."

"What am I supposed to do with him now?" I ask. For this, I left work early?

"Change the scenery," she suggests, still expressionless.

Jolie and Nicky are outside. The Gummi Bears have been cleaned off his face, and Nicky is now holding an enormous bag of Cheez Doodles in his stroller. If this schedule of trying to keep Nicky entertained for an hour each week keeps up for much longer, my otherwise healthy three-year-old will turn into a three-hundred-pound blob of junk food. For now, though, the Cheez Doodles are a much-needed distraction for Willie.

"Yum!" Willie says, grabbing the bag away from Nicky, who must be so stuffed already that he doesn't even complain.

Willie's face is pink, and his eyes are swollen from crying.

"What's wrong with Willie?" Jolie says, looking at him, concerned.

"Bad session," I tell her, shaking my head.

September 19, 1994

Despite his volatility in Dr. Andersov's office, things seem to be going well for Willie at his new school, so far. His teacher sent his homework folder home once, but it didn't contain any homework: only a consent form for me to sign for Willie to attend a schoolwide apple-picking trip.

Willie seems so grown-up since starting his new school, and it's not just the fact that he's shot up two inches in the past month. Every day when the bus picks him up, it reminds me of how separate—physically and psychologically—I am from Willie now. He has a whole life with friends and teachers I don't know. Jolie's arranged a regular play date for Willie with a boy from his class who lives nearby. Considering that many of the children travel from as far away as Long Island and New Jersey to get to this school, we feel lucky to have found a friend who lives a mere six blocks away. According to Willie, the boy is his "new best friend."

The only child Willie seems not to like is a boy whose face, after the first day, he decided he "didn't like." When I asked what he meant, Willie pulled the sides of his mouth down to make a long frown. It occurred to Peter and me that perhaps there's a physical problem or maybe the child just looks aggressive or angry—two distinct possibilities in a school where all the children have some kind of learning or behavioral problem and have been unsuccessful at other schools. Maybe this boy has just been made to feel self-defensive, like Willie, and assumes that school is a place where no one will like him.

I wish I knew more about the kids in his class, but we have to trust that Willie and his teachers can handle it. According to Mrs. Rose, Willie hasn't had any fights with this boy. And of course, there's no rule that says Willie has to like everybody in his class, as long as Willie doesn't pick a fight and behaves himself. "Give it some time," I advise Willie, reluctant to totally give up on the idea that Willie can make friends with this child. "Maybe he'll look happier as time goes by."

September 21, 1994

Dr. Andersov has been able to switch our weekly appointment time so that, instead of meeting on Mondays at 4:15 P.M., we meet on Tuesdays at 5:30. It's much easier for me to get out of the office knowing I won't have to worry about racing back in rush-hour traffic. I pick Willie up in a cab at our building where he's waiting downstairs with the doorman. ("Only a very big boy can take the elevator downstairs all by himself," I explain to Willie to encourage him.) This way, Nicky can stay upstairs with Jolie instead of waiting for us and getting frustrated that I can't stop and spend time with him.

Willie runs out to the cab, and kisses and hugs me—already a much better start than last time. When we get to Dr. Andersov's office, we sit down and discuss what we should do to help him get back in control when he's angry like last time. Willie seems confused that we would bring up last week's outburst.

"But I'm very good at my new school," he says. "My teacher is very good at helping me lose my anger."

Dr. Andersov and I look at each other, with the same sympathetic looks on our faces. Does he think he's here because he's being punished for "bad behavior" at school?

"I'll tell you the worst school," Willie continues, fidgeting on the chair. He's making little snorting noises with his nose—the way he does when he's getting nervous. "The worst school was ——," he says, naming his first play school. "Those teachers should be fired. They were very bad teachers."

I glance at Dr. Andersov, surprised. I guess Willie will never forget the rage he felt at that school, how awful it was for him there no matter how hard he tried. Even though that was almost two years ago, he obviously hasn't forgotten.

"You're in a great school now, Willie," I say to him slowly. "Daddy and I are never going to send you to a school where they won't help you feel proud of all the wonderful things you can do and what a sweet boy you are."

"I know." He nods, courageously. "I'm in a good school now."

Dr. Andersov's turn is first, and she suggests playing some quiet games: Clue, Jr., where we work in teams to solve a mystery, and another board game about Madeline, the little French schoolgirl. (How would Miss Clavel, Madeline's resourceful, implacable teacher, deal with ADD, I wonder?)

Willie has the last turn, and he chooses the toy house by Dr. Andersov's desk. I'm surprised, because I'm expecting him to pick the sand table, as usual. I'm even more surprised when he hands me a boy cloth doll and says, "You be the kid that gets out of control." He sets the table in the kitchen of the toy house with miniature plastic food. There's a cake and roast turkey, salted pretzels, and apple pie. "You want to eat the cake, and I'll be guarding the cake," he instructs me. He picks up a little Alice in Wonderland figurine.

I look at Dr. Andersov, and we have to laugh. Alice, the guard, is puny, about a quarter the size of the out-of-control kid he chose for me. "Look how small the guard is compared to the angry kid!" I say. Poor Willie: That's what he's up against when he tries to keep his emotions in check. A ten-ton anger and a half-inch guard.

"*Stop!*" Dr. Andersov says suddenly, turning to Willie. "What should that kid do to get back in control and not eat the cake?"

Willie smiles, obviously enjoying the excitement and total unexpectedness of Dr. Andersov's interrupting the game.

"Ah," he says. "Try Japanese patience?"

"What's 'Japanese patience'?" Dr. Andersov asks. "Is that like karate?"

"No," says Willie. "Like Shinto religion."

Dr. Andersov looks surprised at his reference, though she knows Willie well enough to realize that he adores displaying his rather sophisticated interests. Dr. Andersov and I watch as Willie demonstrates what he calls his "Japanese patience." He covers his eyes and bends over as if he's praying.

"That's wonderful, Willie," Dr. Andersov says, excited. "Is that what we should do when you get angry, remind you how to have 'Japanese patience'?"

"Yes," Willie says, solemnly. "Now you try it."

Dr. Andersov and I hunch over and clasp our hands the way Willie is showing us. Through the cracks between my fingers I steal a peek at Willie, who looks so serious I have to stifle a giggle. I'm proud of him for thinking up this idea of "Japanese patience," amazed by his innate understanding of what his body needs. His face is hidden in his own hands, concealed from me, and it makes me suddenly sad. He's here to learn how to need Peter and me less—for the inevitable coming of the time when he will grow up and grow away from us. Willie is squinting into his hands, his soft body rocking slowly back and forth.

"Do you see the white light?" Willie asks us in his high voice.

"Yes, I do," I say truthfully, staring at my wonderful boy.

September 24, 1994

There's a new-parents' reception for Willie's school so, even though most of the newspaper staff is staying late to work on a special issue, I'm out the door at 7 P.M., apologizing for leaving "early" but not really meaning it. I duck into a nearby takeout restaurant to wolf down some pasta and a salad (eating right has been hard since I started my new job). The salad takes longer to make, but it's worth it—although I realize I'm running late now and leave a message at Peter's office to let him know I'm going to meet him at the reception at 7:30 instead of 7:15.

The party is being held at the home of some parents on the Upper East Side, which is a twenty-minute taxi ride from my office. As usual, I'm stuck in traffic and don't arrive until 7:45. I see Peter in front of the town house and I wave. When he doesn't wave back, I know something's wrong.

"Where were you? I've been waiting here for almost half an hour!" he says in a voice so loud it makes people passing on the street turn and stare. He doesn't sound angry, only worried, which is worse because it immediately makes me feel guilty. Obviously, he never got my message.

"Oh, you made it," our hosts say to me when I walk in with

Peter. "Your husband was in here looking for you before. He thought maybe you had gone upstairs."

"No, I just got stuck in traffic," I explain, blushing. Great. Now everyone is going to think I'm scatterbrained and unreliable. No wonder her child has ADD, right? I tell myself to calm down. Unlike the parents in the other schools we've been to, the people here aren't looking to place blame about my child. I'm over-wrought from the constant rushing around I've had to do since starting my new job: hurrying to get the boys ready to meet Willie's bus; running around on taxis and subways to get back and forth to my office and Dr. Andersov's. Who wouldn't feel a little stressed under the circumstances?

Our hosts lead us upstairs to a large room where waiters in black tie are serving drinks and hors d'oeuvres. A crystal chandelier glistens over the dining-room table, which is laden with silver trays of petits fours and cookies. We see a heavyset woman with dark hair coming toward us. When we hear her slightly southern drawl, I realize it's the mother of Willie's favorite classmate. I'd just been speaking with her on the phone last night to arrange a play date today for her son and Willie.

"How did it go this afternoon with the boys at your house?" I ask her.

"The boys were so cute together," she says, enthusiastically. "At one point, they were walking with their arms around each other and Willie said, 'You're my best friend in the whole world!'" Peter and I glance at each other, tears already brimming in my eyes. "We've been waiting a long time to hear that," I tell her.

We discuss our previous experiences at Willie's first two schools and she relays similar stories of teachers and doctors saying her son would never learn to read, that they thought he had severe emotional problems.

"Does he have ADD, too?" I ask.

"No," she says, "Tourette's syndrome."

My stomach clenches into a tight ball, and I hope that my shock hasn't been too obvious. I thought Tourette's syndrome was a very serious disease that required constant doctor's attention, even institutionalization. At least, that's the way they always show it on TV. And though I'm embarrassed to admit it, I'm alarmed by the idea of Willie being exposed to the perpetual tics and curses that I associate with the disease.

"What can you do for Tourette's?" I ask, ignorantly.

The other mother shrugs as if it's not a big deal. "He's on medication."

Despite her rosy attitude, I know there must be something she's not telling us. If everything was really as under control as she's implying, her son wouldn't need to be in a special school, right? Or am I just being as prejudiced against Tourette's as other people have been about ADD?

I don't have much time to consider the idea, though, because our hosts are calling us into the living room so the meeting can begin. The head of admissions, whom all the parents in the room know, begins the meeting by discussing the background of the school, how it was started by a group of parents who'd been told that their children couldn't function in mainstream schools. She discusses the dedication of the teachers and administrators, and introduces our hosts and the hosts' son, who will be graduating from the school in June.

The father gets up to speak about what the school has meant to him and his family. His son interrupts him to ask if he can say something. The boy looks about twelve. He's blond, with handsome features just like his father's. But unlike his parent's face, there's something a little bit "off" about his appearance. His head tilts slightly to one side, and his left hand shakes as he cradles it close to his chest.

When the son speaks, it sounds like a lion's roar: full of emotion but not quite familiar. It takes a minute to get accustomed to the slur of his words, the particular cadence of his speech. "Hi, my name is Ron," he says. He's speaking slowly but confidently, commanding the crowd's attention like a seasoned public speaker. Before this school, he says, he couldn't go to a regular school. He has friends now; he feels smart. He jokes that maybe he should have acted dumber so his teachers wouldn't have given him so much homework. All the parents laugh in approval. He reads an essay he wrote that won an award at school last year. It's titled "Hope."

I'm Ron, a ten-year-old boy with disabilities. Cerebral palsy is what I have. It affects my physical skill. In gym, basketball, and other sports, I have to battle myself to play. My hands do not always work as well as other people's. My left hand feels like it is "dead" and I cannot always make it do what I want. Cerebral palsy affects my speech in that I cannot always make myself clear. However, I have been able to overcome these disabilities. This school has taught me hope.

I have been at this school for three and a half years discovering my abilities. When I was in the first grade, I found out about having disabilities. My teachers did not care about me. They did not treat me as a normal person in the class. My parents found out this was happening because of my emotions. Only my feelings showed what really was occurring. I didn't know the words for it then. Later we found this school, the miracle school.

I started learning that I had more abilities than disabilities. Here, the teachers treated me as though I was normal. I felt like I was in a regular school. I didn't feel different. I didn't feel less. I learned that I had things to teach others. I was not afraid of showing what I didn't know. I saw learning could be fun, not always a challenge to me. My goals seemed possible. I thought I would be able to live up to them. I began to have faith that I could have a normal life.

Next year I will graduate. I have come far being a disability kid. I learned a lot from this school. My hope goes beyond those things I got for myself. My hope is that other children will get a lot like me from this school. Their disabilities will become abilities. They will have hope just like me and become a whole person. I have to thank this school and all the people in it for making me feel like a normal kid.

Most of the parents are crying in earnest now, moved and inspired by this boy's words. I bite my lip because I'm afraid that if I start crying, I'll never stop. I'm so furious that all of us have had such a hard time with the mainstream schools, so relieved that we're finally in a place where our children will be welcomed and valued for who they are.

The boy is smiling as all the parents applaud and cheer. His father is hugging him tightly, beaming with pride. Here is a charming boy from a loving family. Despite his physical difficulties, he's upbeat and funny, a high achiever at school and clearly very bright. Maybe he'll be a writer or comedian when he grows up, an educator or even the first president with cerebral palsy someday. And to think where he might have been if he'd been born twenty years ago, when children like him—like ours—would have been shunted off to institutions and asylums.

A feeling of relief washes over me so intensely that I start to shake. I feel like the survivor of a shipwreck who is washed up on shore only to realize, once in a safe place, that she had been close to drowning. Though I'm trying not to, I'm crying—deep sobs that I've been holding back for three years. We're in a safe place, finally. And I, too, have hope.

October 11, 1994

We've started a new game at Dr. Andersov's office about King Kong at the sand table. It's Willie's invention—for the past two visits, he's replaced his usual fences and mountains with a pile of sand that he calls the Empire State Building. Willie likes to play the part of King Kong with a small plastic gorilla, but Dr. Andersov makes sure we all have a turn being the bad guy (King Kong) and the soldiers who are trying to get him off the Empire State Building.

Because there are three of us, there are three roles in the game: the general, who makes the plan to get King Kong down; the sergeant, who carries out the plan with the soldiers; and King Kong. We're trying to make Willie understand that, while it might appear that King Kong is the biggest and strongest, it's actually the general who has the most power.

"Why?" Willie asks, suspiciously.

"The general is the smartest because the general makes the plans," Dr. Andersov says. I'm blinking now, too. This is very Machiavellian for a five-year-old.

"Oh, I get it," Willie says. "King Kong has no brains."

"*Exactly*," I say, pleased.

When Willie plays the general, he comes up with strategies that would've made Norman Schwarzkopf proud. He has my sergeant throw sand "bombs" at King Kong to distract him as the troops sneak around from behind.

"King Kong is just a dumb animal," Willie says afterward.

Dr. Andersov and I smile at each other. Our message has clearly gotten through.

October 23, 1994

Peter and I took a weekend trip by ourselves to our family's place in Massachusetts and, for once, didn't pay the price with Willie while we were gone. Willie was invited to a sleep-over on Friday night at a school friend's house—the friend's mother is the woman who'd said all those nice things about their teacher the first day. Though I was nervous about letting him go, Peter insisted Willie wasn't too young. As it worked out, the boys had such a good time on Friday that Willie's friend came to sleep over Saturday night at our house. Jolie, who was baby-sitting, insisted she didn't mind. I think we're all excited about the idea of Willie having such good friends.

When we came back on Sunday, we brought beautiful, gold-brown leaves from the country, a tic-tac-toe set for Willie, a coloring book for Nicky, and penny candy for both of them. Though Willie seems so big to us now—going on sleep-overs!—his tears, "because he was so happy to see us," made me melt and I picked him up and cuddled him like a baby.

With Nicky, it took a day for his full displeasure to kick in. Maybe he took our departure harder than Willie because he's still dealing with some separation anxiety at nursery school. (Each morning, in a fit of regression, he begs me to carry him to the bus stop and then into school.) Tonight, Nicky had a major temper tantrum, howling over and over that he wanted to stay up late to watch his Power Ranger video.

"Nicky is a major league crab apple," Willie pronounces with the haughtiness only an older sibling can muster.

"N-o-o," I say, pointedly. (How conveniently Willie's forgotten his own tantrums!) "We have to help Nicky learn the right way to act." Peter takes Nicky out of the room to calm him down while I put Willie to bed.

"Cuddle me," Willie says. I've hardly seen him since Peter and I came back from the country. I stare at his face, the way it's changing. His features are getting more distinct, a glimpse of how he will look as a young man. As we stretch out together, Willie makes his last energy-expending wriggles of the night. He sniffles, blowing the air out of his nose loudly, a tic I've always associated with his mild hyperactivity. It's been over a year since he said he was trying to get the "aliens" out this way. His nightmares from last spring have totally disappeared. He no longer dreams of murderous Ninjas invading his home while we're asleep. He feels safer now, more secure that the world is a place where he won't get hurt. His exhalations are fast at first and then slower and more rhythmic as he falls asleep. I'm so proud of Willie, how mature he's getting. This fall has been the best time for him ever. He's got new friends, a new school, a new beginning.

"Sweet dreams," I whisper, knowing his will be.

October 27, 1994

Nicky is definitely angry at me for working late so often this week, or maybe he's still clingy from our being away last weekend. When the boys woke up at 7:30 this morning, Willie was excited because he'd never slept so late before and had to be woken up for school. Nicky, on the other hand, pushed me away, whining "Get out," as he's done almost every time he's seen me since last Sunday. Nicky is surprisingly strong despite the fact that he's as thin as a string bean, not pudgy or soft around the edges like Willie was at that age. Nicky frowns and pouts plaintively as I try to get him dressed. (Do siblings work out ahead of time who's going to be the pain in the neck each day?)

Maybe it's just that three is a harder age than anyone lets on. Neither of my boys had "terrible twos"; it was three that was the challenge. I think back to Willie's first, disastrous play school and wonder how much of his behavior was just an ordinary three-year-old's opposition fueled by the ADD. If Willie had been with better teachers and in a smaller class early on, would we even have realized he had ADD?

When I deposit Nicholas with his nursery school teacher—I literally hand him over to her as a "special delivery" package— she cuddles him and helps him get set up with a game in the dress-up corner. The extra attention and babying is obviously what Nicky needed to separate from me more easily. The difference between Nicky and Willie in this kind of situation is amazing. When Willie was three, how the day started was pretty much how it would end. A tantrum in the morning would lead to another on the bus. He'd have a rocky start in school and just get worse by gym time until things got so bad that the school would finally send him home.

It's wonderful not having to worry about Nicky spiraling out of control after I leave or being beeped from work to come back and get him.

When I get to work, there is a nice message from Dr. Andersov on my voice mail. Because Willie is doing so well, she says, she'd like to give him a special celebration in her office, where he'll get to choose all the turns. She suggests that I check in with his teacher to make sure that today is a day where he did well. If not, we can talk about the idea of setbacks and introduce Willie to the idea that some things (like behavioral changes) take time and practice. I call Willie's teacher toward the end of the day so I can see how things have gone.

"Willie's been great," she says, enthusiastically. "He definitely deserves a reward for his hard work."

Her words ring in my ear like Handel's "Hallelujah."

"For the first time in his life, Willie really loves school," I tell her. "It's night and day from every place else he's ever been."

I'm so glad to be celebrating with Willie at Dr. Andersov's. It seems like he's been growing up so much since he started his new school, not only in terms of his actual size. Our old ideas about his abilities—and disabilities—no longer seem to fit, either.

November 8, 1994

In our presession phone call, Dr. Andersov suggests some new socialization work for Willie she'd like to start this afternoon. The idea is to teach him certain social skills that are second nature for some kids but hard for him because of his Attention Deficit. She wants to start with something basic—helping Willie learn to make eye contact when he talks to people (which will then help him pay attention more to what they are saying and feeling).

As usual, the "lesson" is masked by a game. Willie will start with five poker chips in a cup. When he talks and looks us in the eye, he earns an additional chip. Every time he talks to one of us *without* looking us in the eye, he has to "pay" a chip. As soon as he gets seven chips in his cup, we'll interrupt our turns and give him fifteen minutes to do whatever he wants. If he gets seven chips while he's in the middle of his turn, he'll get fifteen minutes added on.

"Sounds straightforward enough," I say to her on the phone.

"The idea is to make it easy at first and then get a little harder. We'll start with your turn, and you should pick a drawing game. We'll take turns drawing pictures with all of us adding on to the work as we go along."

We've played this game before, and the challenge for Willie is not to get angry as Dr. Andersov and I change his drawing. Switching off enforces flexibility and his not getting things exactly his own way.

"Will he be able to concentrate on looking at us at the same time as he's trying to focus on not getting angry?" I ask.

"That's why it's hard," Dr. Andersov says. "We'll play it by ear. We want him to feel successful at it so if he's having a hard time taking turns, we'll stop the chip game."

Sounds good in theory but, in practice, Willie turns out to be so good at figuring out how to get his own way that we have to revise the rules of the chip game almost as soon as we start. Dr. Andersov had given him the five chips as planned and explained that he'd get one extra chip each time he looked at us when he was talking or when we spoke to him. We sat down for my turn and Willie looked at Dr. Andersov, saying, "Dr. Andersov, do you want to hear something?" He blinks his eyes, mock-innocent, gesturing toward the cup. "Do I get a chip now?"

"Okay, Willie," Dr. Andersov says, putting a chip in the cup. "I see you remember how to get a chip, but we're changing the rules. You can't make up a reason to talk and look at me. It has to come up on its own."

"Rats," I hear Willie say under his breath.

We continue with my turn, and I draw a flower. *"Switch!"* Dr. Andersov says, loudly, and Willie smiles with excitement. He takes the paper and starts to draw a choppy red figure right under my flower. The way he's drawn it, my flower looks like a hat on his scribbly red figure—how Jackson Pollock might have drawn the Tropicana fruit girl.

"What's that?" Dr. Andersov asks, pointing to the red man.

"It's the King of Anger," Willie explains. "Those are bars. He's in jail for two thousand years."

"What's the flower doing there?" I ask. "Is it some kind of hat?"

"It's the flower of self-control growing out of his head," he says, looking at Dr. Andersov.

Good answer, I think, as Dr. Andersov drops another chip in his cup.

"Stop!" Dr. Andersov says dramatically. "It's your turn, Willie. You earned seven chips. What do you want to do?"

Willie rushes to the sandbox, where he grabs the toy soldiers and creates a maze out of plastic fences. I watch him playing, how his face has filled out. He's become so easy in these sessions now. He doesn't complain when Dr. Andersov tells him he needs to finish up, that it's time for the rest of my turn. When I draw a submarine, Willie draws "the Son of Anger" in an ocean jail. When Dr. Andersov draws a goldfish, Willie says he will draw a shark eating the goldfish when it's his turn. But it's not his turn, it's mine again so I draw more "flowers of self-control," a whole undersea garden of them. Willie picks a crayon to start his turn.

"I changed my mind," he announces. "The shark's not going to eat the goldfish. He's going to *talk to it.*"

"Great idea!" Dr. Andersov says, pleased.

After the session, Willie runs zigzagging down the street, re-membering to stop exactly where I told him to wait for me. At home, he eats all his dinner, asking for seconds politely while

Nicky is squirming under the table, trying to avoid eating any-thing at all.

While Peter tries to encourage our finicky younger son to eat dinner, I sit with Willie while he does his homework. His writing exercises still aren't neat, but he's clearly getting there. When he left his old school last June, he couldn't write or read anything consistently except his own name. When he pulls out his reading homework, it looks much too hard. There are pictures next to the sentences and he has to "X" off the sentence that corresponds to the picture. Willie shrugs as if it's easy and taps his pencil on the table.

"The rat is on the pan; the bat is on the can," he reads. "That's dumb! Why would a bat want to be on a can?"

"Willie!" I say, astonished. "You're reading!"

It's been less than two months since he started his new school—less than two years after that first psychologist said she didn't know if Willie would ever be able to handle college. Tears fill my eyes at the thought of how far we've come from that bleak, awful day. My child is reading.

November 11, 1994

Peter and I arrive for Willie's first parents-teacher conference at his new school and, for the first time since he's been in any school, we don't have a sense of impending doom. From the notes that have been sent home in his homework folder, we know he's been doing well academically and socially. There have been no temper tantrums or shouting episodes, and we know from his busy calendar of play dates and birthday parties that he has lots of friends here.

When we get to the school, parents and teachers are bustling all over the small lobby. Although it's Veterans Day and the school is closed, there are a few older children dashing up the stairs to their classrooms. A tall, well-dressed man comes out of Willie's classroom as we're waiting for our meeting to start.

Though we don't recognize him from any of the class events so far this year, he smiles at us as if we're familiar to him.

"You're Willie's parents, aren't you?" he asks, introducing himself as the father of the boy Willie had the sleep-over date with while we were away. He's charming and encouraging about how well behaved Willie was at their house, which is a relief. We've never gotten close to the parents of any of Willie's school friends before—usually because we always felt awkward about what was going on with Willie inside the classroom. For the first time, however, I think maybe Peter and I might make some new friends through this school, too.

It's our turn to go in, and we tell the teacher how wonderful the classroom looks with all the children's writing and artwork up on the walls. She points to a poem Willie wrote about a leaf and, while it's a long way from Walt Whitman, it seems pretty sophisticated to us. Mrs. Rose goes over Willie's progress, how he's learning to work with the other children as a group and be a lot more flexible socially. At the beginning of the year, for example, Willie would say hello only to his best friend. Now, they've taught him how to say "Hi" to the friend and then "Hi, everybody." On his own, Mrs. Rose says, he's been able to extend that principle to " 'Bye, everybody" at the end of the day.

"Have there been *any* problems?" Peter asks.

Mrs. Rose explains that a few weeks ago, Willie got angry when she said jokingly that a Lego toy he was building looked like a toy gun, which Willie knew was forbidden in school. She thought he understood she was just joking, but when she looked at him again, she noticed he was furious, his fists were balled up, and tears were welling in his eyes.

"So what did you do?" I asked, alarmed. This is exactly the kind of thing we've seen from Willie a hundred times before, which can so easily lead to an hour's worth of screaming and crying.

"I brought him a mirror and I said, 'Willie, look at yourself. You're overreacting.' "

I nod, impressed with the way she got her point across while appealing to Willie's sense of pride.

"Now when Willie is playing with Legos he always comes up to me and says, 'Does it look like a gun?' Then he winks to show he's just kidding and gives me this very elaborate explanation of what his Lego thing really is. He's definitely learning how to have more of a sense of humor about himself."

When Peter asks whether Mrs. Rose thinks Willie shows signs of dyslexia or any other learning disability, she says no—he's never had any problems with *b* and *d* confusion or any of the other telltale indicators. Mrs. Rose goes on to tell us a little about Willie's schedule, when he goes to gym, science, art, and speech therapy. She tells us about class projects they're planning for the fall, particularly a class play, which will be *The Shoemaker and His Wife*, the Hans Christian Andersen fairy tale in which Willie is going to play an elf.

There is something so normal about this whole meeting that I feel like pinching myself. So this is what it's like to have a regular teacher's conference: no crises, no expulsions, no tearful scenes afterward. I can see why Willie loves coming here every day. He's learning, making friends, and having fun. "It's such a pleasure to have Willie in this class," Mrs. Rose, the head teacher, says.

"We've been waiting three years to hear that," I tell her.

November 24, 1994

It's Thanksgiving and, this year, I feel we have so much to celebrate: Willie's school, Peter's and my new jobs, Nicky's good adjustment (finally) to his own class, my mother being safe and having sold her house after the robbery. Compared with where we were last year at this time, we're very, very lucky.

It's our last celebration at my mother's house before she moves. I walk through the rooms with a mixture of regret and nostalgia. Since the burglary, I haven't felt she's been safe living here all alone. Her new apartment will have a full-time superintendent living in the building and a twenty-four-hour doorman—a good safety precaution in New York City. But I still feel sad that Willie and Nicky will have so few memories of the house where I grew up. My parents bought this house before I was born. I still know where everything is placed so well that I could walk through the house with my eyes shut and never bump into a single piece of furniture.

I go upstairs to say good-bye to my old bedroom one more time and pass the spot in the hallway where the burglars broke in. The hall has already been papered over for the people who are buying the house. There's no trace of the robbery except for the look on my mother's face when I ask her about it or when she makes a wry joke about how she won't need to pack as much thanks to the burglars.

In my bedroom, I trace the blue-and-yellow butterfly wallpaper with my finger, trying to etch it perfectly into my memory. It's amazing to me how small and old everything suddenly looks— the window frames that need painting, the closet door that is coming off its hinges. Everything in the room has to go into boxes: books, bedspreads, stuffed animals, and sports trophies. I moved everything else out when I got married.

Going downstairs, I hear Willie singing the Shaker Thanksgiving song, something he learned at school. He's been practicing so much, we all know the words by heart. His sweet, little-boy soprano floats up from the living room as if it were being carried on angels' wings.

'Tis a gift to be simple, 'tis a gift to be free,
'Tis a gift to come down where we ought to be.
And when we find ourselves in the place just right,
We'll live in the valley of love and delight.

I hear everyone in the living room "ooh" and "ahh," particularly my mother, who can't believe her five-year-old grandson knows all the words to such a complicated song. I think of Willie's new school every time I hear that song, how Willie is learning the "simplicity" most people take for granted. Willie really understands the meaning of this song. Of all people, he knows how hard it is to find "the place just right."

There is a happy buzz of congratulatory voices, some of which ring above the others: my sister's, my brother-in-law's, that of one of my mother's best friends who is almost like an aunt to us. As usual, my mother invited a ton of people over for the holiday. This year, in addition to extended family, there are three college friends of my sister's.

When my mother first told me of the extensive guest list, I worried I might be too upset about the move to be social. But now I'm glad it's a big, happy crowd downstairs to give the house—and my mom—a proper send-off. What could be more in the spirit of Thanksgiving? Family, friends—all people we love. Our two boys growing up, things on the right track at last.

November 29, 1994

Dr. Andersov calls me for our usual presession conference. She asks how things are going at Willie's school and, when I tell her they're great, she says she's put a call in to Willie's teacher to see if there are any other issues for us to work on with him in session. I'm astonished a minute later when she says that, if the teacher says Willie is doing well—as I know she will—we should start winding down with Willie's therapy, that he'd only need a few more sessions.

"Really?" I say, surprised. I knew Willie would end therapy eventually but I was thinking, at the earliest, this meant next spring or summer.

Dr. Andersov calls me back after talking to Mrs. Rose. As expected, Willie's teacher said she was delighted with his progress. The only issue on her mind is Willie's idolization of his friend—what she brought up in the parent's conference with us before Thanksgiving. When Willie's friend says he's hungry, Willie says he's hungry. When his friend says he's full, Willie stops eating. Dr. Andersov suggests we start making Willie aware of the ways he's mimicking his friend and tell him he's got his own "great brain" and he can think for himself.

"Fine with me," I tell her, realizing it's never too early to battle peer pressure.

When we go into her office for our session, Dr. Andersov tells Willie she's got some important news to discuss with him. "Do you know what the word *graduation* means, Willie?"

Willie thinks a minute, swiveling in Dr. Andersov's office chair. "It's what you do when you're a teenager," he says finally.

"Well, kids your age can also graduate," Dr. Andersov explains. "Graduating means you've finished one thing and you're ready to move on to something else. You've learned so much here about self-control, and we're all so proud of you—your mom and dad, Mrs. Rose, and me, of course. You are ready to graduate now."

Willie smiles until Dr. Andersov says that, once he's graduated, he won't have to come in once a week anymore, that he'll come in for "checkups" or to visit whenever he wants to talk about anything. She says that his last weekly visit will be before Christmas. That's only three weeks away, so only three more regular sessions.

"How does that sound to you?" Dr. Andersov asks.

"Bad," he says, his lower lip starting to quiver.

"Sweetie," I say, surprised, seeing the tears well up in his eyes. "What's the matter?"

"I don't like it. It makes me sad." He says that he never sees his old speech therapist from the East Side after he graduated last spring.

"Would you like to visit her during your vacation?" I offer.

Willie nods.

"Well, Willie," Dr. Andersov says gently. "You're definitely going to see me again because we're going to make an appointment for a checkup right now."

"Okay," Willie says, sniffling. He looks a little cheerier than he did before. "I have to go to the bathroom."

"Are you all right?" Dr. Andersov asks. I can tell she's not sure if Willie's still upset, since the bathroom is his "cooling down" place in her office.

Willie slides off the swivel chair, with a mischievous smile. "I'm fine," he says. "I just have to *pee!*"

When Willie is out of earshot, I tell Dr. Andersov that I didn't expect Willie to get so upset. "Are you sure he's really ready?" I ask.

Maybe what I'm really wondering is if Peter and I are ready. We've been working with Dr. Andersov for so long now that I worry about whether we can handle it by ourselves if something comes up again. I have to remind myself that we won't be totally alone, however. We can always call Dr. Andersov or the people at Willie's wonderful new school.

Dr. Andersov looks at me a minute. "You know, I work with so many kids who have problems feeling connected to the people around them. It's very healthy that Willie can show deep attachments."

I nod and feel grateful for the truth of her answer.

"In honor of your graduation," Dr. Andersov says, when Willie comes back, "you get the first turn today."

Willie takes some Magic Markers and starts drawing a picture. It's an angry-looking man with barlike stripes across his chest. "Is that the King of Anger in jail?" I ask.

"Yeah," Willie replies. "But he's dead."

"Yes, he is," I say, sensing the deeper meaning of his comment. The King of Anger is dead, after all, and Willie's really ready to graduate.

December 3, 1994

Dr. Andersov asks us to sit down before we start playing in today's session. Willie hops up into his favorite leather chair with the rolling casters. At the beginning of the year, I had to pick him up to reach that seat. Now his feet don't even dangle—they nearly reach the floor. It's Willie's last session before graduation. I can't believe we're not going to be coming in here every week. I've started to think of Dr. Andersov as a friend—a typical transfer-ence with the parents of child patients, I suppose. Still, Dr. An-dersov has been through a lot with us. If we hadn't found her, we might still be floundering, getting sent around town by a dozen school administrators out to convince us that Willie had brain damage, oppositional-behavior disorder, or even worse.

"Willie," Dr. Andersov says, "this is your last session before your going-away party next week." Willie looks excited by the idea of a party. He hasn't gotten upset about graduating since the first time Dr. Andersov mentioned it right after Thanksgiving. Dr. An-dersov says how proud she is of all the progress Willie's made.

"I have a lot of friends now," Willie says excitedly. "I had a play date with Steven and he spit at me and I hid near his mom and told her what he did."

"Good using your words!" Dr. Andersov says, enthusiastically.

"What did Steven's mom do?" I ask. It's the first time I've heard of any problems with the boy with Tourette's whom Willie worships so much.

"She gave him a time-out."

"That's using your great brain, Willie!" Dr. Andersov says.

I see her smiling at Willie and know that my deep affection for her is not undeserved. How could I *not* like someone who likes my son so well? Of all the people in the world who know Willie, Dr. Andersov has seen him at his best and at his worst. It must be hard for therapists when patients graduate, too. They only see kids when they're having trouble; they can't keep them long enough to enjoy them when they're back on the right track.

Willie says he wants to play with the encounter bats—plastic sticks with soft foam at the tips. The idea with the bats is to teach physical self-control. I get one and Willie gets one and the rules are that we can't hit each other on our bodies, only on the bats. We start a game with Dr. Andersov keeping score, but we don't play very long before Willie has us in hysterics from the way he creatively bends the rules to win extra points: backing into me, hiding his bat, anything that will make me foul him accidentally and cause me to lose a point.

"Penalty! Penalty!" Willie shouts joyously, jumping headfirst into my bat, demonstrating a playfulness in a competitive situation that we've worked ten months to achieve.

It makes me sad to think that we're not going to be spending this intense, revelatory time together every week. It's been such a privilege to see Willie in Dr. Andersov's office—through all the setbacks and breakthroughs, happiness and tears. Though I'd like to think I'll have the same access to his emotional life as he gets older—into grade school and then adolescence—I know it's not likely. Anyway, what mother would *want* to know everything her teenager is thinking—even if she could?!

Willie's turn is over, and Dr. Andersov starts hers. She picks the invisible-ink pens. I write a note to Willie. "I love you," it says.

Dr. Andersov writes to Willie, "I'll miss you," and Willie reads it out loud. I glance at Dr. Andersov and Willie. The feeling is definitely mutual.

December 20, 1994

I rush, harried but elated, from my office. Our last session at Dr. Andersov's—Willie's finally made it! This time next week, I'll be stuck at my desk, doing serious overtime at the newspaper. My boss is in Australia for three weeks, and I'll be filling in for her—an unwanted but unavoidable added stress over the holidays. But I can't focus on anything negative today. I'm too excited about Willie's graduation. Willie leaps into the taxi with a huge smile on his face when I pick him up at our building. "It's my party today, Mommy," he says, squeezing my hand.

Dr. Andersov looks almost as proud as I feel when we get inside. I look at the sand table and soft, maroon carpet where I've spent so much time playing soldiers, Trouble, and other therapeutic games. I know this room as well as if it were in my own home. Dr. Andersov has us sit down as if it were a regular session. "We're going to do something special today," she says, "in honor of your graduation and all your hard work."

Willie is grinning from ear to ear, his foot bouncing wildly with excitement. Dr. Andersov goes to the sand table, which has its cover on today. From underneath a paper tablecloth she pulls out a plate of cookies. "Are they all for me?" Willie asks, delighted.

"If you want, Willie. I've got the rest of the box here if you run out."

"*Wow!*" Willie says, amazed that Dr. Andersov and I are apparently going to let him eat an entire box of cookies before dinner.

"We've got something for you, too," I say, reaching into my shoulder bag. Earlier this week, I bought Dr. Andersov a silver pen as a thank-you present. When she opens it I tell her, "Maybe you'll use it to write the definitive paper on ADD treatment."

"Oh, it's beautiful," she says, surprised and pleased. "I know just what I'm going to use it for first. Willie, let's decide when we're going to see each other again, and I'll write down the appointment with my new pen."

"Good idea," Willie says, looking serious despite his mouthful of cookies.

We work out a date and chat about what we're going to do on our Christmas vacations. Willie tells Dr. Andersov that he's going to go sledding in Massachusetts. Dr. Andersov says she's looking forward to seeing friends and family over the holidays. The doorbell rings outside, and through the security camera, I can see Jolie and Nicky come into the waiting room.

"Would you like to invite your brother and your baby-sitter in to enjoy the party?" Dr. Andersov asks.

"Okay," Willie agrees.

We open the door and suddenly it seems very crowded inside with Nicky dashing back and forth from the plate of cookies to the jar of plastic soldiers underneath the sand table. "No, Nicky," Willie says, the voice of authority. "Don't run around. I'll help you get the toys."

It's so odd to see Nicky in this room. He's shy with Dr. Andersov, hiding behind me, Jolie, or Willie whenever she smiles at him or asks him a question. It's funny to think that, despite the in-

timate things we've told Dr. Andersov about Willie, she knows little about Nicky and probably never will. I glance at my watch,
realizing it's almost time to go. Willie hugs Dr. Andersov and
I do, too. Though Willie's therapy is officially over, it seems
strangely hard to leave.

It's cold outside, the sky a deep blue-purple. I know I should
go back to work, but I don't want to just yet. "Why don't we get
some frozen yogurt?" I say, despite the fact that it's thirty degrees
out and Willie and Nicky have just eaten half a box of green-and-
red-sprinkled sugar cookies. There is frost in the air, the smell of
snow. It will be a white Christmas; in less than two weeks, a new
year. Christmas lights twinkle on nearby trees and apartment
buildings. In other windows, electric menorahs are still cheer-
fully lit.

Willie wants to run ahead and promises me he'll stop before
the corner. He takes off, receding, a big boy to me in the night. I
close my eyes a minute and picture his strong legs moving, a determined look on his face to go faster. Though I know we'll still
have issues to deal with as he gets older, I feel confident that we
can work with Willie to handle any challenge. When I open my
eyes, there he is, exactly where he promised to stop—panting, ex-
hilarated, waiting for the rest of us.

Where to Get Help

There are now a number of excellent reference guides to understanding and dealing with Attention Deficit Disorder in children—so many, in fact, that it may be hard to sort through them all. Below are the ones that I have found most helpful, though few were available to us when Willie was in preschool. All are written specifically for a general audience (in other words, you don't need to be fluent in psychologese to read them). Most have even more thorough bibliographies if you wish to learn more.

If you suspect your child has ADD, or if your child has already been diagnosed with ADD, the following books and material will be very useful. All provide concise medical explanations of the disorder; most also address hyperactivity and learning disabilities. I cannot urge parents enough to seek out support for themselves as well as appropriate therapy for their child. Nearly all of the more than 650 chapters of Children and Adults with Attention Deficit Disorder (CHADD) worldwide offer such support groups. Many private therapists and psychiatrists specializing in ADD also run workshops for parents and families. The larger, national organizations can provide material for parents seeking special help and/or funding from their school districts for tutors, classroom shadows, and other therapy. Though each district has its own specific regulations, the federal government does provide a helpful brochure, which can help you better understand your child's rights. Last but not least, do not underestimate the help that other parents can provide. Those who have negotiated the system themselves can often offer the most practical advice and remind you that your story, too, can have a happy ending.

Organizations

Attention Deficit Disorder Association (ADDA)
P.O. Box 972
Mentor, OH 44061
(800) 487-2282

ADDA can provide information, reference material, and other information pertaining to ADD in adults and children. The ADDA also publishes a newsletter, *Challenge*. For information about *Challenge*, contact P.O. Box 448, West Newbury, MA 01985.

CHADD
(Children and Adults with Attention Deficit Disorder)
499 N.W. 70th Avenue, Suite 101
Plantation, FL 33317
(954) 587-3700
(800) 233-4050

CHADD is a nonprofit group with more than 650 local branches worldwide, most of which are run by the parents of children with ADD or by adults with ADD. Local groups can give you advice about how to screen therapists or psychiatrists. Many of the larger branches in major cities also offer speakers on a variety of parenting and educational issues. Local CHADD chapters are also good places to obtain preliminary information about getting funding for special programs in your child's schools. CHADD also publishes two newsletters, *CHADDER*—a biannual newsletter—and *CHADDER BOX*—a monthly newsletter for adults with ADD. CHADD also publishes a magazine, *Attention!*, which is specifically designed for parents of children with ADD.

Office of Civil Rights
U.S. Department of Education
400 Maryland Avenue, S.W.
Washington, D.C. 20202-4135
(202) 401-3020

The OCR is the best place to contact for information concerning section 504 of the Rehabilitation Act (1973) and the Individuals with Disabilities Education Act (IDEA), both of which address the rights of children with ADD to a "free and appropriate" education. Even if your child is in private school, you may be entitled to reimbursement for tutoring, transportation, and other therapy.

Other Reference Materials

Barkley, Russell, Ph.D. *Taking Charge of ADHD: The Complete, Authoritative Guide for Parents.* Guilford Publications, 72 Spring St., New York, NY 10012. Barkley is the Dr. Spock for parents of children with ADD. While his previous publications have been fairly technical handbooks for educators and therapists, this is his new "plain English" survey specifically written for parents.

Ingersoll, Barbara, and M. Goldstein. *Attention Deficit Disorder and Learning Disabilities: Realities, Myths, and Controversial Treatments.* New York: Doubleday, 1993. These two call 'em like they see 'em. This is an excellent overview of the unproven and disproven "remedies" offered to parents for treatment of children with ADD.

McNamara, Barry E., Ed.D., and Francine J. McNamara, M.S.W. *Keys to Parenting a Child with Attention Deficit Disorder.* This is the most concise and coherent medical discussion of ADD I've seen to date. Though it's a small brochure, it's full of valuable advice regarding treatment, school, and parenting issues. Available through therapists or ADD WareHouse (see below).

Books for Kids About ADD

Galvin, Matthew. *Otto Learns About His Medicine*. Magination Press, 1988. Available through therapists or ADD WareHouse. A little car named Otto needs to take medicine to control his motor, which "revs" too fast. Recommended ages: under six.

Gordon, Michael. *My Brother's a World-Class Pain*. 1992. GSI Publications, P.O. Box 746, De Witt, NY 13214. Also available through ADD WareHouse. One of the few books written for the siblings of children with ADD. Sibling rivalry, intolerance, re-demption—it's in there. Recommended ages: six to fourteen.

Stern, J., and Patricia Quinn. *Brakes: The Interactive Newsletter for Kids with ADD*. Available from the publisher (Brunner Mazel, 19 Union Square West, New York, NY 10003; [212] 924-3344; $24 a year). A newsletter specifically for children and teens with ADD. If Nickelodeon and *Highlights* made a magazine for ADD kids, this would be it.

Where to Get More Help

ADD WareHouse
300 N.W. 70th Avenue, Suite 102
Plantation, FL 33317
(954) 792-8944

The ADD WareHouse will send you a mail-order catalogue with dozens of books, learning aids, therapeutic games, and other items designed for children and families with ADD. There is a section with self-rating forms to detect ADD, as well as listings of books and information for educators, and children's books. Many of the books mentioned in this guide can be purchased through the ADD WareHouse.